MOTOR SPORT GREATS
IN CONVERSATION

Simon Taylor

From the acclaimed 'Lunch With...' series in *Motor Sport* magazine

Haynes Publishing

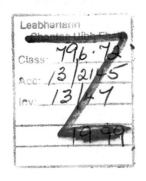

CONTENTS

MOTOR SPORT GREATS
IN CONVERSATION

For Pearl, with love and gratitude.

First published in January 2013

A catalogue record for this book is available from the British Library

ISBN 978 0 85733 250 9

Library of Congress control card no 2012944798

Published by Haynes Publishing,
Sparkford, Yeovil, Somerset BA22 7JJ, UK
Tel: 01963 442030 Fax: 01963 440001
Int. tel: +44 1963 442030 Int. fax: +44 1963 440001
E-mail: sales@haynes.co.uk
Website: www.haynes.co.uk

Haynes North America Inc.,
861 Lawrence Drive, Newbury Park,
California 91320, USA

Designed and typeset by Dominic Stickland

Printed and bound in the USA by Odcombe Press LP,
1299 Bridgestone Parkway, La Vergne, TN 37086

INTRODUCTION

Eating and talking
with the greats

It was back in 2006 that the long-established monthly magazine *Motor Sport* asked me to start taking memorable motor racing names out to lunch.

The idea was that I'd think of characters who had a story to tell, ask them to suggest their favourite pub or restaurant for a good meal and a half-decent bottle, and gently prod them into telling me what it had really been like out there. I hoped to persuade them to go beyond the well-worn tales that we'd all read many times. I wanted them to open up their memories and their opinions with frank and honest insights that might not have been published before, about themselves, about the people they'd known and worked with, about the people they'd raced against. The readers liked the results, and *Lunch With...* has been a part of each issue of the magazine ever since.

There's nothing new, of course, about a journalist carrying out an interview over a meal. What was different in this case was that I asked the editor of *Motor Sport* to allow me up to 6000 words for each interview, and he agreed. These days, when everyone's attention spans are supposed to be so limited, most publishers are scared of long articles. In a desire to reduce everything to its lowest common denominator, they believe that the only thing better than a 1200-word feature is an 800-word feature. *Motor Sport* is probably the only car magazine among the scores on the newsagents' shelves that would have indulged me to this degree. But its proprietor knows that, in an era when news is disseminated instantly via TV and the internet, and even a weekly racing title has to work hard to shed new light on what the informed enthusiast already knows, a monthly has to go a lot further.

Behind its traditional green cover, *Motor Sport* still clings to the character and ethos of the late Bill Boddy, who was its editor for some 60 years, and Denis Jenkinson, who wrote its brilliant race reports for half a century. In those days, no sub-editor was allowed to cut a line of copy. If there were too many words to fit into too few pages, the print was made smaller and smaller to get it all in, until it was barely legible. Fulfilling The Bod's role today, and sharing much of his uncompromising philosophy, is Editor Damien Smith. To him I extend my gratitude for approving my choice of *Lunch With...* subjects month by month, and for not cutting my copy. Jenks' spirit lives on in Nigel Roebuck, who is the magazine's Editor in Chief, and still the best and most respected race reporter of his era.

Several book publishers have approached me wanting to give my *Lunch With...* interviews a longer-lasting home between hard covers. I was delighted that one of these approaches came from my old friend and erstwhile colleague Mark Hughes, Editorial Director at Haynes. For this first *In Conversation* collection he asked me to select just two dozen interviews out of the 80-plus that I have now done. That was an impossibly difficult task, and the selection process was long and agonisingly painful. If your own favourite isn't here, you must clamour for a Volume II.

In every case, we decided to reproduce the articles as they originally appeared, without taking account of what may have happened since. For example, Penske Racing's non-stop schedule in IRL and NASCAR has chalked up yet more victories since Roger and I had our executive breakfast in 2010, and will no doubt continue to do so. When I talked to Andy Green, the fastest man on earth, his plans with Richard Noble to attempt 1000mph on land were barely formed. Now work on the Bloodhound SSC project is proceeding apace. Ross Brawn was taking a year's sabbatical from Formula 1 at the time of our lunch in 2007. It was a very good time to talk to him: away from the relentless pressures of the Grand Prix season he was in relaxed, contemplative mood. After that, of course, he went on to head up Honda F1, turn it into the World Championship-winning Brawn GP, and then mastermind its transition into the Mercedes F1 team.

I usually like to mention where my guest chooses to eat and what he selects from the menu, because it can say a lot about his character. The charismatic Mario Andretti, for example, wanted nothing grander than a cheeseburger in downtown Nazareth, Pa – but he made sure there were a couple of wines from his own Napa Valley vineyard to go with it. In Jacky Ickx's beautiful home in central Brussels we ate delicious native African dishes cooked by his Burundi-born wife Khadja. Jody Scheckter, of course, insisted on feeding me at Laverstoke Park with the superb organic produce from his award-winning farms. Lunch with that wonderful man Professor Sid Watkins was in shirtsleeves around the kitchen table in his beautiful 18th century Scottish manse. But the talk went on all afternoon, over dinner at an excellent local restaurant, and then in his drawing room into the small hours, over several drams of good single malt.

I have travelled far for some of these interviews: in fact, I can claim to have gone to New Zealand for lunch. I was actually in that charming country for a total of 22 hours, but it was worth every hour of the long flight to sit with Chris Amon in a little café in Auckland right next door to where Pop McLaren had his little garage business, living over the shop with his wife, daughters and son Bruce. As for Chris, he uncomplainingly gave himself a six-hour round-trip drive from Lake Taupo to meet me for lunch.

Dan Gurney entertained me to lunch in the All-American Racers building, among the historic Eagles in his collection. Jo Ramirez managed to find a corner of Mexico in Covent Garden to serve us the food he'd loved in his youth. Andy Green wanted to eat in the Bluebird Restaurant in London, because it had once been the garage of a previous land speed record holder, Sir Malcolm Campbell. Keke Rosberg said lunch was bad for his waistline, so we sat in the gardens of his Monaco apartment overlooking the Mediterranean, and one cup of espresso kept him in enthralling voice for four hours. And Brian Redman, visiting from his home in Florida, wanted to go back to his Lancashire roots. That meant fish and chips and mugs of tea in Harry Ramsden's in Guisley.

Sadly, one or two of the people with whom I have sat down to lunch over the past six years are no longer with us. Of those whose interviews are reproduced in this book the urbane, ever-charming Roy Salvadori, a fit and hearty 86 when we met in his Monte Carlo apartment in 2008, was shortly afterwards stricken with the tragic, debilitating illness that finally ended his life in 2012. Dear old Tom Wheatcroft, larger than life as always when we laughed together in his local near Donington, left us in 2009. And in 2012 we said goodbye to Professor Sid Watkins, whose superb work transformed the medical facilities at every grand prix.

Now is as good a moment as any for me to offer my heartfelt respect and thanks to all those wonderful people who have been kind enough to give me so much of their time and tell me their tales. Motor racing folk – drivers, team bosses, engineers, mechanics, designers, organisers, doctors, circuit owners – are all, in their own ways, racers. In their different styles and philosophies, they all believe in grabbing life with both hands and living it to the full. For me, sitting down with each one of them has been, in every way, a privilege.

Simon Taylor
Chiswick, November 2012

CHRIS AMON

*Counting the luck where
it matters*

Today's media like to give our heroes convenient labels. Stirling Moss is "the greatest driver never to win the World Championship" – a glib line which says nothing about The Boy's unrivalled versatility, or his racer's heart. In the same unthinking way, Chris Amon is too often dismissed as "the greatest driver never to win a Grand Prix" or "the unluckiest driver in F1 history". When we meet over an absorbing four-hour lunch in his native New Zealand, I ask Chris how he feels about his entire career being generalised in that way.

He smiles ruefully. "I have a standard answer to that. People tell me I'm the unluckiest F1 driver, but actually I'm the lucky one. I'm luckier than Jimmy, and Jochen, and Bruce, and Piers. Luckier than my team-mates Bandini, and Scarfiotti, and Siffert, and Cevert. And there were others, guys who were my friends, people I raced with every weekend. I had several big accidents that could have killed me. I broke ribs, but I was never badly hurt. Jim Clark never drew blood until his final accident. Jochen Rindt rarely hurt himself, either. But you only need one accident."

The labels his fellow-drivers stuck on Chris were all about his speed. Jackie Stewart calls him one of the very best he ever raced against, maybe one of the most naturally talented drivers of all time. Chris was blindingly quick on the really demanding road circuits: driving the bulky and unloved March 701, he still holds the F1 lap record for the old 8.7-mile Spa, at an average speed of over 152mph. He was also an extraordinarily astute and sensitive test driver, able to detect the effect of the tiniest chassis and tyre changes. And he raced to an old-fashioned set of values: he just didn't seem to know how to behave badly towards other drivers, on or off the track.

Yet his judgements about whom to drive for, and when, were disastrous. He always seemed to join a team when its fortunes were turning down, only to see them rise again after he left. He was 19 when he first raced in F1, and by 23 he was No 1 at Ferrari. But somehow success always slipped out of reach, to be replaced by disappointment and frustration. At 33, after four twilight seasons with minor teams that would have broken the spirit of a lesser man, he went back to New Zealand for good. He has lived happily and quietly with his English wife Tish, worked hard on his farm, raised three children, and never taken a backward glance at the world that consumed him for 15 years.

Today he looks slim, fit and happy. He no longer smokes, and our lunch is just soup and a salad. Having driven north from home on Lake Taupo to meet me in Auckland, and facing a three-hour drive back, he drinks only water. He is relaxed and good-humoured, modest and self-deprecating, a man comfortable with himself. His hair is grey now, his face lined by his outdoor life, but the shy, wide grin that I remember from 40 years ago is unchanged.

As an only child on the isolated family sheep farm at Bulls, south of Wanganui, he read everything he could find about the motor racing that was happening in the far-distant Northern Hemisphere. "I've always had an awareness of history. At one time I could tell you who'd won every post-war GP. When I was seven or eight, a shepherd who worked for my dad propped me up with cushions on an old Ford V8 ute we had on the farm. I soon found out how to slide this thing around on grass and dust. So I learned car control very young."

At 16 he scraped together the funds to buy an ancient midget dirt-track car. "It was absolutely lethal, shed wheels, used to break driveshafts which ran close to your important bits. I only did one race, and fortunately it only lasted one lap. I ran an early single-cam F2 Cooper – those things cost next to nothing out here – and then we heard Tony Shelley had an old Maserati 250F in his yard at Wellington. After the Cooper it was all very different, lots of power, not much traction, throttle pedal in the middle. Peter Collins, Mike Hawthorn and Jack Brabham had all raced this car. I got in and thought, my heroes have sat here. Tony let us have it for £500 plus the Cooper.

"It was very tired, but a really clever guy called Bruce Wilson, who had a little country garage near us, stripped and rebuilt it. In those days everything had to be made because you couldn't get the bits out here. And he did it all for nothing. Without him I would never had got anywhere. I did a season and a half in the Maserati, and it never missed a beat. For the first two or three races I was pretty much a passenger, but then in the New Zealand GP at Ardmore, which Moss, Surtees and Brabham came out for, suddenly something clicked." In heavy rain Chris drove brilliantly among more modern machinery and far more experienced drivers. "I remember Stirling lapping me. I was coping with a huge slide at the time, and he gave me one of his little waves, thinking I'd moved over for him." Watching all this was Reg Parnell, in New Zealand to run the Yeoman Credit Coopers.

For the next year's Tasman races Chris bought a later Cooper, and regularly qualified ahead of several of the visitors. Parnell was there again, running the Bowmaker Lolas, and he took Chris aside. "He told me I'd better get a passport. Months later he called, said he wanted me in London for Easter – four days later! Apart from a few races in Australia I'd never been out of New Zealand. I'd never even seen a jet plane. I got to Heathrow on Good Friday and Reg's secretary, Gillian Harris, took me to the Parnell workshop in Hounslow for a seat fitting in an F1 Lola. Next morning Reg took me to Goodwood for official practice for the Easter Monday F1 race. I couldn't believe how little power those 1.5-litre F1 cars had. I had to change my driving style completely. It was the first F1 race I'd ever seen, and I was in it. I finished fifth."

His first World Championship race was at Spa, no less. On a damp track he held a remarkable sixth place before an oil leak put him out. He quickly settled into the little Parnell team. After finishing seventh at Reims and seventh at Silverstone, he crashed at the Nürburgring when his steering broke. He was unhurt, but more serious was his accident at Monza five weeks later. "This was the last time they tried to use the combined banking and road circuit for the Italian Grand Prix. In practice so many cars broke on the rough surface that they decided to run on the road circuit alone. I went off at the second Lesmo, cartwheeled into the trees and was thrown out. I had broken ribs and concussion, and I was in hospital for several weeks.

"Reg was a no-nonsense guy, almost like a father to me. F1 was very friendly then. I was just the young newcomer, but everyone made me feel welcome: none of the back-biting there must be today. You could talk to anyone, from the World Champion down. Being steeped in motor-racing history, I found myself on the grid surrounded by people I'd grown up almost worshipping. Sometimes I wondered what on earth I was doing there.

"For 1964 Reg had big plans: monocoque Lotus 25s for Mike Hailwood and me, and the latest Climax V8s. Then he got appendicitis, wouldn't go to the doctor – he was stubborn – and by the time they got him to hospital it was too late. He was only 52. His son Tim had to pick everything up. He did his best, but the heart went out of the team. We got the Lotus 25s, but we ended up with customer BRM engines, which weren't so good. Although Mike was pretty much paying for his drive, Tim was struggling for budget. We'd buy secondhand gearbox spares from Lotus, so when you got a rebuilt gearbox it was already tired.

"I'd been living in a bed-sitter in Surbiton, but now I moved into the famous flat in Ditton Road, Kingston, with Mike

Hailwood and Peter Revson. My friend Bruce Harré, who'd come over from New Zealand to work at McLaren, stayed there too, and off and on so did Tony Maggs and Howden Ganley. There were three bedrooms, so we moved around depending on who was doing what and to whom with lady visitors. There was a crashed Cooper chassis propped up in the hall, which somebody was always going to ship back to New Zealand. It was there for months. The poor unfortunate who lived downstairs was a sitting tenant, not paying much rent, and the landlady had wanted to get rid of him for years. The police were always coming round because of complaints about the noise. They'd come in, turn the music down, have a couple of beers and then leave us to it. In the end the man downstairs moved out, so the landlady got her wish.

"I had my 21st birthday party the day after the 1964 British GP, and just about the entire F1 grid came. BP were making a film about Mike Hailwood and wanted to show him relaxing, so they said they'd foot the bill if we let a film crew in. But the crew got so plastered they were incapable of doing any filming. BP had to pay for another party and do it all again.

"Ulf Norinder asked me to share his Ferrari GTO in the Reims 12 Hours. Just before the race he sent me a telegram, saying he unexpectedly had to go to a wedding – his own! – and would I find another co-driver. So I called this promising young F3 racer, J. Stewart. We duly found the Ferrari in the Reims paddock with a rather disgruntled mechanic. Luckily Bruce Harré had come with me for the ride. In practice it did a piston: there was no spare engine, of course, no spares even, and Ulf's mechanic started to pack up. He was reckoning without Harré, who said, 'Hang on, let's pull the engine out and rebuild it.' The New Zealander approach, you see.

"Bruce tore it apart – he'd never seen the inside of a Ferrari engine before – and it hadn't done a great deal of damage, just the piston, a couple of valves, a few other things. Bruce went over to the factory Ferrari guys, who rummaged around in their truck and came up with some bits, and he rebuilt it in the paddock. By now the mechanic had gone off in a huff. During the race we needed some new brake pads, but they were in the boot of the mechanic's car and no-one could find him. Later on we were having a tyre change and could only find one rear tyre. It was a while before we twigged that we'd been racing with the other one still in the back of the Ferrari. But the engine Bruce had rebuilt never missed a beat, and we finished.

"For 1965 Bruce McLaren hired me. He was running the first McLaren sports cars and doing a lot of tyre testing for Firestone, which pretty much financed his operation. As he got busier I took over most of the tyre testing. I did thousands of miles at Goodwood, Silverstone, Snetterton, Brands, even Zandvoort. It was great experience, and with the Group 7 McLarens I was dealing with proper horsepower. In an average day I'd do at least 300 miles. I found I was quite sensitive to a car's behaviour on different tyres and settings, and could feed it all back to the tyre guys."

At Le Mans Chris shared a 7-litre Ford Mk II with Phil Hill. "We had a big speed advantage over the Ferraris, but our gearboxes were weak, and all the Fords retired. After that they got Pete Wiseman involved and ended up with a really strong transmission." In an F2 Lola he won the Solitude Grand Prix, and six days later he won the Martini Trophy in a McLaren from the back of the grid, standing in for Bruce who'd been burned by a petrol fire in practice. Two days after that, back with the daily grind of tyre testing at Brands, the McLaren's rear suspension broke. "I was flat in fourth around the back of the long circuit and it turned sharp right into the bank. It was like an aircraft accident, bits spread for 200 yards, me still in the seat. I was a bit knocked about, so they decided they'd better take me to hospital. The ambulance wouldn't start and they had to give it a tow." Three days later, nursing his bruises, he was off to the Nürburgring to drive a Parnell Lotus-BRM in the German GP.

Chris ran as team-mate to Bruce McLaren in Group 7 races in the UK in 1966 and in the inaugural CanAm Series, but the big event that year was Le Mans, where they scored a famous win for Ford. "All the works Fords were on Goodyears except ours: we were contracted to Firestone. In the wet and dry conditions the intermediate Firestones were terrible, and kept chunking. By Saturday evening we'd had two extra pitstops and were three laps behind the leaders, and Bruce said, 'I'm going to sort this out.' He went to the Firestone people and said, 'We're either going to withdraw the car, or we're going to put Goodyears on it.' So Firestone said, 'Put the Goodyears on.' They called me in, changed the tyres, and Bruce shouted to me, 'We've got nothing to lose. Just go like hell.'

"It rained off and on during the night, but we both drove flat out, and by Sunday morning we were back in the lead, about a minute ahead of the Ken Miles/Denny Hulme car. Ford hung out the EZ sign which Bruce took some notice of, but Ken didn't slow down one iota. Then something weird happened: at the next pitstop, when we weren't due a tyre change, the Goodyear guy, without even looking at the tyres, ordered the mechanics to change one of the fronts, which delayed us. Maybe he didn't want Firestone-contracted drivers winning the race. So Ken was back in the lead. Bruce was getting aggravated now. It rained some more, and it was unbelievably slippery. Bruce got past Ken again, and then Ford told us they wanted to stage a dead-heat. The two cars crossed the line more or less side-by-side, but the French decided we were the winners, because we'd been 20 yards behind Ken in the starting line-up. Afterwards Ken was very bitter, he was literally in tears. The tragedy was he was killed a few weeks later, testing the J-car at Riverside."

That October Chris was summoned to Maranello. "I was absolutely in awe of Enzo Ferrari. When I asked him about F1, he said, 'Do you want to drive for me or not? I know you have F1 ambitions, but I'm not going to put it in your contract.' I signed anyway. The whole thing took about 10 minutes. There wasn't much talk about money, just a standard retainer. Then we went to the Cavallino for lunch. I was on my best behaviour, drinking water, and Ferrari said, 'When Mike Hawthorn signed for me, we came here for lunch and he drank half a bottle of my best malt whisky.'

"Bruce was disappointed that I left him for Ferrari. He'd been my mentor in a way, and saw me as part of his future F1 team. We never quite had the same rapport again – until I went to Indy with him in 1970. We spent the month of May together, which was pretty much the last month of his life, and we got right back onto the same old relationship. I've always been glad about that.

"There were four Ferrari drivers under contract for 1967: Lorenzo Bandini, Lodovico Scarfiotti, Mike Parkes and me. We all went to Daytona for a week in December to test the new P4 sports car. I realised I had to get on the pace pretty quick if I wanted an F1 seat. Lorenzo was very fast, so the other seat was between the three of us. Fortunately my times were about the same at Bandini's.

"Lorenzo had a reputation for being difficult, but I always found him delightful. We did two races together in the P4 – the Daytona 24 Hours in February and the Monza 1000Kms in April – and we won them both. Monaco was my first race with the 312. Lorenzo and I had been practising at Indianapolis, and we flew back to Italy and then drove to Monaco together. In the race he was chasing Hulme for the lead and he crashed near the end, turned over and went on fire. It had been a long, hot race and I think he was exhausted. I was very tired, too: by then I was shivering, which meant I had run out of body fluids and was completely dehydrated. We used to lose five or six kilos in a hot race in the 312. Next day I had to fly back to Indy – I was driving one of the old BRP cars for George Bryant – and when I got to the circuit I heard the news that Lorenzo had died.

"Then Parkes had a huge accident at Spa and smashed his legs. That was the end of his F1 career, and it did for poor old

Scarfiotti, too. He just lost interest and left Ferrari. Ironically he was killed the following year in a hillclimb." Ferrari carried on as a one-car team and, with the entire Scuderia riding on his shoulders, Chris managed four podiums and fourth in the Championship.

"The 312 wasn't a bad chassis, but even before the DFV arrived in June the engines were hopeless. They sounded good but didn't have enough power, couldn't even keep up with the Repcos. But I loved being at Ferrari, loved living in Italy. Modena is a motor-racing city. I got myself a little apartment, I'd go each morning to the Hotel Real Fini for orange juice and coffee, and then I'd get the barber there to shave me. He used to shave Nuvolari. He couldn't speak a word of English, but over my three years in Modena he told me so many good stories. Then I'd go to the factory, and usually there was something they'd want me to try, so I'd go to the Modena Autodromo and do some laps. I was in a car almost every day.

"Often I'd have lunch with the Old Man. It wasn't an invitation, it was a command performance. His old chauffeur, Peppino, had been his riding mechanic in the 1920s. Peppino's job was to keep his car clean – usually the big Ferrari four-seater, like a 330GT – and have it waiting, warmed up, ready for lunch. The Old Man'd get behind the wheel, I'd get in the front passenger seat, and Peppino would squeeze in the back with the Old Man's poodle. In the summer we'd drive up into the hills, where it was cooler. We'd have lunch, me and the Old Man at one table, Peppino at another with the dog, feeding it fruit salad. I'd be sipping water and the Old Man would down a bottle of wine, then a couple of his malt whiskies. The drive back down the hill would be terrifying, horn blasting, goats and peasants scattering. I used to think, 'If I go now at least I'll out in style.'

"I really wanted to win Le Mans in 1967, for Lorenzo. I was sharing a P4 with Nino Vaccarella, the Sicilian schoolmaster, a good guy, very competent. It was going to be hard because

Ford had the Mk IV and we were 20mph short at least. But we thought if we went flat out we would still finish, whereas Ford might have to control their speed to get reliability.

"Just before midnight I was passing the pits when I felt the right rear tyre go flat. The worst place – a whole lap to get back to the pits. I slowed right down, but you think you're crawling and you're probably still doing 100mph. On the Mulsanne there were sparks coming out the back, and I thought, I'm going to have to change this tyre. The Ferraris had a spare tyre and a tool kit with jack, hammer and torch, so halfway down the straight I pulled onto the verge. I was crawling about at the back with cars coming past at 200 miles an hour. I got the back open, found the torch – and the battery was dud. So I just had the passing headlights to see by. I got the hammer and took a swipe at the knock-off hubcap – and the head came off the hammer. So I thought I'd get it jacked up and try to get the wheel off with one of the spanners. Then I found they'd forgotten to put the jack in.

"So I had to drive it back. I tried to stick to about 50 miles an hour, but the tyre flapping around broke a fuel line, and suddenly the whole thing was on fire. I jumped out and rolled into a ditch. The P4 carried on for a bit and then nosed into the ditch further down the road, burning merrily. Marshals and gendarmes rushed up, and they were peering into the fire wondering where the driver was. I walked up and tapped one of them on the shoulder...."

Throughout the 1968 Tasman Series, in an F2 Dino chassis with 2.4-litre V6 engine, Chris had a stirring battle with Jim Clark's 2.5-litre Lotus 49. "There was very little between us in a straight line. The Ferrari maybe handled better, but the Lotus had better brakes. I won the New Zealand GP, and at Levin Jimmy went off chasing me. At Teretonga I spun and Jimmy crashed, but at Sandown we were evenly matched. He could always outbrake me into the last corner, but I found I could nose ahead before the finish line. But on the last lap he must have taken the thing about 2000rpm higher, and we crossed the line with my front wheels level with his rears. It was his last victory.

"We saw a different side to Jimmy in New Zealand. He stayed at my parents' beach house, and was able to let his hair down. People said he wasn't enjoying his racing so much any more, but that wasn't the impression I got. He'd sorted out his tax problems, and was able to go back to Scotland. He was over the Sally Stokes thing, and seemed to be enjoying himself on that front. His death at Hockenheim dented everyone's confidence. He was so good, everybody thought he was bullet-proof. I wasn't alone in thinking, if it can happen to Jimmy it can happen to me.

"Jimmy was brilliant at getting out in front and staying there. Maybe he wasn't so keen on being under pressure – but very few people could put him under pressure. I felt Stewart was Jimmy's equal, but he had to work harder at it. The top drivers in my era were Jimmy, Jackie and Jochen Rindt. And Jack Brabham: he was a hard old bastard, and he drove some cracking races. He got a bit diverted when he was setting up his own company, but his last race, Mexico 1970, he came past me and Denny absolutely going for it, on the grass, up the kerbs like always. He was 44 years old then.

"For 1968 I nearly had Jackie as my team-mate. I tried hard to get him to Ferrari; I thought it would be good for both of us. He was keen, but in the end he went with Ken Tyrrell. The other guy I tried to get there was Parnelli Jones. He was one of the greatest talents I ever saw. It probably wouldn't have been his scene, but I'd watched him in the CanAm and he just flew. A great all-rounder. But they signed Jacky Ickx.

"At Rouen it was decided I would start on intermediates and Jacky would start on full wets. The first spots of rain fell when we were on the grid, and once it became torrential Jacky won with ease, whereas I finished way down. Four weeks later at the Nürburgring it was raining before the start, Jacky and I were on the front row, and Franco Gozzi said to me, 'See if you can hold up Hill and Stewart so that Jacky can get away.' Bugger that, I thought. I got a better start and never saw Ickx for the whole race – until my diff broke and I went off two laps from the end."

With better reliability, Chris could have been World Champion. Eight times he started from the front row, three times from pole: at Spa he qualified 3.7 seconds faster than second man Stewart. In Spain, and again in Canada, he was leading comfortably when the car failed. Always silly things went wrong. At the 'Ring he was almost coming out of the cockpit over the bumps, so for the first time Ferrari fitted a full harness to keep him in the car. Just as well, because at Monza four weeks later he was in second place when a hydraulic union on the moving rear wing came undone, spraying fluid onto the rear tyres. "I had a very big accident, hit the guardrail at Lesmo and it bent back and launched me. I did four end-overs through the trees and landed in a spectator car park. I had no idea where I was, but I undid the belts and crawled out, and there was John Surtees peering at me. He was following, and lost the lot as well."

In the 1969 Tasman Chris won the New Zealand and Australian GPs, and the series, in the Dino. But it was not a portent for F1. "By then Ferrari was in chaos. Italy was riddled with industrial problems, and the Ferrari factory was on strike half the time – not the racing department, but it affected everybody. For much of the F1 season they only entered one car. By mid-year I'd retired in every race except one, usually with engine failure. At Barcelona I was leading Stewart by half a lap when, again, the engine let go. Mauro Forghieri was working on a Flat 12, but every time I tested it it broke.

"I'd signed for Ferrari for another year, but Robin Herd, whom I'd known at McLaren, told me about the March operation he and Max Mosley were putting together. I met them, and Mosley sold me very hard: it would be a one-car effort centred around me, and they had all the money lined up. Of course it wasn't true. But Ferrari's problems were on-going, and I honestly believed I couldn't get anywhere in F1 without a DFV. So I told Ferrari I'd changed my mind. It was the biggest mistake of my life, but frustration does that to people. I said to the Old Man, 'You know how things have been, and I can't go on putting all my effort into this.' 'All right', he said, 'but I'll win a Grand Prix before you do.' He was right about that.

"Robin Herd could have come up with a much better car than the March 701, but they had to have something simple because they ended up with six or seven racing that year. This was the team that was going to be centred around me. The car wasn't bad at the start – Stewart and I tied for pole at Kyalami, and I won at Silverstone in April. But there was no development, so it never got any better. It wasn't bad on smooth circuits, but on bumpy ones like Brands it was appalling.

"At Spa I was leading from Jackie and Jochen, and I could see them getting smaller in my mirrors. Then suddenly there was this bloody BRM looming up. It was Pedro Rodríguez – he'd been eighth on the grid, a good couple of seconds slower than me and Jackie in qualifying. I thought, where the hell did he come from? He just blew by. I stuck with him, and I worked out that the only way I could pass him again was by taking the Masta kink flat, and getting him down the hill. It had never been flat up to then, but on the last lap I hung back, and then I went for it. I did get it flat between the buildings – I was that close to the wall – and I drafted past him down to Stavelot. That was the lap I set the record. But then on the long drag back up the hill he just came steaming past again."

Why did he love Spa so much? "Those corners, Malmedy, Stavelot, Eau Rouge, were wonderful – as long as you didn't look too closely at what was at the side of the track. We all had a lot of respect for each other in those days, because the consequences of an accident could be so severe. Drivers today don't even think about it: they have huge accidents and walk away from them. I fully supported what Jackie and Jochen were doing at that time to get F1 safer, although I didn't necessarily agree with how they were doing it.

"My deal with March was that Mosley would pay me £100,000 in four quarterly instalments. I got the first £25,000, but he still owes me £75,000. Big money then, not small money now. We had a legal meeting, and he gave me this stuff about how I had to stand back so the March lads could keep their jobs. I guess I was too soft.

"It was a difficult year. In May I was back at Indy with Bruce, but I couldn't get to grips with the McLaren. Denny was badly burned when a fuel line came off at full chat and the whole thing went up. That car was spooky – at one stage we put Bobby Unser in it for a few laps, and he came back shaking. But it was good working with Bruce again. Two weeks later I was driving back from the March factory on a sunny afternoon when it came on the car radio that Bruce had been killed testing at Goodwood. I had to stop the car and walk about a bit, trying to get my head round it. It was a very major shock. Piers Courage was killed a couple of weekends later, at Zandvoort.

"About then I had lunch with Jochen in London, and he told me he wanted to stop. He was frightened of the Lotus fragility. A month later he'd won a couple more Grands Prix, he was going to win the title, and he told me he was going to do one more year. Then he was killed at Monza. Looking back, I don't know how I coped with all that. I think there was a lot of stuff being pushed to the back of my mind.

"Matra made me an offer for 1971. Their V12 hadn't set the world on fire, but it was a breath of fresh air being able to leave March. I stayed with them for two years, and I won the Argentine GP, although that was a non-championship race. Did sports car races, too. At Monza I got pole ahead of Ickx's Ferrari, which pleased me. I was leading with nine laps to go and I tried to remove a tear-off from my visor, and the whole bloody thing flew off. While I was coping with 200mph without any eye protection the slipstreaming group came by, and I finished sixth.

"In 1972 we'd had so many retirements that Matra literally ran out of F1 engines, and went to their home GP at Clermont with a sports car engine in my car. But I put it on pole, and led until half-distance. Then I got a puncture. It took nearly a minute to change it – lots of wheel nuts then – and I rejoined eighth. I wasn't happy."

In one of his finest drives, breaking the lap record repeatedly around the swooping five-mile Charade circuit, Chris clambered back to third, and was catching Emerson Fittipaldi's Lotus 72 at four seconds a lap when the flag came out. The French crowd roared their appreciation, and officials insisted that Amon took a lap of honour with winner Stewart. But Chris was downcast.

"Clermont 1972 was a turning point for me. I suppose that was the last time I drove my heart out. Frustration had been building up over several years, and although it wasn't a conscious thing, that was when I said to myself: It's never going to happen. The Matra boss, Jean-Luc Lagardère, asked me if I thought they should continue with F1. I said, 'If you stick with that engine, you're always going to struggle.' It was the end of my Matra drive."

So many stories. Tecno in 1973: two designers building two different cars at the same time. Tecno boss Luciano Pederzani raging at team manager David Yorke over dinner, and felling him with a single punch. The offer to return to Ferrari, blocked by Tecno sponsor Martini. Chris' attempt to run his own team with the Amon AF101 in 1974: the car only ever started one race, and broke. The offer to join Brabham, which Chris refused, because he felt he would be letting down the Amon crew. Then the season with Mo Nunn's Ensign team.

"The Ensign wasn't a bad car, but there was no money. It was all hand to mouth, with two-year-old engines borrowed from Bernie. At Zolder I was fifth when a back wheel fell off and I was wrapped up in catch fencing like a parcel. At Anderstorp I was fourth when the front suspension broke and put me in the barriers, hard. At the Nürburgring Niki Lauda had his accident, and I was shocked by how long it took for help to get to him. I knew the Ensign was fragile, I knew I was planning to stop at the end of the season and I really didn't want to end up on my head. So before the restart I said to Mo, 'I can't trust the car, and I don't want to drive it here.' That was the end of our relationship. Frank Williams asked me to drive in Canada, and I went out on cold tyres in practice and spun it, and got T-boned by Harald Ertl. Then I went home to New Zealand."

In 2003 Chris sold the family farm and retired to Kinloch, but both his sons are farmers not far from Bulls. For 25 years he has been a consultant to Toyota, and helped develop the suspension of the locally-built Camrys and Coronas. Apart from one visit to the Goodwood Festival in 1997, when he was overwhelmed by the welcome he got, he's stayed away from racing. He hasn't been back to Maranello for more than 35 years: "They invited me to the 60th anniversary celebrations, but the invitation arrived three days before the event. I e-mailed Montezemolo and said, 'If I'm still around for the 75th, can you give me a bit more warning?'"

Another wide Amon grin, another self-deprecating chuckle, and it's time for me to catch my plane and Chris to drive back to Tish and his home by the lake. He's right: far from being F1's unluckiest driver, he is truly one of the lucky ones. He was part of a golden age of racing, he has some marvellous and poignant memories, and he's still here.

Chris Amon was talking to Simon in March 2008.

MARIO ANDRETTI

*Always follow
your dream*

Even before you meet Mario Andretti, the bare statistics tell you this man is unique. In a full-time career lasting an astonishing 35 seasons, he was a winner in F1, Champ Car, World Sports Cars, NASCAR, F5000, IROC and even Pike's Peak. These days F1 drivers just do their 18 races a year, but, relying on a punishing schedule of transatlantic commuting, Mario liked to race every weekend – grand prix one Sunday, USAC dirt race the next, endurance sports car race the next.

He's been World Champion, Champ Car champion (four times) and USAC dirt champion, and has been voted Greatest American Driver Ever. He's surely the only man to have won significant races in five decades, from the 1950s to the 1990s. And he still doesn't think of himself as retired. He did Le Mans in 2000, and in 2003, at the age of 63, he lapped Indy at 225mph – until an accident not of his making cartwheeled the car to destruction. This is an extraordinary man who's had an extraordinary life.

He isn't tall, but when he enters a room you know he's arrived. There's a quiet dignity about him which has nothing to do with arrogance or ego, and everything to do with what you know he has achieved. Fangio, on the brief occasions I met him, had just this quality. And Mario's self-deprecating humour amplifies a remarkable recall which can dial up almost any race from that long career, right back to the dirt tracks of his teens nearly 50 years ago.

He can now afford to live anywhere from Connecticut to California, but he has never left Nazareth, the small Pennsylvania town where he fetched up as a 15-year-old immigrant in 1955. Home is a palatial residence built to his specification and standing in spacious grounds on a hill above the town: he also has a vast lakeside estate, Open Woods, deep in the Pennsylvania wilds, and a successful vineyard in California's Napa Valley. In his house the galleried hall is lined floor to ceiling with cabinets housing hundreds of trophies, and the walls in other rooms are covered with photographs, plaques and mementoes, each recalling a moment or a friend from his crowded racing life. The lower ground level is made up of rows of spotless tiled garages, with work benches and quality tools. From the gleaming line-up we choose an orange Lamborghini Murcielago, and he drives me briskly to lunch.

It's a long way from his beginnings. In 1940, when he and his twin brother Aldo were born in Montona in north-eastern Italy, Nazis and local partisans were fighting in the streets. As war ended Montona became part of Yugoslavia, and for three years the Andrettis lived under Communist rule before escaping, with nothing, into Italy. They were billeted in an old monastery in Lucca. "In one big room there were 10 families living, separated only by blankets which we strung up. We lived there for seven years. My dad did odd jobs, always provided for us. We were never hungry, never cold. But as kids we knew it wasn't normal." In 1952 his father applied to emigrate to America. But he heard nothing more.

In 1954 a friend took Mario and Aldo to Monza for the Italian GP. The two 14-year-olds cheered themselves hoarse as the Ferrari of reigning champion Alberto Ascari led the Mercedes team until its engine expired. It made a deep impression. So did the sight of the 1955 Mille Miglia passing by, with Moss and his bearded passenger racing to victory.

Then, suddenly, emigration approval came through. In June 1955 the Andrettis arrived in Nazareth. Gigi Andretti found work at the local cement works, while the boys set about learning English. After school they pumped gas at the local Sunoco station. Within days they discovered that Nazareth had its own half-mile dirt oval on the edge of town.

Unknown to their parents, Mario and Aldo found an old Hudson in a local scrapyard and began to convert it into a stock car. "We scraped together every cent, got some help from local businessmen for parts we needed, and did all the work ourselves." By early 1959 they were ready for their maiden outing. "We painted the Hudson bright red, got ourselves smart overalls – everybody else ran in scruffy T-shirts – and we bought one helmet between us."

The twins were now 19, but local rules stipulated a minimum age of 21. "So we fudged our birth date on our licences. Then the promoter says he can't allow kids with no experience. So we tell him we've been racing in Formula Junior back in Italy since we were 13, and he buys it. We toss for who should race first, and Aldo gets it. Because he's an unknown, they start him at the back for his heat. And he comes through and wins. That's $25 – doled out straight away from the pay window. For the final they start him on the back again and he passes them all, pa pa pa pa, and he wins the race. $150. We couldn't believe it. Next weekend, my turn. I knew I had to do the same, so I did, from the back to the front, heat and final. We went on to run five different local tracks, and we were on top everywhere.

"Our parents knew nothing of this, because we knew they'd try to stop us. Then right at the end of the season, at Hatfield, Aldo was trying to pass the track champion, Freddy Adams, on the outside, and he got into the barrier, hooked his right front on a loose wooden plank. Cartwheeled end-over-end. They took him away in a coma, and read him the last rites at the hospital. I rang my mom and said he was watching the racing and he fell off the back of a truck, just had the wind knocked outa him. Next morning they brought the crashed car back to Nazareth and the word went round like wildfire that Aldo was dead. My dad didn't know what to do, he was so upset, so furious. He didn't talk to us for months. When Aldo regained consciousness, the first thing he said was, 'I'm sorry you had to be the one to face the old man'."

Our route in the Lamborghini takes us past the garage where, half a century ago, two teenagers pumped gas, and then the site of the old dirt oval, next to the now defunct Nazareth Speedway. We arrive at the Newbury Inn – like much of the town, clapboard-clad and dating back to the 18th century – and Mario orders staple American fare: cheeseburger and chips. From the wine list he selects two Andretti wines for me to try: a Chardonnay and a San Giovese. Both are excellent.

As Mario's early reputation grew, he was offered drives: Stock Cars, then Midgets, then Sprint Cars. "Each dirt track was so different, and each would vary totally during the course of a race. You had to learn to read the surface. It was good training for F1 in the wet later on." In 1964 he got a strong Champ Car ride with Clint Brawner, who ran the Dean Van Lines team. But Brawner wouldn't let him make his debut at the notorious Langhorne dirt oval. "In its time Langhorne killed 52 drivers. They used to call it the widow-maker. It was shaped like a big D and you were sideways for three-quarters of the lap, going from lock to lock on the dirt, bunched close at 140mph and steering on the throttle. There used to be a fatality almost every race. One of Brawner's drivers, Jimmy Bryan, had been killed there. So he wouldn't run me, gave my car to an older guy called Bob Mathouser.

"But I was young, all piss and vinegar, and I wanted to race. So I picked up a ride in an old car belonging to Lee Glessner. Unlike the decent cars it had no power steering. But I wanted to beat Mathouser and prove a point to Clint Brawner. My mechanic that day was old Tommy Hinnershitz, who'd been a top dirt racer for 30 years. In practice I was so charged with adrenaline I was coming real close to the wall, not really knowing what the hell I was doing.

"So before qualifying Tommy says, 'Mario, see that post by the entry to Turn 3? No matter how good the car feels, you gotta back off there, set the car up.' Well, come qualifying I was really on it, and as I came to the post it felt real good. Then I remembered what he said, and I did back off a little bit... and I just barely,

barely made it. If I'd gone 10 yards deeper, I woulda gone way out the ball park. They woulda found me in New Jersey. Tommy saved my life that day.

"In the race the surface broke into deep ruts. With no power steering, my hands were hamburger meat by the end. But I passed the Brawner car, finished ninth. It felt good.

"Eventually they paved Langhorne. But it was still tough. It was so quick, and you were turning all the time. You had to feather just before the start-finish line to get through Turn 1. One day I decided to stay flat, thought I'd get it all figured out when I got to the turn. I never did get it figured out, so I crashed after the finish line. But the lap before was a record. It held till they broke up the track for a shopping mail."

In 1965 Mario ran his first Indianapolis. He qualified fourth and finished third, winning Rookie of the Year, and in the pit lane he met Colin Chapman and Jim Clark. Andretti told Chapman his sights were set on Formula 1. "When you're ready", said Chapman, "call me."

That season Andretti beat A J Foyt to become youngest-ever National Champion. He was Champion again the next year. Hungry to race anything and everything, he found sports car drives for the NART Ferrari team and then Ford at Le Mans, going on to win the Sebring 12 Hours three times in six years. He ran in NASCAR and Can-Am, too, yet still pursued a full Champ Car schedule, and raced midgets on dirt if he had a free weekend. In 1966 he drove 14 different cars in 51 races, taking 14 victories in four of them. In 1967 he won the biggest NASCAR race of all, the Daytona 500. "Those guys didn't like an open-wheeler coming down and beating them. Next day a newspaper headline said: *South Mourns Andretti Victory*." In 1969 his 4WD Lotus 64 broke a rear hub during Indy qualifying. Mario escaped with slight burns from the huge fiery accident that ensued, switched to his Brawner Hawk, put it on the front row, and won the race. That year brought his third Champ Car championship title.

"I never had any difficulty moving between disciplines. You get in a car, you switch off everything else and you focus on what you're at. Like I'm doing the Sebring 12 Hours on a Saturday, I fly out Saturday night, Sunday I'm racing a sprint car on a dirt oval. World of difference in the skills required, but the passion's the same."

In 1968, three years after their meeting at Indy, Mario made that call to Chapman. He tested the Lotus 49 at Monza, where 14 years before he'd pressed his nose to the fence to cheer on Ascari. At once he was very quick – "I felt like I was born in that car" – and Chapman decided to run him alongside Graham Hill and Jackie Oliver in the Italian Grand Prix. But there was a problem: on the Saturday Mario was contracted to the Hoosier 100 dirt race. So he qualified the Lotus at Monza on Friday, flew to America, did the Hoosier on Saturday, and flew back to Italy, arriving in the Monza paddock on Sunday morning. Then the FIA invoked a rule preventing a driver from racing twice within 24 hours, and Mario was refused permission to start.

Four weeks later at Watkins Glen it was a different story. Mario made F1 history by taking pole for his first grand prix. He was lying second to Jackie Stewart when his nose aerofoils came adrift, and he finally retired with clutch failure, but it was an auspicious beginning. During the next two seasons there were more F1 races for Lotus, and March with Andy Granatelli's 701, as well as sports car successes for Ferrari. In 1971 Ferrari offered Mario F1 drives when his other commitments allowed. In a fairy-tale debut for the team he won the South African GP, and set fastest lap. Then the Vel Miletich/Parnelli Jones team, for whom Mario ran in Champ Car and F5000, moved into F1 as well, doing a full season in 1975. But the Maurice Philippe-designed car was not a success.

"So 1976 comes along and I'm on the grid at Long Beach, third race of the season, and Chris Economaki puts a mike to me just before the off and says, 'Mario, how does it feel starting your last F1 race? Vel Miletich just told me he's pulling the plug on F1 to concentrate on Champ Cars.'

"No-one had said anything to me. I felt real stupid. I was so upset I almost didn't put the thing in gear. After the race I didn't even want to talk to them, I just went back to my hotel. Next morning I'm having breakfast all by myself, and Colin's having breakfast two tables away, all by himself. He's just had the worst weekend: one of his cars qualified last, and crashed out on the first lap, the other didn't qualify at all. We look at each other, my chin's in my socks, he's even more miserable, and he comes over to join me. So the wheels start rollin', and he says, 'Drive for me, Mario.' I said, 'But you got a car that may just be slightly quicker than a London bus. We got some work to do here.' We shook on that. I felt a horizon opening out. I knew Colin could make me World Champion.

"I called Miletich and said, 'I'll never work for you again. And I'm gonna compete against you in Champ Cars.' He said, 'We have a contract.' I said, 'No we don't, you're in breach. Do what you wanna do, sue me.' Then I called Penske, told him I was doing F1, but I wanted to keep in Champ Car. He said, 'Whenever you're available, I'll have a car for you.'

"I told Colin I wanted to do all the F1 testing, but also I was going to stay in Champ Cars. He said, 'It's impossible. You're crazy.' I said, 'You're probably right, but I have to. There aren't enough races in F1. I can't have weekends when I'm sitting idle.' He didn't argue, he knew I was adamant.

"I'll tell you how the ground effects thing got started. We were sitting round the table at Hethel, Colin, Martin Ogilvie, Tony Rudd, Nigel Bennett. I said what I wanted was downforce without penalty. I remembered testing the March 701 with those aerofoil-shaped sidepods that Robin Herd put on it. We tried taking them off and we lost direction entirely, like suddenly I needed 2.5 degrees extra front wing. So I knew they were working. But it was very inefficient because the air was spilling off them. I said, 'What happens if you have bigger pods, and fences?' The talk went on from there.

"Then we were testing at Hockenheim and in the middle of the Bosch Curve, when the car was on full roll, suddenly I was picking up a tremendous amount of extra grip. I said to Colin, 'something is happening aerodynamically here, when the car gets closer to the ground under roll.' So he sent [chief mechanic] Bob Dance into town to buy some plastic strips and they pop-rivetted them down the side of the car to close the gap entirely. I went out and got under the lap record at once, but as soon as the plastic wore out the grip went away again.

"Colin and I really bonded because he respected my way of working on the setup. He never wanted drivers to be too technical – all he wanted was feedback about what the car was doing. But I had tricks from American racing that were new to F1. I liked to set my cars up with stagger – the left rear tyre slightly bigger than the right rear, compensated with cross weight. I always had the left front and the left rear slightly bigger, even for a circuit that has more left-handers than right-handers. But for a circuit that's counter-clockwise, like Imola, you had to go the other way. And if you look at a circuit with, say, 11 corners, there may be seven or eight that are key for passing, or for speed on the next straight, and two or three that you have to throw away. I always tried to maximise the car for the key corners. I had my own notes and circuit map, and I tried to find the extra angle the others didn't have.

"Aerodynamically the 78 was a brick: on the straights it was dead slow. The 79 was much better, but it had serious brake problems. It had magnesium calipers to save weight, and the inboard rears got hot when the gearbox heated up. The pedal would go to the floor, you had to pump it like hell. In 1978 we won some of those races with no brakes. I complained, but Colin wouldn't have it. There were some things you couldn't convince him about, he'd just hit the roof.

"Colin could be very emotional. I remember him giving Gunnar Nilsson a bollocking about something, thrashing out at him. Then he saw me watching in disbelief, and he said, 'I'm sorry you had to see that side of me.' He would never have dared to talk to me like that. I said to Gunnar, 'How can you take that shit, just sitting there like a little child being scolded by a teacher? You can't get any respect like that.'

"But there was mutual respect between Colin and me. Mind you, I was concerned about the fragility of his cars. He loved titanium, but I insisted on no titanium suspension arms or pedals. That's what paralysed Regazzoni – a titanium brake pedal broke. I used to needle Colin about suspension failures. He didn't take it too well. I didn't want to labour it, he'd lost Jochen [Rindt] because of a brake shaft failure, but I didn't want to die because a suspension part broke. I had a good understanding with the boys on the team. I'd say to Bob Dance: 'If you reckon something doesn't seem strong enough, just tell me. I'll fight the battles with the Old Man.'

"Colin was always paranoid about weight, and wanted you to finish the race with no more than half a litre of fuel left. I used to say to Bob, 'Just put another half-gallon in there.' At Kyalami Colin found out and ordered him to pump the extra fuel out again, right there on the grid! I said to Colin, 'If I run out of fuel I'm gonna take it outa your hide.'" Two laps from the end the Lotus spluttered and started to run dry, and after an unscheduled fuel stop Mario was classified seventh...

"In all my racing, I've always loved my mechanics. That's who you rely on, 100 per cent. Once you understand that, you become a family. I'm still in touch with a lot of the guys I worked with down the years. I always felt they won the races. You earn their respect by going balls out, and they work their butts off to give you what you need to get it done. The wins don't come all the time. But when they do, you all celebrate."

But when Mario won the World Championship for Colin, at Monza in 1978, there were no celebrations. His team-mate and close friend Ronnie Peterson died the following morning from injuries sustained in a Lap 1 pileup. "I've had a lot of team-mates, and not all of them were real friends. Ronnie was a special breed. We worked hard and played hard. We got together with our families, I'd stay at his house, he stayed at mine. We had fun. He had tremendous car control. He could carry a car, overcome its deficiencies. A real raw talent."

For 1978, Mario nearly left Lotus for Ferrari. "I expected to stay for '78, but we hadn't agreed the money. Colin stuck at $350,000 and $10,000 a point, but I wanted $500,000 and the points money. So in September '77 I win Monza for Colin, and then I say I have to go see Ferrari, He says, 'Don't go, we have a deal.' I say, 'Well, we do and we don't.'

So I'm in Ferrari's office, and we get to the uncomfortable stuff, money. That's why people have a manager, I guess, but I've always done my own deals. He says, 'How much do you want?' I say, 'Make me an offer.' And he says, 'Andretti, I can't put a price on your talent.' Very flattering, but also very clever, because it puts the ball right back in my court. So I'm thinking, $500,000 is what I want, so I say to him, '$750,000.' And he says, 'OK'. I think, Man, why didn't I ask for a million? So then I level with him. I tell him I have a handshake with Colin. He says, 'That's what we have lawyers for. If you want to drive for me, I can make it happen.'

So I say to Colin, 'You have to give me $750,000, and $10,000 a point.' He says, 'I can't.' I say, 'Then I go to Ferrari.' So he went back to Player's, they found the money, I stayed, and we won the Championship.

"I was still doing Champ Car, of course, and I won the IROC Championship too. I used to do the red-eye going over and Concorde coming back. I was Concorde's most frequent traveller, 26 crossings in a year. The ground staff were always ready for me, had my *Financial Times* and my brioche waiting. Those days, first class really was first class."

Mario's F1 career lasted 128 races, including a year with Alfa Romeo, a Long Beach ride for Williams, and two swansong races for Ferrari in the turbo era: he sent the Monza crowd delirious by taking pole in 1982, and finished third. At home the wins went on piling up: his fourth Champ Car title came in 1984. In 1993, at the age of 53, he won his final Champ Car victory at Phoenix, and took pole for the Michigan 500 at 234mph, a closed-course world record at the time. He bowed out of single-seaters in 1994 after starting 407 Champ Car races, 67 of them from pole. He won 52 of them, and led 7587 laps.

"I never went racing for the money. I did it because of my passion for it. If you race for money, you're racing for the wrong reason. But I always went for the best deals, because I was trying to justify the risks, for my family's sake. Dee Ann, my wife, used to say, 'Why not take a weekend off, take the kids to the movies?' But I just had to do it. You have no idea how much I loved driving. My son Michael is happy being a team owner, but I never had any of those ambitions. The only part that excited me was the driving."

The Andretti's family record in racing is unique. Aldo raced on after his accident that first year, although his career never rivalled Mario's. Son Michael had a brief, unhappy F1 sojourn with McLaren, but his American career was hugely successful. An Indy winner and an Indycar champion, he now heads up the Andretti-Green IRL team. Younger son Jeff and cousin John, Aldo's son, have all raced at top level: sometimes four Andrettis have been on the same grid.

Now there is Marco, Mario's grandson. In 2006, aged 19, he did his first Indy 500. Mario, Michael and Jeff had all won Rookie of the Year at Indy, so there was huge pressure on the boy. Marco not only followed the script and won Rookie of the Year: he very nearly won the race as well, missing victory by precisely sixty-three thousandths of a second. "He was truly thrown into the lion's den, and what I saw was a complete learning curve happening. He was putting something in the bank every day. He started that month as a boy, and finished it as a man." In December Marco had his first F1 test, for Honda. "I tell ya, he's smart. I say to Michael, he's smarter than both of us. He's gonna go far."

But no-one has come as far as Mario himself. During our lunch, a fan from another table comes shyly over to ask Mario to autograph a paper napkin for her six-year-old son. Mario asks the son's name, and then signs: "To Christopher. Always follow your dream. Mario Andretti".

That's just what Mario did. With self-belief, courage and inexhaustible will, the young boy at the Monza fence followed his dream. It made him the super-hero of American motor sport, and one of the most versatile racers of all time.

Mario Andretti was talking to Simon in December 2007.

DEREK BELL

A team player and an
English gentleman

Derek Bell is, quintessentially, an Englishman. He has raced with enormous success in the USA, where he is a popular figure; his wife Misti is American, and he spends much of the year at his waterside house in Boca Raton, Florida. Many of his greatest victories were scored in German cars, and he has been a works driver at the most famous Italian team of all. But there's always been something frightfully British about his approach to life, which mixes professionalism and a fierce will to win with an old-fashioned belief in friendly good manners towards team-mates, fellow competitors and spectators.

So it's appropriate that we meet in his 17th-century thatched house on the Sussex coast, hard by the family farm where he grew up. He still retains 60 acres around it. Then we walk across the nature reserve of Pagham Harbour and along the shoreline to the Crab & Lobster at Sidlesham, where we sit in the sunny garden eating a stew of locally caught fish and quaffing good English beer.

Even Derek has lost count of how many sports car races he has won, although five Le Mans 24 Hours, three Daytona 24 Hours and two World Drivers' Championships will do for starters. His career has lasted 46 years – so far: last season, at the age of 66, he was running in his umpteenth Daytona, only for his Riley-Pontiac to fail before his first stint. Ask him if he has retired yet, and he says he probably has – then moments later he mentions in passing the Porsche 917 he's racing at Laguna Seca this month, and his likely rides at the Goodwood Revival.

After almost half a century of racing, a life chock-full of different tracks, teams, personalities and happenings good and bad, any chat with Derek can only scratch the surface. We spend more than four hours over lunch, walk back to his house, sit in the late afternoon sunshine by his swimming pool, and the stories keep coming. Finally I have to take my leave and, driving back to London, I remember more dramas, more people, more races we didn't get to.

As a teenager at agricultural college Derek scraped up the funds to take a few Jim Russell Racing Drivers' School lessons at Snetterton, one at a time, driving to Norfolk in his side-valve Morris Minor. Jim Russell himself marked him out as a man to watch. Later he bought a Lotus 7 with a friend, and won his first race, at Goodwood. "It was a handicap, in teeming rain. I started off with lots of much faster cars behind me, like Hugh Dibley's Brabham BT8, and I waited for them to come steaming past, but they all spun off." In 1965 came his first single-seater, an elderly Lotus 22/31 which brought some success in club races, and for 1966, helped by his stepfather Bernard 'The Colonel' Hender, he decided on a serious F3 campaign in Europe. "The Old Man was marvellous. He said, 'Give farming a rest for a bit. You can always come back to it when you're 40, but you can't go motor racing when you're 40.' As it turned out, I was 40 when I won Le Mans for the third time..."

Derek's first choice of F3 car, a Lotus 41, was a mistake. It was never competitive and, trying to beat the Brabhams, he had several accidents. So for 1967 he joined Peter Westbury and Mac Daghorn in a three-car Brabham team and scored some excellent results, including a win at Zolder, third at Monaco, and second at Albi half a length behind the Matra of local hero Henri Pescarolo.

"After that the only way forward was Formula 2. The Old Man had paid for three years of F3, and very reasonably said I had to find the money from now on. I wrote hundreds of letters to prospective sponsors, and had one reply – from Avis, who sent me a badge saying 'We try harder'. In the end the only option was the

NatWest at Bognor Regis. Amazingly they lent me £10,000, but the Old Man had to put up the farm as guarantee." So, armed with a Brabham BT23, his mechanic Ray Wardell and a truck with Church Farm Racing painted on the side, Derek embarked on a European F2 season.

"The first race I actually started was Hockenheim. I qualified fifth on the Saturday, went back to the hotel in Speyer, and found myself having a cup of tea with two of my heroes, Jimmy Clark and Graham Hill. They'd both been having problems with the Team Lotus 48s – Jimmy qualified seventh, Graham 15th – and Jimmy said, 'Tomorrow, when you lap me, don't get too close.' I couldn't believe it, my hero saying that to me before my first F2 race, but he said, 'I've got a really bad misfire, and they can't seem to cure it.' Next day it was wet, cold and miserable. Jimmy and Graham gave me a lift to the track and dropped me off in the paddock, and I never saw Jimmy again. The race was a two-parter, and I finished fourth in part one ahead of Piers Courage. I think Jimmy was lying eighth when he crashed. I knew nothing about it until I saw his mechanic, Beaky Sims, walking through the paddock holding one of Jimmy's shoes, and then the word went round.

"The generally accepted view is that he went off because of a puncture, but my own theory is the misfire did it. You took that long fast corner at 150mph, but it wasn't a critical place. Even in the wet we were going through it two abreast. But if your engine cut out suddenly mid-corner, and you corrected, and then it cut in again, that could send you off into the trees. Years later I talked to Beaky about it, and he said, 'Yeah, we did have a problem with the fuel injection metering unit that day.'

"We were all pretty shattered by Jimmy's death. We didn't seem to be able to get through a month in those days without somebody getting slaughtered somewhere. As well as the chaps at the top like Jimmy, there were kids dying in F3 that nobody ever heard about. At one F3 race, at Caserta in Italy, three people died in an 11-car pile-up – Giacomo Russo, Beat Fehr and Romano Perdomi. Nobody remembers those names now. Three weeks later we were in Denmark, at Djurslandring, and Doug Revson, Pete's brother, was killed. And in F2, three months after Jimmy's accident, Chris Lambert was killed at Zandvoort when Clay Regazzoni collided with him. I'd known Chris since F3. He wore glasses, and didn't look like a racing driver: he looked more like one of those boys at school who always gets everything wrong. But in fact he was brilliantly fast.

"A week after Hockenheim I was third at Thruxton behind Jochen Rindt and Jean-Pierre Beltoise, and third again at the Eifelrennen, on the bumpy Nürburgring Sudschleife. So F2 was going well for me. I realised just how well when I was summoned to Maranello. I had a meeting with Enzo Ferrari, walked across the road with him to the Cavallino Restaurant and had lunch. That was special. Michael Schumacher may have won five World Championships for Ferrari, but he never had lunch with Enzo...

"Then came a test at Monza in the F2 Dino. I was run with several Italian drivers, including Tino Brambilla and Mario Casoni, and fortunately I was quicker than any of them. So Ferrari produced a contract, but I didn't sign it then. I wanted to keep my options open. But they entered me for the F2 Monza Lotteria, and I put it on pole. In the race I was coming out of the Parabolica in the middle of a huge slip-streaming group when suddenly, for no reason, my car spun. There was a huge pile-up – it wrote off three of the four Dinos in the race – and Jean-Pierre Jaussaud was thrown out of his Tecno and quite badly hurt. And I hadn't signed my contract. I went miserably home thinking that was that, but Ferrari got hold of a film of the accident, and they reckoned I was hit from behind – anyway they didn't blame me. Next time I was at Maranello, Franco Gozzi came over and said, 'Il Commendatore was pleased with your pole position' and gave me a bonus cheque!

"I'd also been approached by Cooper, who tested me in one of their Maserati-powered F1 cars at Silverstone. I thought it was a bit of a lorry, but their chap Major Owens, who ran the team for John Cooper, summoned me. An F1 contract at last, I thought, expecting a retainer of at least £10,000. As Owens droned on about how hard times were in F1, I modified my expectations down to

£5000, and then £1000. When he finally got round to making his offer he proposed a three-year contract, with a retainer of £5! For once in my life I was rendered speechless.

"So I signed for Ferrari. The deal was £250 per F2 race, and if they asked me to do an F1 race it would be £500. I did five more F2 races for them that season, and I went to Modena for an F1 test – the old three-quarter mile track, walls and bushes all round. And it was raining. All the wet-weather tyres were on the truck coming back from the German GP, so I had to do it on intermediates, and on the outside of Turn 1 there was Enzo Ferrari sitting in his 250GT 2+2, watching from behind his dark glasses. Mauro Forghieri leaned into the cockpit and said to me, 'You crash, it's the last time you drive a red car.' There were puddles down at the Esses, but the car felt simply wonderful, and the test went pretty well. So they sent three cars to Oulton Park for the Gold Cup, for Chris Amon, Jacky Ickx and me. I ran fifth until the gearbox packed up. Three weeks later I was summoned to Monza. My first Grand Prix – in a Ferrari, in Italy." It was four short years since that wet Goodwood clubby in the Lotus 7.

"I qualified on the third row with Jackie Stewart and Denny Hulme, half a second slower than my team-mate Jacky Ickx. The car had a rear wing that moved hydraulically when you hit the brake pedal, with a manual override switch. But after five laps the engine went, and I had to park it. I was trudging back to the pits when I beheld the shocking sight of my team-mate Chris Amon, flying over the barriers and into the trees. I was sure he'd been killed, and on top of the other crashes that year I began to feel I should get out of this racing business. But back at the pits they told me Chris was OK, so I forgot about it.

"I did a couple more GPs for Ferrari, and that winter Chris and I drove 2.4-litre versions of the Dino in the Tasman Series. It was a lovely seven weeks: Chris, me, Jochen and Graham in the Lotuses, Piers, Frank Gardner. I had some good races. Tom Wheatcroft was down there looking for cars to buy for his collection. 'Any time you need any 'elp, lad,' he said, 'give me a call.'

"My Ferrari contract covered 1969, but that was their disastrous year, crippled by strikes and financial problems. In Formula 1 they effectively only ran one car, and they more or less pulled out of F2 by mid-season. The only F1 race I did was the *Daily Express* Silverstone, when it poured with rain and our Firestones were hopeless. I finished ninth, Chris was 10th. Ferrari released me to drive the four-wheel-drive McLaren in the British Grand Prix, but that was pretty unmanageable, and broke its suspension a few laps into the race."

Twelve months on from his fairytale signing for Ferrari, Derek's career appeared to be beached. It was Tom Wheatcroft who came to his rescue. "We did the Tasman Series in 1970 with his Brabham, using a wanked-out old 2.5 DFV we bought from Lotus. The engine was rebuilt as a 3-litre and we did the Belgian GP, but the gearchange broke on the warm-up lap. Then John Surtees offered me a drive at Watkins Glen if I could supply the engine. Tom lent him the same old DFV and, even though I had to slow towards the end with a terrible transmission vibration, I was sixth – the only F1 point I ever got. But I also persuaded Tom to do an F2 season with a new BT30, run from Church Farm with Mike Earle, and we nearly won the 1970 European Championship: I won Barcelona, and I was third to Stewart and Rindt at Thruxton. It restored my confidence.

"I still wanted to be in F1, of course, and Tom and I went to see John Surtees. But Rolf Stommelen got there first with Ford Germany money, and all John could offer me was F5000, which I thought would be a step back. I drove Tom's March 701 in the Argentine GP, got up to third before that old engine broke again. And the Questor GP in the US, with a Frank Williams March. The suspension broke."

But it was a race that year at Spa which set Derek's career on a new course. Belgian Ferrari importer Jacques Swaters asked him to drive the Ecurie Francorchamps Ferrari 512S in the Spa 1000Kms. He'd never been to Spa before but, even though Derek's co-driver Hughes de Fierlandt was considerably slower, they finished eighth behind the Porsche 917s and the works Ferraris – despite the car catching fire during a refuelling stop. "I couldn't get out because the inside door wire had broken. A mechanic smashed the window with a fire extinguisher, got me out, they put the fire out, I got back in and carried on with singed eyebrows and a scorched face." Although Derek thought of himself purely as a single-seater driver at this point, Spa opened his eyes to the possibilities of sports car racing. "I was going to drive the yellow 512 at Le Mans, too, but when Ferrari offered me a works drive with Ronnie Peterson Jacques told me to take it, even though I felt I owed Ferrari nothing after the way they'd dried up on me in 1969.

"It was my first Le Mans. All the reports, and the official sheets, said I crashed, but I didn't. What happened was I was leading a group up to White House, three 512s, me, Regazzoni and Mike Parkes, all doing 170mph. We came upon Reine Wisell going slowly in his Filipinetti 512. I whistled through the gap with two wheels on the grass, and in my mirror I saw flames and carnage as Regazzoni hit Wisell, and Parkes ploughed in too. I carried on – and about a minute later my engine blew on the Mulsanne Straight. Four 512s out all at once, and of course everybody assumed I'd been in the accident too.

"After the race I stayed on at Le Mans for several months to work on the Steve McQueen film. My first wife Pam and my children Justin and Melanie joined me, and for a while we shared a house with Steve. I was stand-in for one of the actors, driving a 512 Ferrari along with Mike Parkes. Richard Attwood and David Piper were in the Porsche 917s, plus Jo Siffert, Vic Elford, quite a gang. We got $100 a day, $200 a day if it was dangerous work. We had to drive fast, to make sure it looked right. David Piper lost a leg, and I got bad facial burns when the Ferrari caught fire. So it was certainly dangerous. At weekends I'd go off and race my Wheatcroft F2 car. When my mechanic came through with the Brabham I said to Steve, 'Have a go.' He jumped in and enjoyed himself doing several laps of the Bugatti circuit.

"We all got on well because Steve wanted to be a racing driver, and none of us wanted to be movie actors, so we weren't trying to climb on his shoulders. He was a brave guy. Before the insurance company stopped him, he was driving too. Once we were doing a sequence, me in the 512, Steve in a 917, Seppi in a 917. We went through White House at 160mph nose to tail, with Steve trapped between Seppi and me so he couldn't lift off. When we got to the end of the shot and climbed out, Steve was pretty shaken up but he was smiling. Another time Seppi and I came through White House flat out and some idiot was lying on his stomach in the middle of the track with a camera. We were furious, and complained to the director John Sturges. Turned out it was Steve, trying to get a better shot.

"After I got burned I did no more filming, but then John Wyer came on the phone wanting me to test a JW Porsche 917 at Goodwood. There were three of us – Peter Gethin, Ronnie Peterson and me – and somehow I got the drive. The 917 felt hugely powerful but so easy, so light and nimble – this was 1970, remember, when they'd sorted out the early handling problems. By comparison, the Ferrari 512S was like driving a lumbering truck – although the later 512M was much better. So for 1971 I raced the 917, paired with Jo 'Seppi' Siffert. Pedro Rodríguez and Jackie Oliver were in the other JW car. Seppi and Pedro in the same team, what a pair. But they were both killed the same year. It was dreadful. So many people died in those days. It was part of the job description, going to funerals.

"Seppi was dynamic, a real street fighter. Of all the guys racing today, I think David Brabham is most like him. I was so pleased David won Le Mans this year. With Seppi I was the new boy, and he seemed to be happy with me. We won first time out at Buenos Aires, and went on to have a good season, helping Porsche win the World Championship. Seppi was very relaxed out of the car, never wanted to go testing. Pedro was more disciplined, but he could charge even harder than Seppi. Of course, they both desperately wanted to beat each other. When I got pole at Spa that year, three seconds quicker than Ickx's Ferrari, Pedro said, 'Derek, I theenk it is time you drive with me.' When Pedro was killed I moved over to be number one in his car.

"With John Wyer it was like being at school, with him as the strict headmaster, always calling you by your surname. He had all his drivers down to a tee, and we all respected him. It was Frank Gardner who called him 'Death Ray', because of the way he looked at you if you'd displeased him. But he also had a wonderfully dry, sardonic wit. I remember going to the factory one day, and I was wearing a pink shirt and jeans. 'Ah, Bell. A riot of colour again, I see.' David Yorke looked after the drivers, and he was excellent, very clear and decisive. But for 1972 David moved to Martini, to advise them on how to set about F1. His idea was for them to sponsor Brabham, and if it had come off I would've been number two to Carlos Reutemann. But Martini's link with Brabham didn't happen for three more years, because Luciano Pederzani persuaded Count Gregorio Rossi that he should back an all-Italian car. This was the disastrous flat-12 Tecno, and I ended up driving it. Trying to qualify it for its first Grand Prix at Clermont Ferrand the handling was dreadful, and they discovered that four of the nine bolts holding the chassis to the back of the monocoque had broken, so the car was bending in the middle. I only started two GPs with it, and both times the engine blew. It was a useless shitbox." Apart from an unhappy few outings with Surtees in 1974, that spelt the end of Derek's F1 ambitions.

But his sports car career blossomed. New rules outlawed the big 917 for 1972, but Derek stayed with JW, driving the Mirage M6 and its successors, and finishing fourth at Le Mans in 1974 with Mike Hailwood. In '75 his Gulf contract only tied him to Le Mans, so he did the rest of the season with Alfa Romeo in the T33-TT12s, winning at Spa, Watkins Glen and Zeltweg with his old F3 rival Pescarolo. The cars were run by Willi Kauhsen, but the substantial figure of Alfa's legendary racing boss Carlo Chiti was at every race. "Whatever the weather, he'd always wear his three-piece suit. He'd sit in the pits on a hot day in his shirt sleeves and braces, his trousers pulled up over his big gut, stuffing panini into his face, with a handkerchief on his head to keep off the sun, tied with a knot at each corner. A wonderful character."

That season's single Gulf race brought him his first Le Mans victory, with Jacky Ickx. "Jacky wrote to Wyer asking to join the team for Le Mans, and suggesting he was paired with me, which was nice. It was a nerve-wracking race, because for the last six hours the car was clattering and graunching at the back. In the pits they could find nothing wrong, but in fact a rear suspension bracket had broken. We just held on to win from the French Ligier. It was a hugely emotional moment to be on the podium. By then I understood how important Le Mans was."

In 1977 and '78 Derek did Le Mans for Renault – "a great young team, so enthusiastic. In '77 Jabouille and I led for 17 hours, but then the engine let go. Same thing in '78, but our team-mates Didier Pironi and Jean-Pierre Jaussaud won." His relationship with Porsche was renewed with a 924 at Le Mans in 1980, and for '81 he was back with Ickx for a copybook run in the Porsche 936 to score win number two. For 1982 the new 956 had arrived, and with it came win number three. It could easily have been three in a row in 1983, but this time things didn't run to plan. Ickx was taken off on lap two by Jan Lammers' private Porsche 956, but he and Derek worked back up the field to lead by 6am. Then brake discs started cracking. More time was lost but, despite inadequate and unpredictable braking, Derek staged a brilliant late charge back to second place, failing to catch their team-mates by barely a minute.

"Jacky Ickx and I developed a special relationship. Some people said he was a prima donna, but we always got on very well. People think of him as a great sports car driver, but of course he was a brilliant F1 driver as well, runner-up in the World Championship two consecutive years. The reason I liked driving with Jacky was that he was always lucky, always had this amazing good fortune. All the engineers and mechanics loved him, and because they knew he was the best they gave him the best equipment, the best effort. If you were with him you got the best too. I always wanted to be with somebody who was as good as me, if not a little bit better. Jacky was an outstanding professional, brilliant in the wet, and he always pushed the car really hard – yet he had mechanical sympathy.

"John Wyer always used to say: to be a good long-distance racer you have to have mechanical sympathy. You have to treat the car properly. Nowadays there's no worry about wheelspin and over-revving, or missed gearchanges, and they have power steering and even air conditioning. And the cars are more reliable anyway. But you still have to be able to be extremely quick without taking risks, without having accidents. I never had an accident in a works Porsche – I spun a few times, but I never lost a position through driver error. In fact, in my entire sports car career I only once went off the road. That was at Le Mans in a Rondeau: I went out with brand new tyres, forgot they weren't scrubbed in and slid off at the first chicane. But I got myself out and carried on.

"For me, the three greatest long-distance drivers I have ever known were Ickx, Hans Stuck and Al Holbert. Stucky came in when Ickx retired, and actually he was even faster than Jacky – as fast as Stefan Bellof, in my view. He's a vivacious, carefree Austrian lunatic, and he always threw the car around with gay abandon, but he never seemed to damage it. He was far more exciting to watch than anyone else in the rain. When he got pole position he'd come down the pitlane screeching and waving and yodelling with delight. But he never put a foot wrong, and he was incredibly quick.

"Al Holbert couldn't have been more different: quiet, contained, deeply religious, very well-organised and but also brilliantly fast. He was a superb engineer and a wonderful guy, head of a dealership, head of a racing team, ran an Indy operation. In September 1988 we were all in Ohio for an IMSA street race at Columbus. After Friday practice he decided to fly home to take his son to a football match. His Aerostar crashed on take-off because a door came open. He was only 41, and it was a real tragedy.

"Stefan Bellof was the fastest, wildest man I ever drove with. I always thought he would settle down, and that when he drove for Tyrrell, Ken would be able to help him mature. For the 1983 Nürburgring 1000Kms he put our car on pole with a lap in 6min 11sec, the first time anyone had averaged over 200kph around the 'Ring. In the race I handed the car over to him in the lead, and he started to go quicker and quicker. In the pits I said to Professor Bott, 'Don't you think it might be an idea to slow him down a bit?' Then we heard he'd had a massive crash at Pflanzgarten. John Wyer wouldn't have stood for something like that: it was a completely unnecessary accident. But when Stefan got back to the pits, unhurt, he laughed it off. When he had his fatal accident at Spa he was driving for Brun and he tried to pass Ickx's works car for the lead at Eau Rouge. Jacky was completely blameless – he was staying on line, and giving Stefan plenty of room coming down into La Source. But at Eau Rouge it just wasn't on."

The Porsche 956 was replaced by the 962, with more cockpit length to comply with new rules to get the driver's feet behind the axle line. "When I'm asked what was my favourite car, I have to say the 962. In Europe and America I must have won over 30 races with it, and after a bit you stopped realising how good it was – just get in it, drive it and win. It was brilliant. Add together the 956 and the 962 and I just don't know how many races I won. About 37, I suppose. Of course I loved the 917, because it had around 600 horsepower: today's cars have that and more, but they've got so much more grip. When you put your foot down in the 917 you had huge wheelspin, clouds of rubber smoke, you'd be sawing away at the wheel, always lots of drama. And in the rain you'd be going down the Mulsanne Straight with armfuls of lock on... that doesn't happen with today's cars, sadly."

Derek has done Le Mans 26 times in all. His last two victories came in 1986 and '87, both times with Stuck and Holbert, forcing the pace to break the Jaguar XJRs. One race he won't forget in a hurry was 1995. The previous year, after finishing sixth in a Kremer Porsche, he said he'd done his last Le Mans. Yet the following year he was tempted back, at three weeks' notice, to drive a McLaren GTR with his son Justin and Andy Wallace, the Harrods-sponsored car run by Dave Price Racing. The weather was dreadful: Le Mans veterans said it was the worst in the history of the race.

"Unless you've driven Le Mans at night, in heavy rain, you've no concept of what it's like. The Mulsanne Straight is a piece of cake, as long as you don't aquaplane, and the chicanes are well illuminated. But you come out of Arnage, second gear, third, fourth, fifth, over a brow and up to the Porsche Curves, and at 165mph you can't see in the dark where the track ends and the grass begins. That's the worst place. But you just have to keep the power on. That year we'd got the car into the lead, and I'd handed over to Justin at about 11.30 at night, pitch black, the rain coming down, and I hadn't been in the motorhome long when Justin walked in. 'What are you doing here?' I asked him. His eyes were big and round. He said, 'Dad, I've never been so frightened in my life.' Dave Price, to give him his due, saw Justin had scared himself, hauled him out, put Andy Wallace in. Justin felt terrible about it, but he didn't have the experience that Andy and I had. I told him, if he'd crashed it would have been the team's fault.

"During the night I did two and a half hours out there in the rain, and by 4am we were back in the lead. I got out, Andy took over, but after an hour he was back in again. He said he'd had it, he couldn't concentrate. So I took over again. I drove a lot of hours in that race. I was 53 years old, and I was knackered. During the morning it dried out, but JJ Lehto in the long-tail car couldn't get a tenth of a second off me. It really looked like we were going to win. But with two and a half hours to go I started having problems selecting gears. I had to chug out of the pits in top gear and leave it there." The lead was gone, and with it the chances of Derek's sixth Le Mans victory, although he, Justin and Andy did bring the car home third.

Derek has won the Daytona 24 Hours three times, and he believes it's more challenging than Le Mans. "The great thing about Le Mans is the Mulsanne Straight, which – even with the chicanes now – does give you a chance to relax your muscles and move your shoulders around. Daytona has nothing like that. The G-loads on the banking are punishing, and on the infield you have a sequence of very tight corners, usually crowded with cars of widely differing performance. In 1990 I had the biggest crash of my career, in a 962. We'd just refuelled, and I was high on the banking, about six feet from the wall, when a tyre burst. The car hit the wall, went up in the air and flew a long, long way. Then it came down, and carried on upside down. The top of my helmet was scraped away by the track surface. Finally it stopped, and I could smell petrol, so I switched it off and pushed the fire extinguisher button. By the time they got to me I'd passed out from the halon gas, because halon works by taking the oxygen out of the air."

So many other stories – like the Broadspeed Jaguar XJC12s, which Derek and Andy Rouse brought home to second place at the Nürburgring, by far that ill-fated car's best result. Problems and arguments within the works Porsche team, developing the PDK transmission and ABS braking. Formula 5000 in the US and Australia, and the Hexagon Penske F1 car in British events. Helping out with the three-year Bentley Speed 8 programme at Le Mans, which resulted in victory in 2003. Racing Alpine BMW CSLs, Kremer and Loos 935s, IROC Camaros.

For more than 40 years Derek Bell has earned his daily bread by campaigning an extraordinary variety of cars, and always he has believed that his first duty in any race is towards his team. "To be a successful endurance driver, you have to temper your personal ambitions with the requirements of the team. That's how it works, and you must accept that from the first." Had Derek's cards fallen differently, he might have had a great Formula 1 career. But his natural ability to work with people under pressure – team-mates, team bosses, engineers, mechanics – and to display all and more of the speed but maybe not the egotism or arrogance of some of his contemporaries, have helped him become, quite simply, the most successful Briton ever in long-distance racing. It couldn't have happened to a nicer chap.

Derek Bell was talking to Simon in July 2009.

ROSS BRAWN

The architect of intelligent
victory

Among the avalanche of tributes to Michael Schumacher on his retirement at the end of last season were several that named him the greatest racing driver of all time. I have to say that I find greatest-ever titles in motor racing pretty meaningless. Every element of the sport – cars, circuits and technology, to say nothing of levels of reward and acceptable behaviour – goes on changing down the years, so that all-time comparisons become pointless. Therefore, trying to impose some sort of absolute pecking order on the likes of Jim Clark, Tazio Nuvolari, Ayrton Senna and Stirling Moss is like comparing plum jam with tomato soup.

But there can be no argument that Schumacher, during his own era, was indeed the greatest. He won his first F1 victory at Spa in 1992, and his 91st in Shanghai 14 years later. And all through this incredible career runs a consistent thread, for on the pit wall to cheer his first win for Benetton and his last for Ferrari was the same tall, bespectacled figure. Ross Brawn has been an essential ingredient in almost every Schumacher success, and in many ways the architect of every one of his seven world titles.

Ferrari's first season in modern F1 without Schumacher will also be its first without Brawn. After 10 years with the team, Ross is having a year away from motor racing altogether. He still has a house in Italy, but we meet in the picturesque Oxfordshire village where he's had a home for many years. We lunch at his local, the Cherry Tree, where he is evidently a well-liked regular, and where the pub food includes excellent pork and leek sausage and mash.

"It's a strange experience for me, after nearly 30 years in motor racing, not to be part of the new season. But a lot of things came together which helped me decide to take a year out and indulge myself a little, recharge the batteries. Ferrari has been the most enjoyable period of my career. They're a lovely bunch of people. But after 10 years of doing the same thing, I need a new challenge. Whether I get it from Ferrari or elsewhere we'll have to see. The agreement with Luca [di Montezemolo] and Jean [Todt] is that we'll stay in touch, and in July or August we'll reach a decision. Taking a sabbatical gives me a way to leave the company gently if I choose, but also gives me the option to return. I'm open about which route I take – it could be a different job with the same team, or the same job with a different team – but I'll discuss the situation with Ferrari first. If things are running well there and there's no window for me, I'll look to see what other openings there might be.

"So yes, it could be with another team that needs to progress. A period of progression can be very exciting, whereas a period of consolidation – which is what we've had towards the end of my time with Ferrari – is, I think, less stimulating. It's not complacency, because there was never any of that at Ferrari. It's more an unwillingness to make radical change. When you're down near the back of the grid you take risks, because you've still got to prove yourself. Taking risks gets more difficult when you're winning, because you don't want to spoil things that are working well."

Was Schumacher's departure a factor in Ross' timing? "No. I decided what I wanted to do a long time ago, before the issue of Michael or Kimi [Räikkönen] came up. I saw it as my job to structure my succession, and develop the technical organisation to carry on without me. That's been going on for the last 18 months. I really started to reach my decision after we won the 2004 championship almost at a canter [that year Ferrari won 15 out of 18 rounds]. Strangely enough 2005 and 2006, much tougher years when we didn't win the championship, gave me more stimulus. From a technical point of view we get our rewards in lots of different ways. But championships are what we're after, obviously. We're very happy with lots of things from 2006, but we didn't win the championship. Renault did a better job."

Ross is clearly an utterly competitive person, just as much a racer as his star driver. "It's black and white: either you're winning or you're not. It's a horrible feeling when you're not. There are various stages of not winning: it might be because a driver makes a mistake. You can cope with that. It's frustrating, but you can come back from the race thinking we did what we should have done, and it just didn't work out.

"You get situations like at Spa in 1998 [Schumacher was leading the race by over half a minute when he ran into the back of Coulthard], races that are in the bag and you lose them for some stupid reason, and you get angry, but you don't feel frustration for yourself.

"But then you get races when you should have won and you didn't because you haven't done a good enough job, either yourself or someone in the team. If I get it wrong it goes deep, it hurts like hell. It takes me a couple of days to recover from one of those. Outwardly I have to show that we're going to sort this out, we're going to fix everything, but my wife Jean knows not to touch on the subject for a couple of days. It takes me time to come to terms with it. The problem is solved by the need to get ready for the next race, the constant rota of races which drives us all along.

"The peculiar phenomenon in Formula 1 is that we all have different cars, different engines, different drivers, different personnel, and yet the front-runners end up within a tenth of a second of each other. If all of us were working in isolation on a project to those parameters, there's no way we'd come out so close. It's impossible. The reason why we end up like that is because we're driving each other. The catalyst is when you're not fast enough, and when you are fast enough there isn't the same stimulus. You can say you're still putting in the same commitment, making the same effort to go faster. But somehow you aren't. When you're quicker you're not prepared to take as many risks. When you're behind you're pushing the boundaries harder in all the areas. The teams that are behind, provided they've got the resources, will always catch up. That's why the teams that are slower make more progress than the teams that are quicker."

By the mid-1990s Ferrari had become a team that was slower. A Ferrari driver hadn't been World Champion since the late 1970s: Williams and McLaren, and then Benetton, ruled the F1 roost. The young Michael Schumacher had joined Benetton late in 1991 just as Ross arrived, returning to F1 after designing Jaguar's all-conquering XJR-14 sports car. Schumacher was a winner by 1992, and in 1994 and 1995 he won back-to-back titles. But then he quit.

"Michael going to Ferrari was a snub. It was the team's fault that he left. I was totally focused on Benetton. We were a team, Michael, Rory [Byrne, the chassis designer] and me. Then one day Flavio [Briatore] walked in and said, 'Michael's going to Ferrari.' We'd just won two World Championships, we were the strongest team, and Michael was leaving. It was quite difficult for me to come to terms with it. I talked to Michael about it later: there were some problems between him and Flavio, some things which Flavio had done. To be honest, it's the same with Fernando Alonso now – it's illogical for him to have left Renault, but he's left. So why?

"Then I had my own problems with Benetton. At the end of 1995 I'd agreed to stay, on condition that I got total responsibility over the whole engineering side. Flavio agreed to that, but ultimately he didn't implement it. F1 is pretty incestuous, and Michael got to hear I wasn't happy. At the same time, he wasn't happy with the technical structure at Ferrari either. Just before Monaco in 1996 I got a call from Willi Weber, asking if I'd like a chat. That's how it started."

So the initial approach to join Ferrari actually came from their driver's manager. Is that a measure of the power that Schumacher was already wielding at Maranello?

"Well, at Benetton Michael was only a driver: a top-class driver, a winner, but not as deeply integrated into the team as he became at Ferrari, because he'd come into a team that already had a structure. When he arrived at Ferrari the team was at sea; they were looking for some reference points, and Michael was a very good reference point.

"But in the middle and later stages of the Ferrari renaissance Michael always worked through me and Jean, the two senior people. He respected the structure we had. His influence never had a divisive effect, because it came through the proper channels. He'd sit with me or Jean or Rory and give his point of view. He always had a good contribution to make, but he never got stroppy if we didn't choose the path he proposed.

"At Ferrari everybody knew they had the opportunity to contribute to the conclusions we were trying to reach. Take tyre choice for a race: that was always very complicated. I'd chair a committee where all the different elements would present their views. The test team would set out their data, so would the race team, the vehicle dynamics guys, the tyre specialists, we'd have Rory there too. Then I'd decide which was the strongest argument for which tyre choice. And the great thing was that everyone then supported that decision, even if it wasn't their proposal, because they knew they'd been part of the process. Michael always knew that his opinion had been properly heard and properly considered, and if it hadn't been adopted he knew there was a good reason. He's an intelligent guy. It was never: 'I'm Michael Schumacher, I want this'. That was never in his vocabulary. That's how he became a much more integrated, intrinsic part of the team than he had been at Benetton."

What about the role of Michael's team-mates at Ferrari – Eddie Irvine, Rubens Barrichello, Felipe Massa – and controversial races like the 2002 Austrian GP, when Barrichello reluctantly obeyed an order to move aside and allow Schumacher to win?

"The only *contractual* advantage Michael ever had over his team-mate was that he had first call on the spare car, and because of rule changes the spare car has not been an issue in recent years. But we would always take a decision in a race that we felt was best for

Ferrari. Those decisions tended to favour Michael, because he was in the best position to win the championship – but it was never a case of Michael is the No 1 driver, so he has to get this or that.

"We had some difficult times with Rubens, who gave Michael quite a hard time competitively during his six seasons with us. If Rubens had been 20 points ahead of Michael in the championship, it would have been logical for all the strategy decisions to favour him. But it never occurred.

"That race in Austria caused a furore. But you have to remember that at that stage in the championship Michael had 44 points to Rubens' six points, and of course we wanted to maximise Michael's chances of the title. Championships have been lost in the past by a single point. We asked Rubens several laps before the end to concede position, but he wouldn't until the last few hundred metres. These things are all discussed beforehand in the calm of the motorhome, so Rubens knew the score.

"But he's a passionate guy, he was leading the race, and I can understand how he felt. Three races later [by which time Schumacher's championship was almost, but not quite, clinched] we let Rubens lead Michael home in Germany."

Today, Formula 1 races are all about strategy – thinking through every permutation of weather, tyres, fuel and safety-car, and second-guessing other teams' plans too. Ross Brawn is the acknowledged master of this multi-layered game of poker, and his intellectual approach has helped Ferrari to win five Drivers' Championships and five Constructors' Championships in 10 years. We're all familiar with the mid-race TV close-ups of Brawn talking on the radio to Schumacher and, we assume, dictating race strategy on the hoof as a race pans out. But Ross maintains that most of it is envisaged beforehand.

"More and more situations are covered by the computer models and simulations that we work up. We plan for almost every eventuality, because I want to avoid having to make a major decision on the pit wall. I hate those situations when you've suddenly got to pull something out of thin air. If possible, everything's got to be thought through, and every circumstance pre-conceived.

"In the pre-race briefing at Magny-Cours in 2004 Luca Baldisseri, who works on our strategies, said, 'Look, I've got this idea about four pitstops, and it doesn't actually look stupid. It's no faster than three, but it could actually work.' So we looked at how it could be introduced into the race.

"Early in the race we had the fastest car, but we were stuck behind Alonso, and we couldn't use our advantage. On the pit wall I said to Luca, 'Sod it, I'm not going to let him stay stuck like this. Let's do something exciting.' Michael is the guy to make these things work, because he spends time with you and understands what you're on about. So I said to him on the radio, 'Michael, we're getting bored here. We're going to have a go at something.' He knew it was a long shot, but the race came to us and we had the reward."

Magny-Cours has a short pitlane, and its approach bypasses the tight final corner, so pit stops are less costly than at most circuits. Michael's four stops separated him from Alonso, on a lighter fuel load. When Ross demanded a string of qualifying-speed laps to build up enough cushion for the extra stop, Michael delivered. Alonso was beaten by 8.3 seconds.

During a race, what would Ross talk about to Michael? "The systems are quite good now, but they're not 100 per cent. That's why you still see pit boards because – assuming the driver reads them – they are the only 100 per cent system available. The main thing Michael wanted to know was how the race around him was developing, because he was in a little cocoon so he couldn't see the whole environment. Lots of times we'd be giving him targets, telling him how he needed to drive, whether he could consolidate his position or whether he had to push. And we'd talk about what the car was doing and what he, and we, could do to improve it. He was always very active in his discussion with his engineer during a race, and he would do a lot of work with the car because we had lots of adjustable controls that he could play with, plus things we could adjust when he came in, like tyre pressures or wing angle. He could talk to his vehicle engineer, his race engineer and me, and I would be listening in to all of it on both cars."

So being an F1 driver today demands, as well as everything else, high intelligence? "Yes. That's the new era of race drivers. Michael was the first to make that step, and he made the step because he had the ability to do it. It's being able to drive the car on the limit and still have some spare brain capacity to do other things at the same time. As things evolve, the successful drivers will not just be quick. More and more they'll be the ones who can combine that range of skills – really understanding a race, and how to work to get the best from a car. I get the impression that Alonso is in that category.

"Whenever Michael had a new team-mate, he always made them raise their game. They saw the way he worked and learned to follow it. Rubens made great progress when he joined Ferrari, and Massa has too: commitment, approach, fitness. You don't go back to the hotel at six o'clock on Saturday, you stay there with the engineer who's trying to improve the situation."

But Michael did on occasion make mistakes – the aforementioned collision lapping Coulthard at Spa, for example, or his extraordinary behaviour in qualifying at Monaco in 2006. Did he apologise when something was his fault? "The culture in F1 is that you don't apologise for something you've done. If a mechanic cocks up or a wheel stop goes wrong, or if the driver hits the wall, or I make a wrong call in a race, everyone knows you've got it wrong and that's enough. It's not done to go around the crew and say sorry. If Michael made a mistake he'd be very angry, very frustrated. And he'd come back for the next race very quiet, very determined, not jovial, not having a laugh with the guys like he normally did, but totally focused on the race because he wanted to redress the balance. He didn't say anything, but you knew he was thinking, 'I'll make it up to you now.'"

Ross' father worked for Firestone, and he was taken to races from a young age. "I raced karts when I was very young, but I was never much good. There's nothing worse than having the spirit without the faculties to achieve it. Then my father got me involved in slot-car racing, which was quite big in the '60s and '70s, and I raced them all over Europe, won some championships. It was a technical art developing those cars. They weighed three or four ounces and would do 60 or 70mph, so the aerodynamics were quite significant.

"I did a mechanical engineering apprenticeship at the Atomic Energy Research Establishment at Harwell, and then I saw an advertisement in the local paper for a job at Williams. I did a year there as a machinist, but the team was so small that when they discovered I could do other things I did a bit of everything. Frank was having some difficulties and sold out to Walter Wolf, so I left and worked for a season as an F3 mechanic. Then Frank called to say he was back on his feet with Patrick, and was forming a new team. That was in the old carpet warehouse at Didcot. When I joined Frank Williams Grand Prix Engineering there were 11 staff, including me. Today Ferrari's F1 operation is 1000 people.

"I'd been interested in model aircraft, so I understood a bit about aerodynamics. So when Williams started a wind-tunnel programme I got involved almost by default. I found it fascinating. I had a lot of help from Dr John Harvey at Imperial College, who spent more time than he should have done in their wind tunnel showing me how things worked. I'm still in touch with John, He finds us the occasional third-year student he thinks we should take a look at, and every couple of years we take an Imperial College student into Ferrari.

"The Williams years were very formative. We didn't really know what we were doing, but no-one else did either, so we produced a competitive car. After seven years at Williams I went to the Carl Haas Force team. It wasn't a successful project, but it did stretch me; I did the aerodynamics and bodywork. When they folded I went to Arrows for 1987. This was another step into the unknown, because suddenly I was responsible for the whole car. In 1988 we were equal fourth in the Constructors' Championship with Derek Warwick and Eddie Cheever.

"Then Tom Walkinshaw asked me to join the Jaguar sports car programme. We did the first sports car of its generation to use full F1 technology, because some of the engineers I drew into the project had been involved in F1, and our thinking was F1. We looked at the rules and, unlike F1 where you can't be very aggressive technically, there was this formula which had some constraints but was basically incredibly open. It was a playground for us, and we won the World Sports Car Championship in 1991.

"The XJR-14 was the last time I designed a complete racing car because, when I moved back into F1 with Benetton, Rory Byrne took a large part of that responsibility. In the early days at Benetton Rory would do the basic concept and I would help him, but as the team expanded he was happy with that role and I moved more into the engineering and racing side.

"In sports car racing, strategy was a key part of things, but in F1 it was only just getting started then. When I returned to F1 I was amazed how poorly some of the teams used the pit stops to work for them strategically. In 1994 we were often able to beat Williams through simple strategic moves. The fuel rigs were much slower then. We knew we could stay with them carrying 10 more kilos of fuel, and we'd stop at the same time as them but we'd have more fuel left so we could put less in. So our pit stop would be a couple of seconds quicker than theirs and we'd come out in front. All sorts of accusations went flying around, and our fuel cells were stripped three or four times that season. But the calculations were quite simple. It was just something we were more familiar with, because of sports car racing.

"Clever moves can lead to protests, and I got a bit of a reputation, unfortunately. The one I feel aggrieved about was Imola 1994, the traction control issue. The rest you can argue were all about interpretation of regulations and so on, but in 1994 we were simply accused of cheating. The FIA had our ECUs [electronic control units] examined by an outside firm, who found some redundant features that referred back to 1993. All the race data from Imola was available, and it showed no sign of traction control or launch control being used. The menu didn't have those options on it, so although they still existed in the software they could not be activated. All the FIA said was, 'We agree it wasn't being used, but it was there.'

"It was all ensnared in the huge political row going on between Max Mosley and Flavio and Tom, who'd written a letter to the FIA saying Max wasn't fit to be president. Then Flavio said to Rory and me, 'We're going to concede this one, because all Max is going to do is take away our points from Imola.' And I said, 'If you do that deal I will walk out the door, and so will Rory, because we haven't done anything wrong. You won't have a technical director or a chief designer.' So he had to go back to Max and say, 'We'll fight the case, because my guys won't accept a deal.'

"That was the tragedy of traction control: it was like drugs in athletics. Whichever team did well, there was always the innuendo that they had some system that couldn't be detected. All a team principal had to do was have a quiet word in a journalist's ear: 'We hear they've got traction control...' Yet when they made traction control legal and everybody started using it again, the same teams were winning, the same teams were losing. So either everybody had it before, or nobody had it before.

"The more open a formula is, the more stimulating it is technically. I believe that budgetary constraint on Formula 1 has to come from commercial viability, and nothing else. We've frozen the engines, we've got a control tyre, so Ferrari's approach is going to be how to divert those funds that have been saved into other technologies to get a performance advantage. It won't necessarily reduce the overall spend. That's why everyone is building two wind tunnels. When the only variable left is aerodynamics, all the money will be ploughed into that."

Ross believes that F1 can enhance its relevance to the outside world by accelerating technological initiatives for the greater economic and ecological good. "The pressures of F1 mean that things get developed very quickly, but I don't think regenerative braking will wash – I can see it working in town traffic, but it won't help much in a motorway cruise situation. My proposal for F1 is an efficiency formula, where the only constraint is the fuel flow rate. You can use any engine you like, because if the fuel is constrained you'll eke out every ounce of energy. So clever use of energy will win races. We'd probably go for a very small turbocharged engine."

The day after our lunch, Ross and Jean are off to Argentina on a fishing trip. Fishing is a passion for Ross, along with gardening and classic cars. He has a pair of Jaguars, an AC Ace, a 300SL and three beautiful Ferraris: a 275GTB, a Daytona and his "company car", a 430. "But I couldn't turn my back on motor racing and just go fishing and play with my cars. My life needs the stimulus of F1, its energy, its motivation, its structure.

"While I'm away from racing I'm going to miss the adrenalin. During the last couple of races in 2006 I was fitted up with a heart monitor, because Ferrari has a physio who likes to monitor these things. He started with the drivers and then moved on to the rest of the team. In Japan, when Michael was leading, we were in a strong position, and my pulse was 120. The very moment his engine failed – the moment we effectively lost the championship – it dropped to 90. You could plot the exact second it happened from the trace of my pulse. When they say your heart sinks, that's exactly what happens."

So Ross will recharge his batteries this year: catch fish, do the garden, drive his classic cars. But that won't make his pulse race. The lure of Formula 1, which has ensnared him for three decades, remains. Wearing a red uniform or not, Ross Brawn will be back.

Ross Brawn was talking to Simon in February 2007.

DAVID COULTHARD

From karts to TV, a lifetime
in racing

Let's deal with the statistics first. David Coulthard's 13 Formula 1 victories never won him the world title, but he was runner-up in 2001, and took third place in the table no fewer than four times. In his 247 Grands Prix he finished on the podium 62 times – a remarkable hit rate of 25 per cent. And, until the new scoring system came in for 2010, his career total of 535 championship points was more than any other British driver in F1 history.

But mere figures paint an inadequate picture of the intelligent, thoughtful racing driver known to everybody in the sport as DC. Since 1995 he has lived in Monaco – his long career in modern F1 has put him well into the multi-millionaire bracket – and for 10 years one of his business interests was a hotel chain which included the posh Hotel Columbus in Monte Carlo. He sold it last year but still uses it for meetings, and that's where we sit down to a healthy lunch of pumpkin soup, sea bass with plenty of spinach and green beans, and mineral water.

He's 40 now, still wiry and slender, still lantern-jawed. "When I was in F1 I would do cardio every morning, cycling hard around the mountains, then in the afternoon a couple of hours in the gym, mixed with swimming in the sea in the summer and skiing in the winter, based at my chalet in Switzerland. Today I still train, but it has to fit in around everything else. In fact I'm lighter than I was – F1 neck muscles weigh heavy – but I'm racing in DTM now, and those cars are hard work. The cockpit heat is high, and you lose a lot of fluid in the car."

David admits that as a karting youngster he became obsessed by his weight, getting on the scales several times a day and swimming or skipping for an hour to burn off every increase, even making himself vomit if he thought he'd eaten too much. His father ran the family transport business from the little Scottish village of Twynholm, near Kirkcudbright, and with an elder brother and a younger sister he had a happy middle-class childhood. He was karting seriously by the age of 11, and success came quickly, with three Scottish Junior titles and then a punishing schedule all over the British Isles: leave school on Friday afternoon, into the motorhome with his parents and helpers, drive all night, a hard weekend's racing at one of the circuits down in England, back up the M6 during Sunday night and back at school on Monday morning. Monday evening clean out the motorhome, Tuesday evening strip and clean the kart, Wednesday evening clean the helmet and leathers, Thursday evening pack up the motorhome again in time to hit the road on Friday evening. It left no time for kicking a football around with his mates and all the other things normal kids do.

"But I never felt I was missing out on anything. It gave me something extra, a discipline at an early age, a focus, I spent hours ensuring my kart and turnout were spotlessly clean, and I kept a notebook in which I recorded every race I did, giving myself marks out of 10. I never gave myself a 10, even if I'd won all my races that weekend, because in my mind I felt I'd made a small mistake or missed an opportunity somewhere. I always thought I could have done better. I suppose it showed I had the right make-up. There were probably better drivers than me, but driving is only one element. There's also preparation, determination, resilience – the ability to pick yourself up when things go against you. I was learning all those lessons. Crucial in this was Dave Boyce, who tuned my karts, but also gave me a lot of guidance. He's a legendary figure in karting: he looked after Allan McNish before me, and now he's helping young Harry Newey, Adrian's son."

As David progressed up the karting ladder he raced all over Europe, and even in Australia. "When my father said it was time to move up to Formula Ford I was reluctant. I was comfortable in the karting environment, and I needed to be pushed into the next one. At first FFs seemed soggy and imprecise after karts, but in the end I really enjoyed it. Like Allan McNish before me and Dario Franchitti after me, I came under the wing of the Leslies, father David and son David. It was a wonderful way to take my first steps into the world of car racing. I'd travel to their base in Carlisle, work on my car, go testing with them. Father David was a man of few words, but what he did say meant a lot. Son David's death in 2008 in that tragic air crash with Richard Lloyd was just a dreadful, dreadful thing."

David's first car season was pretty sensational. As well as having the most highly polished car and the shiniest helmet on the grid, he scored 22 wins out of 28 starts, winning both the Star of Tomorrow and P&O Ferries titles, and then scooping the first McLaren/*Autosport* Young Driver award. He was still only 18. "That first year the Autosport Award wasn't a proper shoot-out, it was just decided by a judging panel, and if I'd had six or seven other young drivers to compete against it might have been a different story. I was still a naïve lad from a Scottish village, very shy, very green. The first time I took a flight alone, from Glasgow to London, I came down the escalator at Heathrow in my little sports jacket and tie thinking, what is this big scary world? Some 18-year-olds are street-smart, they've been ducking and diving for years, but that wasn't me. I took time to adapt.

"Then Jackie Stewart phoned up with an offer to join Paul Stewart Racing. Jackie was tremendously helpful to me, and he, Helen, Paul, Mark, they're all close friends to this day. But I didn't have a good first year with PSR. I was in Formula Vauxhall Lotus, and I lacked maturity and experience: I no longer had my family around me, plus I had a very smart team-mate in Gil de Ferran. At Spa I got nudged into the barrier and was hit by another car, which broke my leg. That's the only time I ever missed races because of injury. When they cut off my overalls in the medical centre, with Jackie and my parents looking on, my lucky underpants were exposed to view, which was hugely embarrassing. I'm not particularly superstitious, but since my karting days whenever I won I seemed to be wearing a particular pair of pants. So I'd taken to wearing them for every race. By now they were full of holes, and no longer doing the job underpants are meant to do. After that I stopped wearing my lucky pants, but I have to admit I continued to take them to every race, in a little black bag along with a four-leaf clover somebody gave me, and a gold coin. Years later, when I was at McLaren, somebody was getting my stuff together for me, discovered the pants and threw them away. Just as well, probably.

"In 1991 I was doing F3 for PSR and battled with Rubens Barrichello for the championship. In the final round I tried a half-hearted move on Hideki Noda and he turned in and bent my front wing, and I lost the championship on that. It was silly, because I could have passed him later. But I won more races than Rubens, including the F3 Masters at Zandvoort and Macau, which meant a lot on that round-the-houses circuit against really international opposition.

"My year in Formula 3000 with PSR, 1992, was terrible. We tested well all winter, but in the races our Judd engines never seemed very strong, and the results weren't there. PSR wanted over £500,000 for 1993, and there was no way I could raise that, so I went to Pacific, a much lower-budget set-up. I had to go round borrowing bits from Reynard and Cosworth. I was still shy and no way was I a hustler, so that was difficult for me. But I won at Enna, and going into the last round I was in the running for the title. But the throttle pedal broke on the first lap. That left me third in the championship.

"Also in 1993, I got a last-minute call from Tom Walkinshaw to do the Le Mans 24 Hours in one of his Jaguar XJ220s, with David Brabham and John Nielsen. During a pitstop the car fell off its jack onto David's foot, so it was down to John and me to do the rest of the race. I was used to driving flat-out everywhere, but we had to hold to a set lap time to conserve fuel, plus we had a gearbox problem. I found it quite boring, because I was too young to appreciate the opportunity and the history of it all. But we won the GT class and had the podium thing, with the crowds and the British flags waving for Jaguar. So I always say I won Le Mans, and only if you push me do I admit it wasn't an overall win! We were disqualified a week later anyway, because Tom had left the catalytic converter off the car. But I've still got the trophy.

"By now I was doing F1 testing for Williams, working with the driver I'd always admired most, Alain Prost. That winter I tested with Williams' new signing, Ayrton Senna, and later with Nigel Mansell. I had so much respect for those guys, it was a case of 'speak when you're spoken to', but it was fascinating to watch how they worked. Prost would be out of the car after every run, having an espresso and talking to the engineers. Nigel was all about setting a time and then heading for the golf course. Ayrton wanted to get into absolutely everything, every smallest detail. Our first test together he did a couple of days and I was told to turn up for the third day. When I got there early he was already there, so I thought he'd decided to do the third day after all. But he just wanted to listen to what I thought of the car, to know if my impressions accorded with his. I was going to be testing a lot of elements with the car, and he wanted to know whether he could trust my judgement. Once he felt comfortable with that, he left.

"My time with Williams taught me how to approach testing for the rest of my career. In those days we did massive amounts of testing and, whenever there was a test, I wanted to be in the car. For two reasons: I wanted to influence its development myself, and I wanted to stop somebody else getting in and showing potential.

"For 1994 my F3000 ride was with Vortex, run by Ronnie Meadows: he's team manager at Mercedes F1 these days. By now I had no money left. The first round was at Silverstone on May Bank Holiday Monday, and I qualified third and finished second. But we had no budget for round two, so my season would have run into the sand after that. But that weekend Ayrton Senna was killed at Imola, and the world changed.

"By now I'd done a lot of testing with Williams, I was familiar with the car and the team. I'd done it for nothing in 1993, and in '94 they were paying me £20,000. At Monaco, two weeks after Ayrton's death, they ran a single car for Damon [Hill] and then they summoned me to Jerez for a test. The press were touting Patrese, Barrichello, Comas, even Johnny Herbert for the drive, and I turned up at Jerez expecting lots of them to be there. But it was only Damon and me. And, just as Frank Williams arrived, I crashed the car. There was a silly little tyre chicane where Martin Donnelly had his accident, and I clipped it, spun into the gravel and damaged the rear wing. That's blown that, I thought. But back in the garage Frank said, 'I'm not going to hold that against you. I'm here to tell you you're driving for us in Barcelona next weekend.' The deal was on a race-by-race basis shared with Nigel Mansell, who had an Indy contract. I was paid £5000 per race – not what you'd expect to get as a Grand Prix driver, but of course I didn't care about that. I was just delighted to have the drive. I learned later from Julian Jakobi, Ayrton's manager, that Ayrton told Frank and Patrick [Head] he liked what he'd seen of me as a test driver, and said, 'This guy needs an opportunity.'

"All my testing had been in the '93 car, and in Barcelona there was a drivers' strike and Friday practice didn't happen. So qualifying was my first run in the FW16, and it certainly felt more difficult to drive. I qualified ninth, and I was running sixth when an electronics problem put me out. In Canada I finished fifth: I got terrible cramp in my back and lost all feeling in my right foot, so I wasn't very strong there. Mansell was in the car for France, and at Silverstone I finished the race stuck in sixth gear, but got in the points again. During that race my radio crackled into life: 'Dave?' 'Yes?' I shouted, waiting for a key piece of strategic info from the pitwall. 'Dave, can you do a 2.30 pick-up at Towcester?' Somehow a local mini-cab firm's radio had got onto the Williams frequency...

"By the time we got to Monza, my seventh race, I was starting to go well. I wanted to secure my place in the team, Damon wanted to win the championship, so our approaches were different. He must have been under immense psychological pressure: he was 10 years older than me, a family man, he'd been number two to Prost, number two to Senna, he'd seen his team leader killed, and now here was a young team-mate showing no respect. Well, not that, because I like to think I showed respect to all my team-mates, but a young team-mate on a different agenda. My engineer, whom I'd inherited from Senna, was David Brown, who'd engineered Mansell and Prost to title wins. When I arrived at Monza I was told that my engineer was now John Russell, because Damon had insisted that, as number one driver, he should have the number one engineer. It wasn't a problem for me, because John was also an excellent engineer. Anyway, at Monza I was leading after the mid-race pitstops and I got the call on the radio to move over for Damon. I didn't think he was close enough, but of course he was challenging Michael Schumacher for the title – Schumacher was serving a two-race ban at that point – so I did as I was told. Then my car ran out of fuel in the Parabolica on the last lap.

"I was second to Damon in Portugal, having led, and then for the last three races Mansell came back. I was in the TV commentary box at Jerez when he spun, and [BBC director] Mark Wilkin tells the story that when I saw him in the gravel I found it hard to contain my delight."

That October, as David was negotiating a two-year deal with Williams for 1995/6, Ron Dennis made a determined approach to get him to McLaren. Then, just as the Williams contract was about to be signed, Frank Williams reduced his offer to one year. Disappointed, David signed a letter of intent with McLaren, and Frank referred the matter to the Contracts Recognition Board in Geneva. The upshot was that David remained with Williams for 1995, on a retainer of £500,000, but committed to McLaren for 1996/7 at roughly four times as much per year. "My racing career up to that point had saddled me with about £300,000 of personal debt, and my father's overdraft with his local branch of the Bank of Scotland had to be cleared. I really needed to get things balanced out." At this point he decided to move from a shared house in Chiswick to become a Monaco resident.

The 1995 season, David's only full year with Williams, brought him his first victory at Estoril – with pole and fastest lap – plus seven podiums. "I felt I fitted in well there. Frank is a remarkable individual. I never knew him before his accident, but the way he leads the organisation, makes the decisions that he does, his focus and clarity of thought, is extraordinary. I always found him straightforward to deal with, and I had enormous respect for him. His sense of humour can be disconcerting: he said to me once, pointing to his feet, 'You as a Scotsman will appreciate this. I've made this pair of shoes last me 15 years.' It amused him that I looked shocked when he said that. And Patrick I loved working with, because he has so much energy and enthusiasm. With Patrick there's no such thing as a discreet conversation. He'd come up and boom: 'Keep this to yourself, David,' and his voice would carry through office doors or across the garage."

So for 1996 David found himself in the very different atmosphere of McLaren, where he was to remain for nine seasons. For six of them his team-mate was Mika Häkkinen. When David arrived Mika, after five years in F1, had yet to win a Grand Prix, and was just recovering from his dreadful accident in Adelaide. "There's no question that Mika was the favoured son at McLaren. Ron Dennis is an honourable man and utterly loyal, to his team and to the people in his organisation. But I think he's better at the honeymoon than the marriage. Within a team you can give both your drivers equal equipment in every way, but if one is given a little bit more psychological support it does make a difference. I'm only human, and it did erode my self-confidence. You need to be in an environment that allows you to perform to your ultimate.

"You could argue that Ron made the right judgement, because Mika won the team two World Championships, and maybe he was less susceptible to variations in performance during a season than I was. But you couldn't have argued that with me while I was there. After all, it was me that broke McLaren's long drought. They'd gone 49 Grands Prix without a victory until I won in Melbourne in 1997, and then I won again in Monza. When Mika finally did win in Jerez, it was only because I was told to move over for him, which at the time I was very unhappy about. To be honest, my personal preference would be to drive for a single-car team, so that all the energy within the team can be used positively. Whenever you have a World Championship battle fought out between team-mates – like Senna and Prost at McLaren, Mansell and Piquet at Williams – it's destructive.

"That's why Fernando Alonso left McLaren at the end of 2007. Some thought he behaved like a spoiled child, but I admire him for having the strength of character to leave. He joined the team believing he'd be the number one and the whole team would be behind him, and suddenly Lewis was the rising star and Fernando felt like a sort of negative distraction.

"As an individual Mika was very clever. He realised early on that the less you say, the less you have to explain afterwards. He would never publicly be involved in any controversy, he kept his thoughts to himself and didn't expend energy unnecessarily. He was incredibly energy-efficient. While we were team-mates it was very much a cool business relationship. We both lived in Monaco, we'd leave at the same time for each GP, get in our separate private aircraft, take off, land within minutes of each other, then go in separate cars to the circuit. It wasn't because we had a bad relationship, it was just what we did. We had a couple of disagreements down the years which I see as the normal sporting speed-bumps that you have, but we never actually fell out. Now we get on really well as neighbours; in fact we share an office down here with [Häkkinen's long-time manager] Didier Coton, and we do a number of things together.

"Financially I was a lot better off at McLaren than at Williams, of course, but from sitting on the Adelaide front row in November '95 to 13th on the Melbourne grid in March '96, that was when the penny dropped that I'd opted for money over performance. There was a lot of unreliability at McLaren then, and I seemed to pick up more of it than Mika." So David's first season with Ron's team was fairly fruitless. But the next year, helped by those wins in Australia and Italy, he was third in the championship, two positions ahead of Mika. By now Adrian Newey had arrived from Williams, and the first McLaren that was entirely his own project, the MP4/13, was devastatingly quick for 1998.

There was more controversy in Melbourne, when three laps from the end David was again ordered to move aside for Mika, who'd lost the lead after mishearing an instruction to pit. "Two races later, in Argentina, I put it on pole, led from the start, and Schumacher got inside me at the hairpin, hit me and spun me round. I have a photograph of the incident on my office wall, and Michael has all four wheels on the grass. I said to him afterwards, 'You were off the track.' He said, 'No I wasn't.' He won the race, I got going again and finished sixth."

Then at Spa, when Schumacher was leading in heavy rain and David was running well down after earlier problems, the Ferrari crashed into the back of the McLaren and tore off a front wheel. "A lot of people still think that was a deliberate attempt by McLaren to finger his race, but we weren't that devious, or that smart to work out exactly where he was on the track. It was raining hard, visibility was bad, and I knew he was about to lap me, so I moved off-line and lifted off, which was when he hit me. After the race he came storming into my pit, with little Jean Todt and Stefano Domenicali trying to restrain him, shouting, 'You tried to f***ing kill me!' It was nonsense, of course, and it's the only time I can remember Schumacher losing his cool. At Monza two weeks later we shook hands in front of the cameras, and then we talked about it in private. He still said it was my fault, so I remarked, 'Michael, have you ever been wrong?' His reply was, 'Well, not that I remember.'"

All of which made David's win in the French GP in 2000 all the sweeter. "Michael and I were first and second on the grid, and I got away better than him, so he turned across me, chopped me. I had to come right off the throttle." David recovered, got past Rubens in the other Ferrari and then caught and passed Schumacher to lead. After the stops the Ferrari was back in front, but the McLaren was soon challenging. "I got alongside him at the hairpin and he drove me off the road. I was as angry as I've ever been in a racing car. I got alongside him again a few laps later and we banged wheels, but I got the job done. I gave him the finger from the cockpit – which was a bit ridiculous, because he couldn't see me from where he was sitting, but it made a good photo. Michael was a lot more aggressive than other drivers have been – you could say Senna was cut from the same cloth – but there are rules for a reason and you have to follow them. I'm always getting on my high horse about driving ethics, and there may be times when I've done things people don't agree with. But driving standards, sporting conduct, call it what you will, all that was important to me.

"Actually, I've got two of Michael's helmets. He has a helmet collection, and in 2006 he asked to swap signed helmets with me. And in '96 at Monaco I had a problem with my visor misting up, and we have the same-sized heads, so he lent me his spare. Look at a picture of me at Monaco that year and you'll see I'm wearing Schuey's helmet, with the sponsors' stickers covered up.

"McLaren were a hugely innovative team. The second brake pedal, for example: it was on the 1998 car and nobody knew about it until a photographer, Darren Heath, popped his camera into the cockpit after Mika had stopped on the circuit and walked away. It allowed you to work one rear brake individually, selecting left or right with a solenoid switch, so in a corner it could help turn the car, the way a tank turns. It was tricky to use, because you had to power through it, accelerate at the same time, otherwise it could flick the car sideways. Mika and I never discussed it, but we ended up using it independently: you could see it on the data. We used it all the time, even coming out of hairpins to control wheelspin. McLaren's technology and innovative thinking were on another level from Williams."

David never owned his own aircraft, but during his F1 career he usually travelled by chartered executive jet. On May 2, 2000 he was flying from Farnborough to Nice in an eight-seat Lear 45 with his girlfriend Heidi, his trainer Andy Matthews and Heidi's Maltese terrier, plus a crew of two pilots. Over France the plane had an engine failure and diverted to Lyon. The emergency landing did not go well and the plane crashed heavily and caught fire. Both pilots were killed. Somehow David, Heidi and Andy escaped the burning wreckage with only minor injuries, and the dog survived too. Two days later David was in Barcelona for the Spanish GP. With broken ribs he qualified fourth, and finished second to Mika -- only after being chopped again by Schumacher when he got alongside him on the pit straight. He passed the Ferrari a lap later.

"It sounds silly, but all through my teens I never thought I'd live past 30. I didn't necessarily think I'd die in a racing car, I just thought something would get me. So when I was sitting in the plane aged 29 and two months and it was going down, I thought, well, there you go. Not until I was in bed in my apartment in Monaco that night did it really hit me. After that dreadful experience I did think, briefly, about reshaping my life altogether, but – and this is where Ron Dennis showed his true colours – he was just fantastic, very protective, very understanding. The next day we went to his house in Mougins, north of Cannes. He had a medical specialist check us over and a physio, and he said it was up to me whether or not I raced in Barcelona. But there was never any doubt in my mind.

"Ron never lets his drivers keep any trophy they win, it's a contractual obligation that they all go back to McLaren. But after I finished second Heidi said to Ron, 'You should let David keep that trophy.' Ron couldn't bring himself to give it to me, because that would have created a precedent, but he gave it to Heidi, who gave it to me. For all the others I had to get replicas made."

At the end of 2004, after nine seasons, McLaren replaced David with Juan Pablo Montoya. "At the time I was struggling with one-lap qualifying, and maybe I'd been with the team too long." But the Columbian's time with the team lasted only a season and a half before he left F1 for NASCAR. David refers to Montoya as "the chubby little fella" and keeps his affection for him well under control. "As a competitor he wasn't always respectful of others. But I'm sure he's a wonderful chap, and that he'll make lots of money, live his life, be happy and put on more weight...

"When I knew I was out of McLaren I wanted to remain in F1. I felt I had more to offer, but I wasn't going to stay at any cost. I talked to Frank Williams and Sam Michael, and I was already negotiating with Jaguar when Red Bull took it over. So I met with [Red Bull boss] Dietrich Mateschitz. He told me what he wanted to achieve and what his financial commitment was; I told him where I was at, and how I thought I could help with the team beyond just driving. Then we shook hands. He is a remarkable guy. He delivered on everything he said he would, and I believe I delivered on everything I said I would. I knew Christian Horner from karting – he'd come along a couple of years behind me – and I'd seen what he'd done with his F3000 team.

"In Red Bull's first race, Melbourne 2005, I was fourth, and the hug Christian gave me when I got back to the pits – I don't think I've ever been hugged so enthusiastically. In '06 we had a lot of car problems, particularly with the cooling system, but I got the team its first podium at Monaco. And I got involved in a lot more than just the driving. Adrian Newey was on Christian's hit list of people he wanted to bring into the team, but as Adrian and I had worked together so much I made the initial contact.

"One race I won't forget was Fuji 2007. I'd never been frightened in a racing car, but that was scary. You were driving into opaque balls of spray with no way of knowing what was inside. Visibility was zero. The standing water was shocking too, rivers running across the track, and when the race started behind the safety car most of the drivers were of the same mind. We were on our radios saying, 'You can't run this.' Massa and Räikkönen spun on their way to the grid. Alonso, Wurz, Vettel, Webber, Heidfeld, they all went off. I started 18th and finished fourth, which was my best result that season, and I was proud of it. Colin McRae had died two weeks earlier in a helicopter crash with his son Johnny, and the memorial service was that day, so I raced wearing one of his helmets. I got all the F1 drivers to sign it and sent it to [Colin's wife] Alison as a mark of respect from all of us."

David's last F1 podium came in Canada in 2008, and that November in Brazil he raced his 247th and final Grand Prix. "Life as a retired F1 driver is very different. When I was racing, the dishwasher, microwave and oven at home were never used, because I never ate in. Now I have a normal family life. I met Karen [his partner Karen Minier] in 2003 when she was covering F1 for the French TV station TF1, and we got engaged in '06. At first, because of her 12-year-old daughter's schooling, she was living in Belgium and I was in Monaco, but now we're all together down here as a proper family. Our son Dayton Coulthard – he's DC too! – was born in 2008. I have various businesses to take care of, including a TV production company with Sunil Patel and Jake Humphrey, which is fun and interesting. But I did find I missed the racing. There was a little void. And now DTM, which I started doing in 2010 for the Mücke Motorsport Mercedes team, nicely fills that void. The challenge is learning how to drive those cars, which is a very different technique.

"I had 15 seasons in F1, and it seems to have passed in a blink. Now, when I go back to the same paddocks, the same races, in many ways I don't remember being an F1 driver, because I'm concentrating on trying to do a good job for television. It's a completely different set of skills." But the single-minded focus, the painstaking attention to detail, all that hasn't changed. He's in his third season as a BBC TV paddock pundit, and this year he moved up to the box to be Martin Brundle's co-commentator. He would say his technique is still developing, but most of the Sunday sofa population seem to agree that Martin 'n David make up a brilliant duo who've raised informed race coverage to a new level. The enduring relationship between F1 and DC looks set to last a long time yet.

David Coulthard was talking to Simon in May 2011.

EMERSON FITTIPALDI

*Racing with his gods over
three generations*

In terms of youthful success, Lewis Hamilton rewrote the record books in his first F1 season in 2007. But his meteoric progress didn't diminish the achievements, 36 years earlier, of a Brazilian tyro called Emerson Fittipaldi. Emerson was already 22 years old when he arrived in a cold and unwelcoming England in February 1969. Two months later he had his first Formula Ford race: and 15 months after that he was in Formula 1 with Lotus.

Hamilton won his sixth Grand Prix, but Fittipaldi won his fourth – restoring morale to a team that was reeling from the tragic death of their No 1 driver. In his second full F1 season he became the then youngest-ever World Champion. A year later he switched to McLaren, and straight away he was World Champion again, scoring McLaren's first Drivers' and Constructors' titles. Then, at 29, he turned his back on the easier challenge of driving for a top team to run his own Brazilian F1 operation. It was a failure. He retired disillusioned and demoralised, saying he never wanted to race again. But at the ripe old age of 37 he was persuaded to get back in the cockpit and try CART in the USA. His glittering second career lasted 12 seasons. He won the Indy 500 twice, and was crowned CART Champion in 1989.

Emerson is 61 now, a grandfather who has just become a father again, and is working harder than ever. Finding a lunch date in either of his home towns of Sao Paulo or Miami proves difficult, but eventually we manage to coincide in a hotel restaurant near Amsterdam. Slim, spare and bright-eyed, he is bouncing with energy and good humour despite two consecutive nights of long-distance flights. He's flown to Holland to cheer on the Brazilian team in the opening round of the A1 GP series at Zandvoort, but he left Sao Paulo two days earlier for Detroit, where he had a high-level meeting with General Motors. GM are striving to develop greener cars, and one of the Fittipaldi businesses is producing ethanol from sugar cane. In Brazil four million of the nation's cars run on ethanol , and Emerson sees a great future for it on a worldwide basis.

He's a New Age man in other ways, too. He lives on a strict macrobiotic diet, and before his abstemious meal of swordfish and salad he orders a cup of very hot water, gets a small tin out of his pocket, spoons an enigmatic brown substance into the cup, and drinks it. It's concentrated Japanese miso, made from fermented soybean, and Emerson likes to have several cups a day. Wherever he is in the world he has a daily session in a gym, and he seems indecently young and healthy for a man in his seventh decade – let alone a man whose spine is held together with titanium rods and screws.

Emerson's grandfather emigrated to Brazil from southern Italy, and his Russian mother fled to Brazil in the 1930s. His father Wilson raced motorcycles and was a journalist and commentator, going on to become Brazil's Murray Walker. When Chico Landi, the only Brazilian F1 driver of any standing before Emerson, won the Bari GP in a 2-litre Ferrari in 1948, Wilson was there to describe the race to his radio audience at home. He was still commentating on F1 when both his sons, Wilson Jr and Emerson, were in F1 in the 1970s.

The brothers grew up surrounded by motor sport, and Emerson, younger than Wilson by three years, was racing motorbikes in his teens. You had to be 17 to race karts then, but Emerson helped build and prepare his brother's kart, and that of a friend called Carlos Pace. As soon as he was 17 Emerson started winning kart races, and sales of replicas of the machines he built, called Minikarts, helped finance his racing. Then he moved into Formula Vee with a self-built car, winning the Brazilian FV championship and selling 28 customer replicas. There was a Porsche-engined Karmann-Ghia VW coupé and, later, a remarkable twin-engined VW Beetle, whose fibreglass silhouette hid two 1600cc flat-four engines in tandem behind the driver. With 350 horsepower in a car weighing 550kg it was devastatingly quick, and in Emerson's hands this unlikely beast outpaced the wealthy local racers in GT40s and Lola T70s at Jacarapagua.

When Emerson arrived in England in 1969 he could speak almost no English. Like so many young drivers from abroad, he learned the words for gear ratios and camber angle before he learned the words for bacon and eggs. He bought a Merlyn Formula Ford: "I had enough money to buy it and get to the races, but no money to mend it if I crashed." He towed the Merlyn behind an old Land Rover, and lodged with a family in Wimbledon for £7 a week – "Mr and Mrs Bates, they were very kind to me. Always I was very lucky to meet the right people that help me, like Denis Rowland, he had very good engines, knew the right set-up for the car. Then Jim Russell and Mike Warner. Then Peter Warr, and then Colin Chapman. Everything happened in a few months."

The right people wanted to meet the Brazilian newcomer with the strange name because, just like Ayrton Senna da Silva a dozen years later, he was winning everything. His first race was actually at Zandvoort: he put the Merlyn on pole and led until his engine disintegrated. Rowland gave him the parts to rebuild it. They took the finished car to bleak, windy Snetterton for a test, and the gearbox broke. "I cried that day. I thought I would go back to the sunshine in Brazil and forget about Europe." Rowland persuaded him to persevere, and he returned to Snetterton for his second race – and won. More FF wins followed, and in July Jim Russell, who'd been watching his progress, engineered a deal with Mike Warner of Lotus Components, and the Merlyn was exchanged for a Lotus 59 F3 car. Emerson was fifth in his first F3 race, second in his second, and won his third. He won seven more in the next three months, and on the strength of half a season took the British F3 Championship.

The first F1 offer had already emerged. "By September I was living in Norwich. Frank Williams, who was having flying lessons, flew up to see me with his instructor. He said, 'Next year I will have two de Tomasos in Formula 1, and you can be No 2 to Piers Courage.' I said, 'Thank you, Frank, it is an honour this invitation, but I am not ready.' Then later in the year Colin Chapman called me into his office. My legs were shaking, I was thinking of Jim Clark and Graham Hill, all that history. It was a very emotional day for me. He said, 'I want you to drive for me next year in Formula 1.' I told Colin I need more experience, I want to start in F2 and see how things go.

"F2 was so good in those days, because you raced against all the F1 drivers with equal cars and engines. So I did six or seven F2 races in the first half of 1970, and I got to know Jochen Rindt. He was the king of F2 then, and I ran close with him sometimes. Then Colin said, 'We want to put you in the Lotus 49 for the British Grand Prix, a No 3 entry.' I sat in the car for the first time in a test at Silverstone in May. Colin flew there from Hethel in his Navajo, with me sitting in the back. I never flew in a private plane before. Jochen was there testing the 72, but Colin sent him out in the 49 for a few laps to see it was OK, and then I jump in the car. I do five or six laps and then I come in and say, 'The car is understeering a lot.' 'The car's fine', says Jochen. 'Don't change anything. Just use more power and the understeer will go away!' But they put on more front wing for me, and I started to set good times. Jochen was pleased – sometimes a driver doesn't like to see another driver going well, but he was happy about it. He even hung out the pit signals for me himself."

At Zandvoort a few days later Piers Courage was killed. Frank Williams approached Emerson again to offer him the de Tomaso drive, but Colin responded with a proper contract. The record books show his Brands Hatch F1 debut resulted in a steady drive to eighth, but in fact he had lost fourth gear, and the car also had a broken exhaust manifold. Before its problems Emerson's fastest lap was only 0.9sec off winner Rindt's best in the 72, so Chapman must have been well pleased with his young No 3. Two weeks later came his first points with a fine fourth at Hockenheim, and then in Austria he drove the 49 for the last time, slowed by mixture problems.

Team Lotus arrived at Monza with three 72s for Rindt, John Miles and Emerson, including a brand new 72 chassis for Rindt. In Friday practice Emerson was sent out to shake it down. "Colin say at Monza we must run with no wings on the car. I was taking it easy, bedding it in, and I saw Jack Brabham coming up in my mirrors. I didn't want to get in his way. Then when I look back at the road I am 100 metres past my braking point for Parabolica. I lock the front wheels, and I hit the back of Giunti's Ferrari, fly over it and finish up among the trees, with the car standing on its nose. I had to stand on the pedals to get out. Colin was extremely pissed off, it was a brand new car. On Saturday morning I had breakfast with Jochen, and he asked me to replace him in the F2 team, because he wanted to stop F2 now. We shook hands on that. Then a few hours later he was dead."

Jochen Rindt, the World Champion elect, was killed when his Lotus 72 veered left under braking for the Parabolica, almost certainly because one of the shafts to its inboard front brakes sheared. The car nosed underneath the poorly located Armco barrier and hit one of the retaining posts, and was dreadfully damaged. It was a crushing blow for the Lotus team, who withdrew at once from the weekend. No 2 driver John Miles believed running the 72s without wings at Monza to maximise their straight-line speed made them unstable, and he had a ferocious argument with Colin Chapman in the pits just before Rindt's accident. He left the team immediately.

"It was a very awful time, for me, for everybody. Piers and Bruce [McLaren] had been killed that summer, and now Jochen. In those days the cars were very weak in an accident. Everybody in the team, everybody, was so sad. Colin rang me and said he was withdrawing from the next Grand Prix also, that was Canada, two weeks after Monza. He said, 'Emerson, I don't know what I'm going to do. I'll let you know.'

"Then a week later he call me again, and he say, 'I want you to be No 1 driver for Lotus. We are going to Watkins Glen.' I thought he would be getting someone more experienced. I had only done four Grands Prix, and had one crash! Coming out of the tragedy, the ambience in the whole team was very difficult. Jacky Ickx still had a chance of winning the championship for Ferrari if he won the last two races, and Colin said I had to beat the Ferraris because it had to be Jochen's championship. There was big, big pressure on me.

"Ickx qualified on pole. I was third on the grid behind Jackie Stewart. Then the night before the race I was very sick. I had a high temperature, sweating, cold. Colin walked into my room and said, 'Can you drive tomorrow?' I said, 'I don't know, depends how I wake up.' I woke up dizzy and went to the track, and then it was time for the warm-up, and I got in the car and the adrenaline started to work. I came into the pits after the warm-up and I said to Colin, 'I feel great.' "

Emerson made history that day: he won the United States GP, ensuring that Jochen Rindt was posthumous World Champion, and also clinching the Constructors' Championship for Lotus. He is the first to admit it was a lucky victory: late leader Pedro Rodríguez ran low on fuel in the closing stages. But that victory, and new recruit Reine Wisell's third place in the other 72, did much to restore Lotus morale.

"I couldn't believe it when the pit signals said P1. When I came to the finish flag I saw Colin run into the road and throw his hat in the air. When I was a kid in Brazil I used to see pictures in magazines of Colin doing that for Jim Clark. Now he was doing it for me.

"Then Enzo Ferrari called me. He offered double what Colin was paying me, but he wanted me to drive sports cars too. It was difficult to say no to Enzo Ferrari, but I wanted to concentrate just on Formula 1. I stayed with Colin for three more years."

In 1971 Lotus failed to win a Grand Prix for the first time since 1959, partly because the 56B turbine car deflected a lot of Chapman's attention. Emerson raced it four times, in three non-championship races and at the Italian Grand Prix, where because of legal proceedings following Rindt's death it was entered by World Wide Racing. Despite two cracked brake discs he brought the unwieldy car home eighth. The other problem was that the new slick tyres were showing up handling problems with the 72. "The '71 season was the first year for slicks, and they had much more grip. The 72 was too flexible, and on the high-grip tracks we were in trouble. On the low-grip tracks like Monaco it was not so bad. I did the whole race there with no clutch and finished fifth." In June he and his first wife Maria Helena were badly hurt in a road accident and, having missed Zandvoort, he was still heavily bandaged when he came through to third in the French Grand Prix. He repeated the result at Silverstone two weeks later, and he was second in Austria. But it was not a happy season.

"Colin didn't believe us when we said the cars weren't handling. But for the non-championship race at Brands Hatch at the end of the year, the one when Jo Siffert died, we had reinforced suspension, a whole new package, and the car felt so different. Now we were looking good for 1972."

With the red and gold colours of Gold Leaf replaced by the black and gold of John Player Special, it was an amazing year. In 12 championship rounds Emerson hit reliability problems in four, but in the other eight he had five wins, two seconds and a third, to be crowned World Champion at 25. The way Colin and Emerson worked together recalled his relationship with Jim Clark a decade earlier. "One evening we were having dinner, talking, and suddenly Colin said, 'I don't want to get closer to you, Emerson. Friendship is dangerous for me, because of what happened to me with Jimmy and with Jochen.'

"I always say Colin was a genius. I never worked with anybody who had so much intuition about how a race car is working, how to design a car, build a car, set up a car. He taught me so much about testing and development, he was the best school a driver could have. Sometimes if it wasn't working right we go for dinner, I tell Colin exactly what the car is doing, he goes back to the garage to change the car, and next day it is improved. His solutions to problems always came so quick. And he always want to win, always so committed."

Emerson's team-mates – Reine Wisell, Dave Walker – were clearly No 2s, but the arrival in 1973 of Ronnie Peterson meant that Lotus had two winners on the team. Between them they won nine races, and Lotus romped home Constructors' Champions. But the Drivers' title went to Jackie Stewart, with Emerson second and Ronnie third. Journalists looked for friction between them, but found none.

"Ronnie was my best friend in Formula 1. I had been close to him ever since Formula 2 in 1970. I stayed with him in his house in England, he stayed with me in Switzerland. We had a strong working relationship." This was tested by what happened at Monza that year, with the Championship in the balance. "Colin, Ronnie and I talk about it before the race, and decide we will not race against each other. But near the end, if Ronnie is leading and I am second, Colin will give a signal to tell Ronnie I can come past him. So in the race we are easy one-two and I am waiting for the signal from Colin, and it never come. I am going crazy, because I still have a chance in the championship. So I start chasing Ronnie, and Ronnie start racing too. You can't blame him for that, because there was no signal. At the line he beat me by 0.8sec. After the race I went to Colin, I was very disappointed, and Colin said, 'Well, I decided not to give the signal.'

"So next day, Monday, I begin to talk to other teams for 1974. I had been four seasons with Lotus. I went to see Brabham, where Bernie was now, and Tyrrell, because Jackie was retiring. And McLaren. Marlboro were finishing with BRM and they came to me and said they would go with me to whichever team I chose. It was a big responsibility. I knew Brabham could be very good because, technically, Gordon Murray was on the edge. Tyrrell had won so much with Jackie. McLaren had never won a championship, but I liked the feel of the team with Teddy Mayer. So I said to Marlboro, 'I am going to McLaren,' and they said, 'OK, we'll back you up.' And Texaco came with us too. Then Colin called me, he said, 'Emerson, I don't want you to go.' I said Colin, 'Thank you, I am going to miss you, but I have to go.' I felt sad because I was one of Colin's greatest fans, after four years working together.

"McLaren was such a committed team. Four good people at the top: Teddy was the boss, very well organised, very good at planning everything. Phil Kerr, who'd been with Bruce McLaren since the beginning, and Alistair Caldwell as chief mechanic. And Tyler Alexander – he's still there, at McLaren, after 40 years! Gordon Coppuck designed the car, the M23, which was a simple, straight-forward car."

Emerson's first race for McLaren, in Argentina, was beset by minor problems, and it was won by his veteran team-mate Denny Hulme. But the second race, in front of a delirious home crowd at Interlagos, he won. There were only two more victories that season, but a string of podiums racked up the points. He took the Drivers' title, and McLaren their first Constructors' crown.

Emerson had always been concerned about the avoidable dangers of Formula 1, following the lead of Jo Bonnier and Jackie Stewart in this regard. "Jo was killed at Le Mans in 1972, and Jackie retired at the end of 1973. In 1975 I was reigning champion, so I had to say what was right. The whole safety structure was bad in those days. At some tracks the medical care was terrible, with no proper equipment to keep a driver alive. When I arrived for the Spanish GP in Montjuich that year, I went for a run around the circuit to have a look at it. I could see the Armco barrier was just sitting there, with no bolts to hold it in some places. It was a disaster. I talked to [FIA President] Balestre and the circuit director, they promised it would be finished properly, but nothing happened. In qualifying I just drove slowly round in second gear. Marlboro had guests there from all over the world and I had to make a welcome speech to them on Saturday. I said to John Hogan of Marlboro, 'I know I'm under contract, and defending World Champion, I accept the risks of motor racing, but this is beyond what I should accept. I am not driving tomorrow.' I said it in my speech to the guests as well.

"Then the organisers said they would impound the McLaren transporter if I refused to drive. So I told Teddy I would do one lap in the race and then stop. That's what I did. Balestre had a meeting with the FIA commission right there and they took away my licence, suspended me for three races. Balestre said that if the FIA passed the track as safe then the World Champion had to race. I left the circuit as soon as I'd done my one lap of the race, went straight to the airport and flew home to Switzerland.

"When I landed at Geneva airport there was a TV crew waiting to interview me. I assumed it was because I'd walked away from the race. What I didn't know, what they wanted to ask me about, was Rolf Stommelen hit the barrier and was launched into the crowd. He had broken legs, wrist and ribs, but four people in the crowd were killed. We wasted four lives for nothing. Montjuich was never used again, and of course I heard nothing more from Balestre about my suspension."

Marlboro were to stay with McLaren for 24 seasons, but after 1975, with two more victories and another second place in the Drivers' Championship, Emerson astonished the world by moving to the Copersucar Fittipaldi team. Wilson and Emerson had first talked about setting up their own team in 1973 and, with sponsorship from a giant Brazilian sugar co-operative and an adventurous car designed by Richard Devila, it came into being during 1974. But in 1975 Wilson had a miserable first season with it, and neither car nor team seemed capable of winning races.

"It was a challenge for me. Looking back, it is a decision I regret now. I don't know if I would have won more championships." (Emerson's replacement at McLaren, James Hunt, won the title in 1976.) "Maybe. But If, the word If, doesn't mean anything in motor racing. My time with the Fittipaldi F1 operation was very tough, very frustrating. Can you imagine how difficult it was trying to build a car in Brazil, on Brazilian money? But I learned a lot from the experience. I learned a lot for my life and for my future."

From being a winner and a champion, Emerson was an also-ran. There were non-qualifications and retirements, and only the occasional lucky point. In 1977 there were three fourth places, and in 1978 a rousing second place in front of those Brazilian fans, this time at Jacarapagua. But that was to be the zenith.

The team struggled on through 1978 and 1979, and when Walter Wolf's F1 team was wound up Fittipaldi Automotive took over the remains for the 1980 season, inheriting designer Harvey Postlethwaite, team manager Peter Warr and driver Keke Rosberg. The young Adrian Reynard joined straight from University the same year. Keke got on the podium for the season-opener in Argentina, and Emerson did the same two months later at Long Beach. But Fittipaldi Automotive never looked like becoming a serious player. At the end of 1980 Emerson stopped driving, but continued to manage the team.

"For two years I tried to get enough finance to run the team properly, but I couldn't. For a Brazilian team to design and build a Formula 1 car was fantastic in my opinion, but the media in Brazil didn't understand why we didn't get race-winning results right from the start. They criticise us and bombard us, and that drove away potential sponsors. It was very demoralising for me.

"Also I didn't like the ground-effect cars that were coming in by 1980. There was not so much finesse in driving them. You just had to have big balls. Every extra kilometre you carry into the corner you increase the downforce, but then when you lose it there is nothing. In 1982 we stopped the team. I believed then that I had retired from motor racing for ever."

He ran his businesses in Brazil, and went back to kart racing for fun. In 1984 promoter Ralph Sanchez asked him to drive a March-Chevrolet GTP in his three-hour round-the-houses Miami race. "I said no to him. I told him I was retired, I was happy with my life in Brazil. He called me again, and again, and finally I said yes. I'd never been to Miami – sometimes I'd just slept in the airport there on my way home to Brazil – and I said to myself, I like this place. So I got in the car, and it was so good to get back in a cockpit. I put the car on pole. In the race we were challenging for the lead when a driveshaft broke. I went to Disneyworld the next day, and a local guy called Pepe Romero was trying to get hold of me. He said, 'I am putting together a CART drive for you.' I called Chris Pook, who ran the Long Beach Grand Prix, he was an old friend, and I say to him, 'This guy want me to run in CART. You know everybody in the USA, can you handle it for me, like a driver manager?' He say OK, and we start working together."

Indianapolis had held a fascination for Emerson since he was a kid reading the magazines in Brazil. "At Lotus I used to ask Colin to tell me about going to Indy with Jim Clark. Then it nearly happened with McLaren. I tested Jimmy Rutherford's winning 1974 McLaren-Offenhauser at Indy, and it was beautiful to drive, but those cars were fragile then. Texaco wanted me to do an Indy programme with McLaren in 1975, but the clash with the F1 calendar was difficult. I was concentrating on the World Championship, and I didn't want to do it that way. I only wanted to go to Indy if I could do it properly, and if I felt safe in the car.

"Now the cars were using carbonfibre, and were much stronger. And I found that I loved the challenge of the ovals. It was the mental approach, the technical approach, setting the cars up right. I always liked fast corners, and the ovals suited my driving style. You never feel comfortable on an oval if you are going fast enough, but you have to be very smooth. It was so different from the ground-effect days in F1. I felt like I was reborn."

Emerson's first CART season saw him drive for three different teams, eventually standing in for the injured Chip Ganassi with Pat Patrick. Staying with Patrick, he won the 1985 Michigan 500 by a tenth of a second from Al Unser Sr, and after three more strong seasons he won the 1989 Indianapolis 500 after a awe-inspiring last-ditch battle with Al Unser Jr, leaving the Indy lap record at 224mph. With four more victories that season, he was crowned CART Champion. For 1990 he moved to Penske, where he was reunited with his old McLaren team manager Teddy Mayer. There were more wins, including Indianapolis again in 1993. In 1996, now aged 49, he decided that this would be his last season. "The day before the Michigan 500 I called Roger Penske and I said, 'Roger, I've decided to retire at the end of this season.' He said, 'As a team owner I'm going to miss you, but as a friend I'm very happy.' Then in the race next day I crashed.

"I qualify fourth, second quickest of the Mercedes engines behind Greg Moore, who was third. He was a rookie then. Jimmy Vasser and Alex Zanardi with the Hondas were in front. I ran very strong on full tanks in the warm-up, and I didn't want to get stuck behind Greg, I wanted to get the slipstream from the Hondas, I knew they would pull me away from everybody. So I decided to go high above Greg at the start. It worked perfect, and I was three-quarters past him when he lost a little downforce at the front. He slide up into my car, and I go backwards into the wall. I was doing between 190mph and 200mph. According to the black box, the impact was 160G. It was a big hammer. I broke vertebrae, I had a collapsed lung, internal bleeding."

Doctors said only Emerson's fitness saved him from more serious injury, or death. One medic said such deceleration was "not really compatible with survival" and that his fitness levels were comparable to an athlete in his late 20s rather than a man in his fiftieth year. During complex surgery his spine was rebuilt with titanium. But his racing days were done. "I thank God", he says now, "that I am still here."

Just a year later he had another brush with death when, flying his microlight aircraft over the Brazilian wilds with his six-year-old son Luca, he crash-landed into a swamp. He suffered further spinal injuries. For several hours until rescuers arrived little Luca, who was almost unhurt, had to flap his arms to ward off the circling vultures, which were attracted by Emerson's blood-soaked clothing.

He was briefly tempted back into the cockpit for the Grand Prix Masters series last year, and had a good battle with his old CART sparring partner Nigel Mansell at Kyalami. "It's a shame it hasn't got the finance now. I hope it happens again." For now he has his ethanol business, his fruit business – with 600,000 orange trees in a huge plantation 200 miles north of Sao Paulo – his car accessory range, his performance car exhibition.

"I was so lucky in my career because I work with all these good guys – Denis Rowland, Colin, Peter Warr, Teddy. I was always learning with these people. When I left Formula 1 I believed I had retired for ever. I never thought that one day I would drive Indianapolis. Or win Indianapolis, I never dream that. I raced against three generations: when I start in F1 there was Graham Hill, Jack Brabham, gods to me. There was my generation, Ronnie, Jackie, Lauda, all those. And the next generation too – I remember an incredible dice with Jacques Villeneuve, my last year in CART. I have been so lucky in my life."

Emerson Fittipaldi was talking to Simon in September 2007.

DARIO FRANCHITTI

From Scottish export to
American hero

In today's Formula 1-obsessed world, the name of Dario Franchitti does not loom as large as it should. All those reference books and websites that believe motor sport starts and ends with Bernie's fortnightly round will list the smallest career detail of any driver who has achieved a few faltering laps of a Grand Prix. Yet this Scotsman, who has been Indycar champion three times in the past four years, is far less familiar.

In North America it's different. There Dario is a hero with a big fan following who appears good-humouredly on TV chat shows and, with his Hollywood actress wife, makes up a golden couple. Despite career earnings in the multi-millions, and in marked contrast to some current F1 drivers, he is utterly unspoiled by success. He remains a friendly Scottish lad, modest, down-to-earth and lacking in any air of self-importance. After 20 years in racing he retains a boyish delight in being able to spend his life doing what he loves. And, most unusually for a 21st-century racing driver, he has a well-educated fascination for the sport's history. In his houses in the USA and Scotland his collection of books and memorabilia, much of it covering periods long before he was born, is remarkable. In one house an entire room is devoted to his hero, Jim Clark.

So, appropriately, he suggests we lunch in the historic Royal Automobile Club in Pall Mall. He's on a flying visit from his Tennessee base to be inducted into the *Motor Sport* Hall of Fame, the first non-F1 name to receive this accolade. He notes with delight that an ex-Clark Lotus 21 F1 car is on display in the foyer, and then we take lobster ravioli and sea bass in the Great Gallery.

Dario is one of a remarkable clan that has its roots in Italy but ended up in West Lothian, that nondescript area between Edinburgh and Glasgow under the shadow of the closed Leyland factory and the defunct Polkemmet coal mine. The Franchittis made and sold ice-cream, and the di Restas had a café. "The families are related – my dad George and Louis di Resta, [Force India driver] Paul's dad, are second cousins – and it's made more complicated by how close we all are. Dad started racing karts in the 1960s, and then did some Formula Ford at Ingliston. Of course I'd go with him. As a kid the only things I ever read were racing magazines. My dad helped Louis, who's 10 years younger, into karting, and then at the age of 10 I got into a kart, and I won my first race. I just went out and did it, it came naturally with no thought."

By the time he was 11 Dario was Scottish Junior Champion. Then the clan ventured south and he won back-to-back British Junior titles. "My parents made a lot of sacrifices. The business was seven days a week, so Mum would stay behind to run that while Dad was away racing with me. By 1987, when I was 14, I was doing the World Championships, up against a lot of names: Rubens, DC, Fisichella, Jan Magnussen. One year, when I was the only British guy to qualify for the final, I started 17th and got up to sixth behind Christian Fittipaldi. Then Luca Badoer took me out.

"When I was about to leave school – this was 1990 – David Leslie's father suggested I should go to the races with his team, polish the cars, do odd jobs, watch and learn. It taught me a tremendous amount. For 1991 Formula Vauxhall Junior came in. I was 17, and it was time to do it for myself. At the time Dad's business wasn't going so well, so he decided to remortgage the house. That raised enough to pay for one season. He didn't tell my mum until after he'd done it. They both had so much faith in me it was unbelievable, but in the end it turned out not to be too bad an investment."

In his first season of car racing Dario took the Vauxhall Junior title, and Paul Stewart Racing offered a Formula Vauxhall test. "Graham Taylor, the engineer, had to do a report for Jackie Stewart on how I went. Years later he showed me his notebook from that day: scribbled across the bottom of the page was 'Sign immediately'. Of course I now had no money at all, but Jackie said, 'You drive the car and I'll find the money.' Essentially we did a future earnings deal, no interest, no life percentage, just paying back when I could what it had cost them to run me. But Jackie didn't like talking to prospective Scottish sponsors about a driver with an obviously Italian name. He wanted me to change it to Jock McBain – I still wonder if he was serious about that...

"Jackie found the money, but for the first time, instead of being with my family, I was in a professional team, there were sponsors involved, and it was all rather daunting. I struggled to learn how to drive the car properly, and it got so I was telling Graham Taylor how to engineer the car and he was telling me how to drive it. I said to Jackie, 'I don't think I can work with Graham any more.' Jackie said, 'Graham's a good guy, I think you should work things out between you.' So Graham and I sat down over a cup of tea and we sorted it out." They are still friends today. At the end of that difficult season came a big confidence boost when Dario won the McLaren/*Autosport* Young Driver Award – and in 1993 he was FVL champion.

"The cash from the Young Driver award all went on my racing, and I still had literally no money, couldn't even buy myself a shirt. When I wasn't in the car I'd do anything to keep body and soul together, instructing at racing schools, doing circuit days for BMW and Nissan: you'd get £100 a day, but it was often absolutely terrifying, sitting in the passenger seat next to some complete wally. A lot of young drivers were doing the same. We were all skint but we had a lot of fun, we lived the life.

"Another way to earn money was delivering cars. You could get £20 a day doing that. I was driving a truck for an Edinburgh Mazda dealer when I had a call from Jackie Stewart: 'Come now to Milton Keynes, because King Hussein of Jordan is arriving to view the facility. Put on your team gear and look smart.' So I turn my 7.5-tonner south down the M6, and it's 4am when I fall asleep and go over the centre barrier. Somehow I manage to get it back to the hard shoulder, but I'd blown the front right tyre. I had to struggle to change this big truck wheel, and I arrived at Milton Keynes with my team gear no longer looking so smart. I don't know what the King thought."

After his storming year in 1993, the pendulum swung away again in '94. "Stewart moved me up to F3 with Jan Magnussen. In Vauxhall Lotus I'd usually beaten Jan, so I was happy about that. And I won the first round. But after that Jan could do no wrong, won 14 out of 18 races. For me nothing seemed to go right: various problems, odd failures. I scored enough points for fourth in the series, but whenever it was going well something would happen. It was soul-destroying.

"Then I was on a train and a girl with a strange German accent called me and said, 'Norbert Haug of Mercedes-Benz vant to speak to you. Call ziss number.' I was sure it was one of my mates winding me up, and I didn't even bother to write down the number. Then one of the *Autosport* journalists called me and said, 'Have you heard from Norbert? He asked us who we'd recommend as young talent for the Mercedes International Touring Cars team, and we said you.' After a frantic struggle I got Norbert's number, called him, and he said, 'Be at Hockenheim next Tuesday to test our ITC car.'

"The car was phenomenal: nearly 500 horsepower, sequential gears, ABS brakes, active aero, active rollbars. The pokiest thing I'd driven up to then was an F3 car. I loved it. I must have gone reasonably well, because they asked me back, but Jan Magnussen showed up too. That was bad news, because I knew there were two places in the team. One was going to Giancarlo Fisichella, and I expected Jan to get the other because he'd just landed a McLaren-Mercedes test contract. We set just about identical times and Gerhard Unger, who was running the team, was happy. But when I got home he called and said, 'Sorry Dario, the drives are going to Giancarlo and Jan.' Shit. I didn't have the money to go F3000, I was going to get further into debt if I stayed in F3 and, although I think Jackie still believed in me, the engineers and mechanics at PSR probably didn't. Then Gerhard called again: 'We've fallen out with Fisichella. Get over to AMG at Affalterbach and we'll see if we can do a deal.'

"They put a contract in front of me, and I signed it. It was a huge amount of money to me then, six figures, the first time I'd ever earned any money out of racing. Plus I went from driving around in old borrowed bangers to my own Mercedes C36. I went back to Milton Keynes and told Jackie I was leaving. I didn't handle it well – I should have told him before I went to Germany – and he was a bit pissed off with me for a couple of months. Then he went back to being the same old Jackie.

"As soon as AMG finished the first of the new cars for 1995, back to Hockenheim, and I was the first driver they put in it. I went out on new tyres to put in a time, lost the back end going up to the first chicane, hit the barrier and flipped over backwards. The car was totally destroyed. It was like Armageddon. The biggest thing they found was half a carbon-fibre door. The steering wheel was bent, the pedals were bent, the inlet trumpets were torn out of the centre of the Vee. I was a bit concussed, so I got a lift back to the pits, and the team went out to the wreck and couldn't find me. They thought I'd run off into the forest to hide. I almost lost the whole drive there. But I qualified on pole for the first race, thank God."

During his first season with Mercedes Dario finished third in the international series, the ITC, and fifth in the German series, the DTM. In the 26-round combined series in 1996 he finished fourth, winning at the final event in Suzuka. "I loved racing those cars. They evolved at a tremendous rate: semi-automatic gearboxes, movable ballast, trick aerodynamics. They talk about flexible wings in F1: we had them in ITC 15 years ago. At one point I was qualifying a car with full ground-effect, full skirts,

Chris Amon is the fastest racing driver ever to have come out of New Zealand, but cruel luck and unfortunate team decisions dogged his career. (LAT)

Amon's Ferrari rounds Druids during the 1968 British Grand Prix. He finished second. (LAT)

From humble beginnings as an Italian immigrant, Mario Andretti rose to be one of the most successful, and versatile, American racers of all time. (LAT)

Andretti's Formula 1 World Championship title came in 1978 with the Lotus 78. One of his six victories that season was in the Belgian Grand Prix at Zolder. (LAT)

Derek Bell is the UK's most prolific sports car racer ever, campaigning with success in all the great classic endurance races for Ferrari, Porsche, Alfa Romeo, Renault, Mirage and others. (LAT)

Bell won the Le Mans 24 Hours an extraordinary five times. This was his 1986 victory for Porsche, co-driven by Hans Stuck and Al Holbert. (LAT)

Impassive behind his pit-lane screens, Ross Brawn has directed winning Formula 1 campaigns for more than 20 years, at Benetton, Ferrari, Honda, Brawn and Mercedes. (LAT)

Celebrations at Suzuka in 2003, when Michael Schumacher clinched his fourth consecutive Drivers' title, and Ferrari their fifth consecutive Constructors' title. Left to right, Schumacher's team-mate Rubens Barrichello, Brawn, Ferrari team chief Jean Todt and Schumacher. (Ferrari)

David Coulthard scored more than 500 F1 World Championship points in an F1 career that lasted 15 seasons, before finding a new career as a TV pundit. (LAT)

Coulthard takes a tight line in the McLaren MP4/17 on his way to a superb victory in the 2002 Monaco Grand Prix. (LAT)

Emerson Fittipaldi retired in 1980 as a double World Champion, then returned to racing in the USA, becoming Indycar champion and winning the Indianapolis 500 twice. (LAT)

Fittipaldi's first World Championship was with Team Lotus in 1972. This is his Lotus 72D in an opposite-lock slide in the South African Grand Prix in 1973. (sutton-images.com)

Dario Franchitti, born in Scotland, has become a superstar in America, with four Indycar championship titles in five seasons, and three Indianapolis 500 victories. (James Mitchell)

Pitstop for Franchitti's Chip Ganassi Racing Dallara-Honda on his way to another great win in the 2010 Indy 500. (LAT)

Wing-Commander Andy Green is a qualified fighter pilot who somehow found time to beat the speed of sound and become the fastest man on earth. (James Mitchell)

Thrust SSC streaks across the Black Rock Desert in Nevada on that historic day in October 1997 – at 766.035mph. (Jeremy Davey, SSC Programme Ltd)

and a button to raise the car hydraulically to beat the ride-height test. By the end of the year it had all got too expensive, and the series died.

"At the end-of-season dinner in Stuttgart I sat next to Paul Morgan of Ilmor, who built the engines Mercedes were running in Champ Car. Lovely guy, died in that plane crash in 2001. He said, 'What are you going to do next?' I said, 'I'd love to try Champ Car.' Paul said, 'Maybe I can help you on that.' Next thing I know, Norbert's sending me to the Homestead track in Florida to do a test for Carl Hogan. That was a wake-up call. The DTM cars had power steering, and in terms of upper body strength were not difficult. With the Champ Car, when I took one hand off the wheel to change gear, I couldn't hold it in a straight line, the thing would weave all over the track. And God, it was quick. I'd come from 500 horsepower to over 900, big heavy car, loads of downforce. Jimmy Vasser was testing there as well, and I remember thinking, 'How am I ever going to get near his times in this thing?' But after two days I got within a second of him, and Hogan said, 'Right, let's do it.'

"I'd already had a run in an F1 car at the end of 1995. Because of the Mercedes relationship I got half a day in the McLaren MP4/10B at Jerez. After about 50 laps my neck was gone, but it went fine. David Coulthard was there having his first run in a McLaren, having just quit Williams, and I ended up about a second slower than him.

"But now I'm focused on Hogan and Champ Car for 1997. Then I get a call from Norbert. 'Ron Dennis wants to see you in Woking, just for a chat.' I've never told anybody this before. I turn up at the McLaren factory, and Ron says, 'We want to give you a test contract. You'll drive the Champ Car at weekends in America, and fly back and test the F1 McLarens during the week. We'll pay a good part of your American budget, and we'll also pay you a test driver salary. If one of the regular drivers gets hurt you could become a Grand Prix driver.' Then he hands me this 60-page contract. You can guess the sort of thing: I'd be locked into a seven-year deal, but they could dump me any time they chose. I took the contract home and ploughed through it, and then I called Ron and said, 'Thanks, but no thanks.' I think that was the start of the end of my relationship with Mercedes, but I just didn't feel comfortable with that. But I always got on well with Norbert. He liked to take a gamble on young drivers, and if it hadn't been for Norbert I wouldn't be sitting where I am today.

"So, there I am in Champ Car. And my second time in the car I'm doing an oval. That was a massive shock. It was bloody scary. These days I left-foot-brake on ovals, although I still right-foot-brake on road courses, much to the surprise of the younger guys. But then I was right-foot-braking everywhere. I qualified in the top 10, next to Michael Andretti, and I did OK in the race until the leader, Gil de Ferran, came up to lap me. I tried to leave him lots of room, got on the marbles and went off. I didn't make that mistake again. But I got pole in Toronto, and led three races that year. In my sixth race, on the oval at Gateway near Carl's home town of St Louis, we were in front with 20 laps to go when the gearbox broke. Our Mercedes engines were strong, the car was quick, but the team was pretty disorganised and we had lots of problems.

"I had various offers for 1998, but Honda and Firestone seemed the way to go, so I joined Team Green. Paul Tracy was my team-mate, and we got on really well: a fun guy to hang out with, a good team player, no mind games, no bullshit. But in the car, phew, unbelievably aggressive. I was now being measured against a top guy in an identical car, and I hadn't really done much over there at that point. But I'd got it figured out a bit now."

He certainly had. Five poles, more than any other driver; nine front-row starts; storming wins at Road America, Vancouver and the wet Houston; only a blown engine in the final round robbed him of second place in the championship. "The Vancouver win was cool, because they had a thing called the Marlboro Pole Award. If you won a race from pole position you got $10,000, but if nobody won from pole the money rolled on to the next race.

Before Vancouver nobody had won from pole for 33 races. So I got $340,000 added to the rest of the prize money. We had a good party that night.

"Most of that season I was fighting Alex Zanardi, who won his second title before going back to F1 and Williams. Alex was incredible on the road courses: he had this attitude in his head, he just didn't comprehend that he could be beaten, ever. Even today, after the accident in 2001 when he lost his legs, he still has that attitude. At Long Beach he was a lap down, and he came back and won. Ten years later he was still talking about it: he said to me, 'Did you have any mirrors that day?' Funny he should say that, because at Long Beach the glass vibrated out of both mirrors, so I could see nothing behind. 'Thought so,' he said. 'You didn't put up much of a defence when I came through.'

"I was still enjoying the road courses more than the ovals. On the ovals I tried to follow Greg Moore. He was the master, you never saw anything like it – and at that stage those cars were beasts on the ovals. He became my best friend. We'd travel together, train together, chase girls, go skiing in the off-season. That period was one of the happiest times of my life. In 1999 I had a great battle for the title with Juan Pablo Montoya. On the ovals Greg would give us a hard time, but on the road courses Monty and I kind of separated ourselves from the rest. He was always quick, and always looked quick – all arms and elbows – whereas my style makes it look like I'm not going that quick. In qualifying I beat him 10 times, he beat me 10 times. We both made mistakes during the year, and at Surfers Paradise I had to qualify on pole, lead the most laps and win the race to stay in contention. I did that, and Monty crashed. But in the last round at Fontana I had a wheel-nut problem in the pits and lost a lap. We ended up dead level on points, but Monty had more wins, so he was champion."

In the early laps of that Fontana final, Dario's friend Greg Moore perished in a massive crash. More than a decade later, Dario goes quiet when he thinks of it. "I'm glad I didn't win the title that day. His death took away the enjoyment of racing, it burst the bubble. He was from Vancouver, and when I finally managed to win the Vancouver race in 2002 it was good to be able to dedicate the victory to him. I did the same thing when I won the championship in 2009, because it was the 10th anniversary of his death. It's important that people don't forget about him. An unbelievable driver – on the ovals, the quickest of all – and a special person.

"I told Barry Green I had to get away for a bit, took the winter off, and the next time I got in a car was February, testing at Homestead. Into Turn 3 on the oval at 190mph, the spindle holding the right rear wheel to the upright failed. I don't remember any of this, but I hit the wall with such force that it cracked my pelvis in three places. My head somehow missed the cockpit surround and hit the wall too, so I had a massive head injury. I was back in the car four weeks later, but the brain contusions took me several years to get over. It affected my mental concentration, my balance, my memory, my fatigue levels. It also changed my personality: I became more serious, although Greg's death may have been part of that."

Soon after the Homestead crash Dario had another F1 test. "The Stewart team was now Jaguar, but Jackie was still close to it. In a throwaway remark I told him I'd quite like a run, and he said he'd make it happen. But because it was F1 it was terribly complicated: contracts, clauses, sub-clauses, all that crap. It was at a full two-day test at Silverstone, and if a journalist spoke to me I had to have my lawyer there, because he'd read all the small print and knew what I was and was not allowed to say. I'd already got a bad feeling about it when I went to the factory for a seat fitting, because one of the mechanics started telling me what was wrong with the team and who was doing a bad job. I did the first day and struggled a bit but it wasn't too bad, and I knew I could build on that on day two. But next morning my car had Luciano Burti's name on it. They put me in another car which was a dog, play in the steering rack, wouldn't even brake in a straight line. It felt as though the team didn't really want me there. I went back to America, relieved it was over. I hadn't made a good impression, and at that point I decided that F1 wanted to forget me.

"I'd had two ambitions as a kid: to do F1 and to win the Indy 500, like Jimmy had done. F1 was now a closed book, and at that time I was in CART and Indy was IRL. But in 2002 Team Green had a separate Indy programme too, and I did the Brickyard for the first time. I tried to be nonchalant, treat it as just another race, but the emotion and magic of the place got to me. At the end of '02 Michael Andretti bought into Team Green and they switched to the Indy Racing League. At that time IRL was all ovals, no road circuits. But I trusted the team, and decided to stick with them. In the end I did 10 years with Barry Green.

"By now the effects of the head injury had gone away, and I felt I was back to my best. Then I broke my back. I was in Scotland, riding my MV Agusta, when an oil line came adrift and sprayed onto the back tyre. I had to stand the bike up and put it through a hedge. The other side there was a six-foot drop, the bike dug in and I took off. Back in the US the brilliant Dr Terry Trammell fixed me up, with titanium rods in my back which are still there. But I missed most of the 2003 season.

"In 2004 I won Milwaukee and Pikes Peak, and I qualified third at Indy. I was still learning those IRL cars – a bit less power than the Champ Cars, a higher centre of gravity, and on the ovals you had to run them with more oversteer. And I don't like oversteer. With a Champ Car, if you got a wiggle on and you didn't catch it first time, you were in the wall. With IRL you had to run loose, with the rear end dancing away. It took me a while to get comfortable with that. By '05 I'd got it all figured out, and the IRL was now running road courses as well, which made me feel a lot better. We led several races, won Nashville and Fontana. But '06, for various reasons, was just a bloody disaster, and I decided to make a big change. I did a deal with Chip Ganassi to go to NASCAR. We're about to sign and Chip calls and says, 'Nobody else could have taken this drive from you, but I've just signed

Montoya.' That was a blow. Back with IRL and Team Green, I went into 2007 with low expectations."

But this time everything went right. Dario fulfilled a dream by winning a rain-interrupted Indy 500 with a brilliant mix of storming pace and clever strategy. "I'd hit one of my life's goals, and it changed the way I went about racing, it relaxed me. After that I had a run of poles and wins, and it was as though I could do no wrong. I thought, 'This is too good, something's going to happen.' And it did, at Michigan Speedway.

"I'd stalled in a pitstop and fell to last, but the car was a rocket ship that day, and I came through and caught the leader, Dan Wheldon. I got alongside him and he tried to side-draught me. You can do that in NASCAR: if you get really close to the other car's rear quarter you can slow it down. But in open-wheelers there's just no margin for error. His right front clipped my left rear, and I looped high in the air. The engine was bouncing on the rev-limiter, and on the radio I heard my spotter, Dave, say, 'Aw shit.' I thought, 'That's the last thing I'll ever hear.' It seemed to go on for ever. I open my eyes and I'm still way off the ground, with cars flashing past beneath me. Then I land and flip again, that's when the roll bar snaps off and my head's going r-r-r-r-r-r down the track. When it finally stopped and the marshals rolled the car over I just had a bruise on my nose from the helmet. Thanks, Mr Dallara.

"Then, six days later, it happened again. This time it was my fault. At Kentucky Speedway I was coming back after a problem, nobody told me it was the last lap, and I didn't see the flag. I'd just shifted into sixth as Kosuke Matsuura slowed after the finish line. I hit him, looped up into the air, hit the wall hard. I was pretty shaken up, and I hurt my knees, but I flew my helicopter home that night. We had more dramas towards the end of the season, but I beat Scott Dixon by 637 points to 624 to take the title.

"So I'd won Indy, I'd won the title – and I decided to go to NASCAR for 2008. Strange decision, I know. The Team Green guys were really upset with me. People said it was because of those two accidents, but it was nothing to do with that. I was straight back in the car after those two loops. I suppose I was looking to accomplish something else, a new challenge. I signed with Chip Ganassi, flew to Talladega, got in this huge great barge, steering wheel this big, pulled out of the pits and thought, 'What have I done?' I did the first Nationwide race and qualified on the front row, which wasn't too bad, but then they put me in a Sprint Cup car for the first time at Atlanta, which is the fastest oval they run. I was a fish out of water. It's a totally different technique driving those cars. I like to be tidy, keep the car working in shape, but you can't do that with NASCAR. Those things spin their wheels at 190mph coming off a corner. I didn't have a clue what I was doing. I had glimpses of getting it together, and then I broke my ankle in a crash at Talladega. Coming back I started to qualify the Cup car in the top 10, and I had a Nationwide pole at Watkins Glen and a good fight with Jimmie Johnson. But at the end of June Chip said there was no sponsorship for my car, and he closed it down. I was reigning Indycar champion with nothing to drive.

"In August I went to watch the IRL race in Detroit, stood at Turn 1 as the cars went through, and thought to myself, 'What have I been doing?' I went to Chip and said, 'I want to do IRL with you.' Chip said, 'Fine, I'll pay you this much.' I said, 'No, I want this much.' He said, 'OK, you're on.' That was it. And as soon as I got into the Target Ganassi Dallara Honda it was like coming home,

"My worry was whether, after a year away, I'd be able to keep up with my new team-mate Scott Dixon, who was starting his eighth season with Chip as reigning IRL champion. Luckily I was able to get the job done." Five poles, five wins, and his second IRL title 11 points ahead of his team-mate: it was as though he'd never been away. And in 2010 he was champion again, after a torrid battle with Team Penske's Will Power which went down to the final race. High point for Dario was his second Indy 500 victory.

"I led 155 of the 200 laps, but I wish it'd been as easy as that sounds. The track temperature went up 10 degrees between qualifying and the race, and my car was a real handful, dancing all the way through the corners. I was really marginal on fuel. My crew were saying, save fuel, save fuel, I was going as slow as I dared and Wheldon was second and getting closer. I decided to let him creep up on me, and on the last lap go all out. But with a lap to go there was a caution, so we queued up to the finish, and I'd won it with a gallon left.

"This season Dixie and I are in the Target Ganassi cars again. Everyone is in Dallara-Hondas these days, although that changes for 2012 when Chevy and Lotus come in. So it's pretty much a one-make formula, but that puts more emphasis on race preparation and organisation, and the Ganassi guys are really good at maximising that."

In 1999 Dario was introduced (by Greg Moore) to the actress Ashley Judd. Despite the pressures of their wildly different careers – Ashley has now appeared in over 30 films – they managed to spend time together and in 2001, in a memorable Scottish ceremony, they were married in Skibo Castle. "Ashley is a fantastic supporter. Her own life is incredibly busy – she's involved in a lot of humanitarian activities, she's a global ambassador with Population Services International for education and prevention of Aids in young people, and recently she went back to Harvard and got her master's degree. But she still gets to a lot of races. We live in the middle of nowhere and, although there's a bit of fuss when we turn up together at one of her events or one of mine, most of the time we manage to stay below the radar.

"When Colin [McRae] was killed I lost enthusiasm for my helicopter, and I sold it. But I've had my Ferrari F40 for 12 years, I've got a 355, a Mini-Cooper, a Porsche turbo. I like Porsches. I've got a 964 Speedster, a Carrera GT with straight pipes, and a 993 RSR replica, a real hooligan's car. Among my racing stuff – helmets, overalls, paperwork, I never throw anything away – I've bought back my original Formula Vauxhall Junior, I've got a Reynard Champ Car, I've got the Corvette pace cars from my two Indy wins. And the Jim Clark collection is growing: I have the actual chalk pitboard that was used when he won at Indy in 1965, and I've just got the entry forms for his first race, Crimond, June 16, 1956, in Ian Scott-Watson's DKW.

"A real thrill was driving Jimmy's winning Lotus 38 around Indy just after Classic Team Lotus had restored it for the Ford Museum. It's hard to put into words what that meant to me. I had a replica set of Jimmy's overalls made for that day, and a helmet – we got a special paint sample made up so the blue was precisely right – and the correct goggles. And I had the pitboard sent over from my Clark room.

"I love sports car racing. I've won the Daytona 24 Hours for Chip, got second overall and first LMP2 at Sebring, and I'd love to do Le Mans. I couldn't do it justice right now, but that's on the list. [Dario's brother Marino, five years younger, is a successful sports car driver in the ALMS.] Historics, too: winning the TT at the 2006 Goodwood Revival was a blast, with Emanuele Pirro in the ex-John Coombs E-type. Not so good in '07: the E-type went backwards into the bank at Fordwater on my second lap of practice – I still maintain a wheel came off. I woke up in hospital in Chichester next to Adrian Newey, who crashed his E-type in the same session.

"I want to keep going in IndyCar for as long as I can. Now I'm almost 38, and nearer the end of my career than the beginning, I realise how much I love it. I'm winning more than I ever have, but it's a results business, and if I don't perform I'll have to retire. I wouldn't like to step back and drive for a team that isn't top-notch. I've been lucky enough to drive for some great teams, none greater than the team I'm with now. And no regrets now that F1 didn't work out for me. I wouldn't trade any of what I've had."

It must be something in the water in Scotland. That rugged country of a mere five million souls bred Jimmy Clark, Jackie Stewart and Colin McRae; it bred David Coulthard and Allan McNish; it bred Ecurie Ecosse. And it bred Dario Franchitti, an export of which it can be very proud.

Dario Franchitti was talking to Simon in March 2011.

ANDY GREEN

*The fastest man
on earth*

In the 1920s and 1930s, the World's Land Speed Record was all about heroes. Men of courage like Sir Henry Segrave (231mph), Sir Malcolm Campbell (301mph), George Eyston (357mph) and John Cobb (394mph) were feted by their country. More famous than the top circuit racers of their day, their faces smiled down from news-reel screens and their names were familiar to every schoolboy.

Today, Wing Commander Andrew Green, OBE is not as well known to the general public as were his LSR forbears. In the 21st century it's Formula 1 drivers who are the media heroes, and few can really grasp the concept of a man driving a car across a lonely piece of desert faster than the speed of sound. Fewer still would understand that he risked his life doing this, for no payment. Or that he did it as a matter of nationalistic pride, and to underline the excellence of his country's engineering prowess. Andy Green's heroism is the old-fashioned sort, one that doesn't make a fuss, and doesn't produce good fodder for the tabloids. As a serving RAF officer, he had to use his normal annual leave to take part in the attempt, and he was back at work serving Queen and Country three days after setting the record.

A Phantom and Tornado pilot, he has seen service in East Germany, Bosnia, and more recently Afghanistan and Iraq. He has been part of the Defence Research Agency team at Farnborough, working on future generations of fighter aircraft, as well as RAF Attachment Commander in charge of the Harrier Squadron in Kandahar. Currently his role on the Air Staff Directorate involves crucial high-level strategic planning of on-going military operations. His normal lunch routine is half an hour in the gym in the basement of the Ministry of Defence, or a brisk run along the Embankment, followed by a sandwich at his desk. But, 10 years almost to the day since he became the fastest man on earth, I persuaded him to have a proper lunch and to talk about it.

Andy revels in the heritage of the Land Speed Record. So his chosen venue, the Bluebird Restaurant in London's Kings Road, was entirely appropriate: during the 1920s it was a garage, and Malcolm Campbell based his cars here. Tall and clean-cut, with a firm handshake and a steely eye, Andy is visibly very fit. His choice is healthy (scallops and sea bass, with a half-bottle of dry white Bordeaux) and then more indulgent (cheesecake).

His is an unusual mix of talents. He was 15 when he decided he wanted to be a pilot: his father had been in bombers in World War II. But from boyhood he was also a brilliant mathematician. In the same week he was offered a cadetship in the RAF and a place at Oxford. So the RAF sponsored him through University, and he duly got a first in mathematics. The year he did, 1983, he was fascinated to read about a fellow called Richard Noble breaking the Land Speed Record.

In the LSR's prewar heyday, oil and tyre companies were delighted to sponsor record attempts, and bask in the reflected glory of each new mark. But by the 1950s record-breaking on land had gone out of fashion. There was a flurry of mainly American activity in the 1960s, punctuated by Donald Campbell's oft-thwarted but ultimately successful efforts, and then in 1983 the brave Richard Noble brought the record back to Britain with Thrust 2's 633.47mph.

With extraordinary determination and persistence, Noble continued to pursue his dream of a car that would beat the speed of sound, even though he had endless difficulties raising the money to do it. Companies happy to spend huge sums putting their logo on back-of-the-grid Formula 1 cars could not see the attraction of attaching themselves to the world's fastest car. Most didn't believe it would ever happen, or reckoned it would end in tragedy and the worst sort of publicity. Fortunately many members of the public felt differently, and much of the funding that kept Noble's project alive came from donations to the Thrust website.

In 1994 Noble let it be known that he was looking for a driver for his supersonic car, and Andy, now a fully-fledged jet fighter pilot, applied. "I knew that the sound barrier would be the last great challenge in land speed record-breaking, and I believed it was very important for a British driver to be the first to do it. It was irresistible."

There were 30 serious applicants. A sophisticated series of interviews and tests, including technological and psychological exercises and a day in a rally car on the loose, whittled them down to eight, all pilots of one sort or another. In February 1995 Green, then 32, was chosen.

Thrust SSC used two Rolls-Royce Spey jet engines slung either side of a narrow cockpit, riding on four solid wheels that had no tyres, because no tyre has ever been made that could begin to cope with supersonic speeds and forces. There were two wheels in front, conventionally spaced, and two mounted centrally at the back, in slightly staggered tandem, which steered.

"Think about a car weighing 10 tons. A car 54 feet long. With one hundred thousand horsepower. And with rear-wheel steering. Lots of people said it would never work. Professors of aerodynamics said a supersonic car couldn't be done, and the assumptions they were making meant their reasons were entirely valid. Our task was to explore those assumptions without making something inherently dangerous."

Finance was a constant problem throughout the project. "Everybody is amazed that we achieved what we did on so little money, and so are we. It was a five-year project involving a core team of 30 people, not all of whom were being paid, plus a lot of volunteers. Richard managed to run the whole project for £3 million. The thing was never properly resourced. We bought nothing we could borrow, and we borrowed nothing we could steal.

"Of course I didn't expect to be paid. This was amateur motorsport at its absolute best. If you were driving a friend's hillclimb car at Shelsley Walsh for the weekend, would you expect to be paid, or would you do it for fun? The RAF couldn't give me any time off: I'm paid by the taxpayer, after all, and you can't expect the taxpayer to fund a motor racing project. So I saved up my holiday over a year and a half to give me the days to do it."

Richard Noble had started working on the Thrust SSC project in earnest in early 1994. The car first turned a wheel on a British runway in September 1995, but it wasn't until October 1996 that it first ran on a desert.

"For that first test we flew SSC to the Al Jafr Desert in Jordan, 93 tons of kit in a chartered Antonov, and we managed four runs in four weeks. One end of the desert to the other, stop, five days while we re-engineer the car, one more run the other way. An F1 team may do 10,000 miles of testing in a season, to say nothing of wind tunnel work and so on. We needed four weeks to do what an F1 team could do in an hour.

"First off, the rear-wheel steering didn't work. We hadn't got the geometry right. Then we found this huge wheel shimmy problem. We adjusted the geometry, and put dampers on the wheels. We were faxing designs back to England, and new bits were being engineered overnight and flown out to Amman in pilots' hand luggage. We were doing a lot of rapid prototyping, and developing the team skills out there in the desert. We got up to about 300mph, enough to show up the steering weaknesses, and then the rains came. So we loaded up again and flew home. When we got back we cut off the back of the car and re-engineered it completely.

"We went back to Jordan in May 1997. We got everything unloaded, got the desert marked out and cleared, and we managed nine runs in 13 days, which was a huge boost to the team. We were getting into summer temperatures, so we'd start at 5am and stop at 9am: after that it was too hot. The computer bays on the car were getting up to 100deg C. We started to use some quite high-end acceleration, and on the first full afterburner run I'm taking it nice and steady, 200, 250, 300, max burner, and suddenly it's going all over the place. I just cannot keep it in a straight line.

"Driving a normal car, if it diverges, you respond to correct it. But I was getting into what in an aircraft you'd call a pilot-induced oscillation. The vehicle diverges, you put in a response through the steering wheel, it responds, you put in another, but at that point the vehicle is reversing its response, so you get a double input. You and the vehicle are working out of phase. Every time there's the slightest input, say from irregularity in the desert surface or a crosswind, you've got to correct it. But if you start steering at the frequency of the car it gets worse, not better. I got out of the car that day and I said to myself, I think this project has just finished. The car's unstable. I think we're stuffed.

"I didn't feel I could talk to Richard or anyone else about it, so I spent the night thinking it through. And I came up with the conviction that I was simply going to have to bully the car into being stable, go very high frequency with my steering movements to keep it under control, coupled with lower frequency inputs to steer it. I'd have to steer it at two separate frequencies, simultaneously. So that's what I did, and it worked. I'd found a way to drive the thing. The downside was that I was never going to enjoy it. Imagine taking all the hairiest bits out of a three-hour sortie in a Tornado and doing them all in two minutes. It was the hardest thing I've ever done: like trying to balance the point of a pencil on the end of your finger."

In September 1997 the team arrived at Black Rock Desert, Nevada for the official attempt. Unlike Bonneville, which is a salt surface, Black Rock is made up of a fine alluvial dried mud. If you pick up a chunk of it, you can crumble it into dust as fine as talcum powder. This slightly compliant surface works much better with the solid wheels than Bonneville's salt, which is harsher. Over a five-week period Thrust SSC's speed gradually increased.

"The figure that counts is a mean of two directions, and the rules say you have to do your two runs within an hour. So in real terms you have very little time to get everything turned round, download all the data, refuel, run the checks, get set up and then do it again. Our track was 14 miles long: the measured mile was in the middle, with 6.5 miles to accelerate, 6.5 miles to slow down.

"The acceleration is very slow to start with, because the air intakes are optimised for Mach 1, so at lower speeds they can't get enough air to develop full power. Zero to 100mph takes about 20 seconds, winding the engines up to full power takes another eight seconds, and after that you're putting on another 100mph every four seconds. So 200mph to 700mph takes 20 seconds. That's over 1G: if you dropped a golf ball from the top of a building and jumped after it you'd be overtaking it. So it takes less than a minute to go supersonic from a standing start, and you're supersonic for about four miles.

"At that speed it takes about 4.69 seconds to cover the measured mile. We couldn't have boards marking the start of the mile, because with my narrow field of vision from the cockpit between the two engines there was no way I could see them at that speed. I was steering along a white line painted on the desert, and through the mile we had a second white line running parallel to it to show me I'd got there. A line painted across at the Start and finish would have been invisible – we were covering well over 1000 feet per second,"

On September 25th Andy did a two-way mean of 714.144mph, breaking Richard Noble's 14-year-old record by over 80mph, much to Richard's delight. Then on October 15th – 50 years and one day after Chuck Yeager's Mach 1 in the Bell X-1 aircraft – Andy's two-way mean was 766.035mph, and Mach 1.02. Ten miles away in the little town of Gerlach, the sonic boom broke plates and took pictures off walls, and set off fire extinguishers in the local school. History had been made.

"It wasn't deafeningly noisy for me. Jet engines make their noise out of the front, which is the high-pitched whine, and out of the back, which is the roar. I was sitting between the two, in an incredibly strong safety cell with a fireproof bulkhead. I was using a flying helmet because I needed the air supply, and it's quite difficult to get a long-duration air supply into a driving helmet. I'd had a lot of input into the design of the cockpit, and instead of a steering wheel I used an aeroplane yoke, with steering geared about one turn from lock to lock. Throttle under my right foot, brake under my left. We could have had a hand throttle like on a jet fighter, but we decided I'd need both hands to steer it. Just as well we did...

"We had active suspension because every time the aerodynamic neutral point moves you have to alter the pitch of the car to compensate. And plus or minus one degree of pitch on the car equals plus or minus 10 tons of load on the front wheels. Running the active fully up through the trans-sonic region increased the load on the front wheels by almost 10 tons. The wheels started to plough into the desert. If you ran the back end one degree from the down position you would create 10 tons of lift, and it's a 10-ton car with 6.5 tons on the front wheels, so that would make the car fly very quickly. You need to find that aerodynamic neutral point incredibly accurately.

"We were finding a lot of things in the high trans-sonic region which we could not explain. Like the toe-in at the rear wheels was moving from half a degree toe-in to half a degree toe-out. It could have been distortion of the back end, or steering wind-up, but distortion of the structure under the heat and load of high speed wasn't something we'd modelled.

"And we were generating some very powerful shock waves in front of the car. We found the wheels were actually going round less fast than the ground speed: we were ploughing the surface in front of the car. The shock wave was digging up the desert, so the four individual wheel tracks disappeared, and we started to get a single ploughed trace 12 feet wide.

"Things change so much between Mach 0.8 and Mach 1. When the shock waves start to form, depending on the shape of your vehicle, you've got a mixture of sub-sonic and supersonic flow. If you're doing Mach 0.95 and the air accelerates locally by another five per cent, over the cockpit or the curve of a wheel arch, it will form its own little shock wave there. In the trans-sonic period it's doing that in various places around and underneath the car. The pressure difference where the air goes from sub-sonic to supersonic is so great that if it happens underneath the car it can lift it off the ground.

"And the car may be fractionally different in shape from one side to the other. It's a hand-built car. We measured it as accurately as we could, but the tiniest difference, the thickness of a few coats of paint, can make the shock waves form earlier on one side. It happens with aircraft when you take them supersonic, but tiny corrections with the controls can fix that. With a car, it's the wheels that have to take the differences in load, and you start to realise the magnitude of the forces involved when a tiny difference can translate to an extra ton of load on one of the front wheels. Once you get well over Mach 1, life gets much easier. It's getting there that's the challenge."

The inevitable question: to what extent did he have to come to terms with the fact that this exercise could kill him? "It's not so much the driver's problem. Everyone else on the team has to sit there living with the knowledge that, if they get their bit wrong, the result could be catastrophic. Once the car starts to roll they have no control over it. The driver can say, that doesn't feel right, and he can throttle back. And if it's something he can't spot, a structural failure which he can't see or an aerodynamic failure he can't respond to, ultimately he won't be living with the consequences. The engineers will. We talked it through as a team, what risks we were willing to accept, and the answer was we wouldn't accept any avoidable risk. But then, all risks are avoidable if you don't run the car..."

The achievement of that record, for Andy, for Richard Noble, for the whole team, was immense. Then it was back to normal life. The team dispersed: Andy put record-breaking behind him and continued to pursue his high-flying RAF career. Then in 2005 JCB decided to go for the Diesel Record, and approached Andy.

"JCB build their own engine, the 4-4-4, which is a four-cylinder, four-valve-per-cylinder, four-litre unit designed for earth-moving work and developing 80bhp. Sir Anthony Bamford is a car nut, and he wanted to know how much power his engine could produce, and how fast it would go in a car. Ricardo, who'd helped develop the engine in the first place, told him they could take it from 80bhp to 750bhp using turbochargers, intercoolers and water injection – an increase of nearly 1000 per cent." Bamford looked up the diesel record and found it was 235mph, and he talked to Richard Noble. But Richard pointed out that a diesel truck had done a one-way pass of 280mph, and to do the thing properly they needed two engines and 1500bhp. The result was Dieselmax.

"JCB went outside their comfort zone with no guarantee of success. If BMW had done it, it wouldn't have been such big news, but this was a digger company setting out to build the world's fastest diesel car. The whole thing was done in a year. John Piper of Visioneering, an ex-F1 guy, built the chassis, and Goodyear developed the tyres, and we went to Bonneville and stayed on after the Speed Weeks last year. We had a tyre limit of 350mph, but I got straight up to 365mph, and I had to throttle back to stop the car accelerating. We took the record at 350.092mph. New tyres are being developed which should be good for 450mph: Goodyear has learned a lot about high-speed tyre behaviour, and it has changed the construction. So we'll go back and find out what Dieselmax can really do."

Naturally, Andy drives a British car – a Jaguar XK8. To relax he flies a Pitts Special aerobatic plane, and he's a keen sky-diver. "Flying your own body, using your own arms and legs, is a very skilled sport and takes a lot of learning. It's good to force your brain to do something different. The Pitts is the same: I can do it safely because I recognise its limits. I've just taken my Yachtmasters, and some time in the future I'd like to be teaching people how to sail. The discipline and team-work in sailing has a valid military application."

If the right team of people, with the right budget, wanted to take the LSR beyond 800mph, would he be interested in being the driver? "It's not worth doing if it's just showing off and trying to get your name in the record book. The reason for doing it would be the same as with Thrust SSC: to demonstrate how great British engineering is. And to do it genuinely for the British public, get them excited, get them involved. That's harder than it sounds, because this area of motorsport is hard to explain. You need to get to a whole generation of 12-year-olds in order to inspire the engineers of tomorrow. I was seven years old when Neil Armstrong walked on the moon, and I remember that day very clearly. It's too big a subject to try to assess the illnesses in our society today, but there's a need for inspirational projects to fire the imagination of the young. I don't know whether something like this would get to a disturbed 13-year-old and give him some interest, but if you only reach one tenth of one per cent of the kids and inspire them in some way, it's worth doing."

Patriotism is thought by many today to be a dated concept. Not by Wing Commander Green. "It's hugely important to me, as a serviceman, and as a Brit. Without patriotism it would be difficult for me to do my job, which is to serve and protect my country. Patriotism was a major motivation for me doing the Land Speed Record. It gave me the chance to stand on a global stage and say, here is a great piece of British endeavour."

A proper hero of the old-fashioned sort, Andy Green: a worthy follower in the wheeltracks of Campbell and Segrave. Britain should feel very proud of the achievements of Messrs Green and Noble. So it's to be regretted that so few of their countrymen seem to know and understand how much they've done for us.

Andy Green was talking to Simon in August 2007. In 2008 he and Richard Noble announced the rocket-powered Bloodhound SSC project, aiming to beat 1,000mph by 2014.

DAN GURNEY

America's greatest motor-racing
ambassador

Ever since this "Lunch With..." caper began, at the top of my Wanted list has been Daniel Sexton Gurney. This is a man who drove for Ferrari in the 1950s, who spearheaded Porsche's foray into Formula 1, and who won Le Mans for Ford. A patriot who built and drove the first American F1 car ever to win a Grand Prix. A victor in F1, sports cars and USAC – sometimes in the same season – and also in Can-Am, Trans-Am and NASCAR. A race car manufacturer too, who ran front-line teams in Indycar, Champ Car, Formula 5000, Trans-Am and IMSA. And a racer acknowledged by his peers to be one of the very best: famously, the man whom Jim Clark regarded as his most serious rival.

I knew Dan Gurney to be a courteous and deep-thinking man who would make a wonderful lunch guest. The problem was, he didn't want to have lunch with me. Or, rather, he was very happy to invite me to lunch at his Eagles' eyrie, but he wouldn't be interviewed. The reason was a good one: for a while now, Dan has been working on his autobiography. There have been other books about his extraordinary life, but none authored by him. This will be the real story, and an important addition to racing's written-down history because, throughout a golden era, Dan was there. So he has decreed: until the book is done, no more interviews.

But Dan's a long-time *Motor Sport* reader. So, with typical generosity, he decided that he would, after all, talk to me about his career, but would keep back some of the detail. We agreed that my piece had to be an *amuse-bouche* for the autobiography. And he vetoed questions about his friends who are no longer around – Jimmy Clark, Peter Revson, Bruce McLaren, Swede Savage, Ken Miles, Phil Hill, Denny Hulme, Cliff Allison and many more. It's a melancholy list, and he still feels their loss too keenly. He will say what he wants to say about them in the book.

The neat, unobtrusive facility in Santa Ana, south of Los Angeles, has been the centre of Dan's working life ever since he set up All American Racers in 1964. Today it is humming with precision engineering and prototype work, and also development of the revolutionary Alligator motorcycle that has been a Gurney project since the 1990s. Dan is 78 now, but he likes to go to work "just about every day": he remains president of AAR, with his son Justin as general manager. For 40 years a key member of the team has been Dan's wife Evi, whom he first met when he was racing for Porsche. She was PA to competitions boss Huschke von Hanstein, and later ran Porsche's press office. One of his 85 staff is the legendary fabricating genius Phil Remington, who was with Eagle throughout its heyday and still works there full-time, aged 88. People tend to stay loyal to Dan.

His big office is crammed with memorabilia, but it's a measure of the man's modesty that many of the framed photographs that cover the walls are not of him but of friends, fellow drivers, men he worked with, people he admired or wants to remember –like the iconic shot of Fangio drifting his 250F Maserati through the downhill curves at Rouen. There's also a small museum of significant Eagles down the years. On the patio lunch is laid out in the sunshine: fresh salads, good Californian wine and coffee.

Dan was born on Long Island, New York – his father was a leading bass baritone at the Metropolitan Opera – but when he was 17 the family moved to California. His father set up an avocado farm, ironically not far from where the Riverside circuit would later be built. But for Dan, first it was hotrods. "In my teens I put a Mercury flat-head in an old Model A, took it to

Bonneville and went 130mph on methanol. We were proud of that." There was impromptu drag racing too, but in 1955, home after a spell in the Korean War as a gunner, he decided that road racing held more appeal. So he bought a Triumph TR2, and had his first race at Torrey Pines.

Soon, looking for more speed, he bought a Porsche Speedster. "I was working at an engineering firm for $1.12 an hour, so I went to the bank for the money. In those days you could do that." Soon the money was gone, and Dan realised he'd have to rely on talking his way into other people's cars. "One day I was up at Willow Springs and these two fellows with a Corvette were having trouble getting in a good lap. So I offered to show them how." Dan beat the class lap record, and found himself co-opted to drive a Corvette at the inaugural meeting at the new Riverside track. He won conclusively, beating the fastest 300SL Mercedes by almost half a minute, and finished sixth in the main event against proper sports-racers. The Corvette's owner, Cal Bailey, worked for millionaire building contractor Frank Arciero, who had a big 4.9-litre Ferrari with an evil reputation.

"It had been rebuilt after a wreck and ended up not very user-friendly. Arciero asked me to try it at Willow, so first I spun it around on the pit apron to get a feel of it. I had to modify my driving style to deal with what the car wanted – not the first time I'd had to do that, or the last. Then I went out and got under the outright lap record. I was lucky because it wasn't a car everybody was clamouring to get into, but it was certainly fast."

A string of wins in the big Ferrari got Dan noticed, but it didn't go down well at his place of work. "I was in line for more responsibility, but they told me I'd have to stop racing. I didn't, of course, so I got fired. I had a wife and two small children by now, and I found myself standing in line at the unemployment office. I felt like a gigantic failure. My problem was I wanted to do road racing. In oval racing you could make a living, but there were no professional road racers in the US then. Things were looking pretty bleak. Then I got a phone call from Luigi Chinetti, Ferrari's man in New York who ran NART [the North American Racing Team]. In baseball they have the farm system, where top teams watch the minor leagues for any new talent coming along. Well, I didn't realise it, but Chinetti was doing that, following the American races and keeping Enzo posted about what was going on. And he offered me a drive at Le Mans."

So Dan flew to Europe for the first time. In the 24 Hours he was paired with Bruce Kessler in a NART Testa Rossa, and in dreadfully wet conditions they got the car up into fourth place. Kessler was at the wheel when the Jaguar D-type of Jean-Marie Brousselet crashed fatally on the Dunlop Curve. The remains of the D-type cannoned into the path of the Ferrari, which rolled and caught fire. Two weeks later, in the Reims 12 Hours, Dan shared a Ferrari 250GT with André Guelfi, and they got up to second place before Guelfi crashed.

Dan stayed in Europe for several months, travelling with Troy Ruttman and his wife Beverley in a Renault Dauphine. "We had a wonderful time. Troy was a charismatic guy who'd won the Indy 500 at the age of 22 – the youngest winner ever. He was a gifted racer, did the Carrera Panamericana in a Mercury sedan too. But winning Indy at that age was more than he could cope with, and he fell in with the wrong people, did a lot of drinking and carousing. He was sampling F1 in a Scuderia Centro-Sud Maserati 250F, and we used the Dauphine to learn the 'Ring. It was OK for the downhill parts, but uphill it was hopeless! Bernard Cahier fixed me up with a little Osca for the sports car race before the German GP, and I was down to drive an Ecurie Ecosse D-type at Silverstone, but Masten Gregory crashed it. And I got to test a Centro-Sud Maserati 250F at Modena."

Back in America he continued to race for Arciero and NART, but then Chinetti came on the phone again. Ferrari had lost Peter Collins and Luigi Musso in fatal accidents and Mike Hawthorn to retirement, and Dan was summoned for a test at Modena. "I drove a 2-litre sports car, then a 3-litre sports car, then an F1 car. Two days later, at Monza, they put me in a Testa Rossa. It was raining, and [Ferrari test driver] Martino Severi, who knew every inch of the place, set a time first. I had a wad of 10,000 lire notes to keep me alive in Italy, and I didn't want to leave them in the pits, so I stuffed them in my driver's suit. I didn't fit the seat very well anyway, and the pressure of those banknotes was just in the wrong place, so my right leg went to sleep after a few laps. I managed to get through it, equalled Severi's time although I didn't beat it. Then, on my coming-in lap, I spun at the Parabolica. I didn't hit anything, and drove on to the pits, and they never knew.

"I flew back to the US not really knowing what to make of all this. Then a telegram arrived from Ferrari. It offered me a ride in the 1959 World Sports Car Championship, for a retainer of $163 a month." Joining a team that included Tony Brooks, Jean Behra, Phil Hill, Olivier Gendebien and Cliff Allison, Dan shared the winning car at Sebring, led the Targa Florio, held second at the 'Ring until clutch trouble dropped him to fifth and, teamed with Behra, led Le Mans for five hours. And he was called to Monza for another F1 test. "It was the latest 246. Enzo was there, and Behra had just got under the lap record with it. I did about 10 laps, and then they changed the 15-inch front wheels for 16s. They told me *'Guarda'*, watch out. After a couple of laps to warm the tyres, I went down to my usual braking point at the Parabolica and the fronts locked. I lifted and tried again, and they locked again, and by now I was pretty far in. I managed to spin the car, but it hit the bank, almost spat me out as it banged and bounced, and ended up pretty bent. I figured, OK Dan, you've really done it now. Back at the pits they said, 'Too bad. By the way, in those first 10 laps you equalled Behra's time.' Three weeks later I was driving in my first Grand Prix."

That was at Reims, where his engine blew. But he did three more for Ferrari, and amazingly finished second (Avus), third (Monsanto Park) and fourth (Monza). "The Portuguese race got people's attention because I was quickest Ferrari on what was thought to be a tricky road circuit. Phil was coming into his own then, but Tony Brooks was rightly considered to be team leader, and I had the utmost respect for him. You're always searching for a measure of where you stand. That was what mattered to me."

At Reims Behra had his famous argument with Romolo Tavoni, threw a punch and was sacked from the team. "I liked Tavoni. He was a big tall gangling person, worldly in an appealing way, and you sensed that if you worked for Enzo you'd better pay him some respect. When he and Behra had their difficulty I didn't understand it, because I really admired Jean. Enzo seemed to foment that sort of trouble: one of his weapons was to frighten people if he could. Four weeks later Jean went over the Avus banking in the rain during the sports car race.

"There were a lot of unknowns at Avus. The height and contour of the banking meant you'd be in trouble if you lost it there. I'd heard the bricks got very slippery in the wet, but we didn't run in the rain."

Dan's F1 career had got off to a great start, and he was hailed as the discovery of the season, but for 1960 he opted to go to BRM. "I realised mid-engined was the way things were going: Cooper had proved that. At that point Enzo was still saying the horse should be in front of the carriage. The BRMs looked beautifully made, lots of nice machining, and I assumed they would be as strong and durable as the Ferrari, I thought all racing cars were like that. But I was wrong."

That season with the new rear-engined BRM was a disaster. Dan retired from every championship round except Silverstone, where a long pitstop delayed him. And at Zandvoort the hydraulic pipe to the single rear transmission brake ruptured as he hit the brakes at 160mph. The BRM leaped a sand dune, went through a barbed-wire fence, and killed a young spectator. Dan was lucky to escape serious injury. "At the time Stirling was the acknowledged deep-braking guy, and I was trying my best to equal him. After that I altered my braking technique, never went quite so deep any more."

The same year, paired with Stirling Moss in a Camoradi Maserati Birdcage, he scored a great victory in the Nürburgring 1000Kms. Moss said later, "Along with Fangio, Dan was the best co-driver I ever had." Dan returns the compliment. "Stirling was the superstar, without any question. When I wasn't racing myself I'd go out and watch how he drove. Sharing with him was a huge privilege. You want to know how you measure up, you share a car with Stirling." In treacherous conditions of drizzle and fog, Moss handed over to Gurney with a full minute's lead, which Gurney was consolidating when the Maserati broke an oil pipe. "Suddenly the cockpit was flooded with hot oil, sloshing forward when I braked and back when I accelerated. I nursed the car seven miles back to the pits – building hotrod engines as a teenager had given me mechanical sensitivity – but when [Maserati chief mechanic] Guerrino Bertocchi saw all the mess there was quite a bit of Italian opera. I persuaded him the engine might still be OK, they just had to mend the oil line and clean it up." The stop lost nearly six minutes, but after a brilliant charge back up the field Dan retook the lead from the Hill/von Trips Ferrari, before handing back to Moss.

With the advent of the 1500cc F1 he moved to Porsche, which was embarking on its first full Grand Prix season. "I really learned how to drive at Porsche because, unlike at BRM, the cars always went the full distance." With its air-cooled flat-four the car wasn't the fastest, but Dan was second at Reims, Monza and Watkins Glen, and ended up third equal in the championship with Moss. For 1962 Porsche had its new flat-eight. "Still air-cooled, still only two valves per cylinder, but still pretty reliable. And they were great people. I'd expected them to be all Teutonic and serious, but they weren't at all. Very hard-working, but with a sense of humour." At Rouen Dan scored Porsche's only victory in a championship round, and two weeks later, in front of 300,000 people, he won the non-championship

Solitude GP. Three weeks after that he took pole for the German GP, finishing third after a race-long battle with Graham Hill's BRM and John Surtees' Lola.

Also in '62, Dan paid his first visit to Indianapolis. He'd never seen the place before, and took his driver's test in an old Zink Offy roadster. "I told Zink's chief mechanic, Denny More, that the car felt like it was going to spin all the time, I had no confidence that it wasn't going to bust the tail loose, and could he give me a little bit of push – which is what they call understeer at Indy. And he just said, 'No'. One of those old-time chief mechanics, they were in charge, they didn't have to do anything they didn't want to. It was a shock to me. I flew to Europe to do the Targa Florio for Porsche, flew back, and tried one of Mickey Thompson's new cars, with an alloy pushrod Buick V8 in the back. Right away it felt good." He qualified it eighth, and ran in the top 10 until the transmission failed. The Gurney fascination with Indy had begun.

"I knew a mid-engined car was the way to go at Indy. Colin Chapman had never been, so I bought him a round-trip ticket so he could take a look. Then I introduced him to some Ford people in Detroit." Out of that came a deal for two Lotus-Fords in the 1963 race. During March testing, to the consternation of the Indy establishment, Dan sensationally lapped at over 150mph. But in qualifying in May he hit the wall. "The Dunlop ally wheels were cracking. Part of why I hit the wall was because we didn't have enough wheels to go round, and I had to go out on Jimmy's set. He was using more negative camber than me and his tyres were worn differently. I did the race in the spare car, finished seventh." In 1964, with the new Ford four-cam V8, the team's Dunlop tyres weren't up to the task, which put Gurney and Clark out.

In sports cars, Dan scored the Cobra's first FIA Championship win in the 1963 Bridgehampton 500Kms, and in 1964 he was part of Carroll Shelby's effort to wrest the GT Championship from Ferrari. At the Targa Florio the leaf-sprung Cobra wasn't ideal for the bumpy, tortuous 45-mile circuit, but Dan and Jerry Grant got up to second place. "Once you got used to all the banging and crashing, the Cobra had good brakes, a lot of tyre on the road, lots of horsepower. The aerodynamics weren't great, but we raked the windshield right down, so Jerry and I looked over the top, and that was worth 10mph. On the straights in Sicily we were pulling 160. It wasn't too predictable when you had to move to the edge of the road to overtake another car, but power-on cornering with the tail out was a lot of fun." Eventually the rear suspension broke, but Gurney heroically nursed the car home eighth, going the full distance to take the class win. "When I finally crossed the line the pits were deserted. I found the team in a restaurant having dinner. They couldn't believe I'd made it to the finish. I just looked at them, turned round and left. I wasn't terribly pleased." At Le Mans that year he had the more slippery Daytona Cobra coupé, taking the GT class and a fine fourth place with Bob Bondurant, and he won the GT category in the Goodwood TT with third overall.

When Porsche left Formula 1 at the end of 1962, Dan signed for Jack Brabham's new team. "Jack ran a tight operation – we had one mechanic per car – but Tauranac produced a car that was awfully good, handling-wise. I've been accused of constantly tinkering with the handling of my cars but, with the Brabham, my mechanic Tim Wall and I hardly ever changed anything. Slow tracks, fast tracks, it was good everywhere. Spa was a great place to learn your level, compare yourself with the others. I think I was the only guy then who could get through the Masta kink without lifting, because I'd learned at Indy how to deal with really high-speed corners. At Spa in 1964 I was leading by over half a minute – and I started to run out of fuel. I dived into the pits and yelled at Tim: 'Gas! I need gas!' But he'd loaded everything back in the transporter to go home. No gas. I drove on, but I ran dry half a lap later, and Jimmy won." In three seasons, Dan led a lot of races for Brabham, but only won two: at Rouen – the marque's first victory in a championship round – and in Mexico City.

His timing was not always ideal. Soon after he left Ferrari, it won the championship. Same with BRM; same with Brabham. But when the new 3-litre rules were announced for 1966 he laid plans for a Formula 1 challenger of his own. He'd set up All American Racers with the blessing of Goodyear, and run his own Lotus at Indy in 1965. Now the idea was to build and run cars in USAC and F1 using the same basic design, one with the four-cam Ford V8, the other with a new V12 commissioned from Weslake in England. Exquisitely engineered, the cars were called Eagles, and boasted a distinctive beak-shaped air intake.

The F1 car, after using an elderly 2.7 four-cylinder Climax as a stopgap, got its new V12 late in 1966. "The guys at Weslake did a terrific job with the budget I was able to generate. The engine was basically very sound, although its oil scavenge system wasn't up to it. And it was less powerful than we'd hoped – the most we ever saw was 393bhp, which was a bit shy of the early DFV's 420." But in 1967, despite its power handicap, the F1 Eagle started to go really well. In the Race of Champions at Brands Hatch Dan took pole and won both heats and the final, holding off Lorenzo Bandini's Ferrari.

Racing in F1, USAC, sports cars and Trans-Am all at once required incredible stamina, and Dan's schedule from late April to mid-June that year bears repeating. He flew to Texas to drive a Mercury Cougar in the Green Valley 300 at Smithfield, and won. Back at Indy, his Ford four-cam-powered Eagle set fastest practice lap at 163.8mph. Then the flight to Europe, to Rye to check on the V12 engine programme at Weslakes, and to Monaco for the Grand Prix, where he ran third until the injection pump belt broke. Overnight flight back to America, straight to Indy qualifying, and at 167.9mph he was just pipped to pole by Mario Andretti. Race day at Indy, a Tuesday, and Dan was running second to Parnelli Jones' STP Turbine when rain stopped the race. It was re-run on Wednesday, when Dan should have been on the plane to Zandvoort for the Dutch GP. He took the lead when Parnelli spun — only to be delayed by a jamming fuel tank valve, which led to engine failure. By Friday morning he was at Zandvoort with a lighter, magnesium-monocoque F1 Eagle, and qualified second behind Graham Hill in the new Lotus 49. In Sunday's race he was holding fourth when the metering unit failed. Monday he stayed at Zandvoort for a test, Tuesday he was back at Rye, Wednesday he crossed to France for the Le Mans 24 Hours. Sharing a Ford MkIV with AJ Foyt, he won at record speed. Tuesday another Goodwood test, Thursday to Belgium for the next GP – and a historic win with the Eagle.

So the two greatest victories of Dan's career happened on consecutive weekends. "AJ was a superstar, a damn fine engineer and a great race driver. He hadn't been to Le Mans before; it was my tenth time, and I persuaded him it wasn't a race, it was an endurance contest, and we had to be kind to the car. He left it to me to set the car up — the key was how little spoiler you could get away with at the back and still take the Mulsanne Kink flat. So we were sensible in practice, and only ninth-fastest. The Ford people were going nuts: 'What's wrong with the car, Dan?'. I said, 'The car's fine.'

"By the second hour we were leading, and by five in the morning we were six laps ahead of the Lodovico Scarfiotti/Mike Parkes Ferrari P4. I knew that the Ford's Achilles heel was its brakes. You did 213mph down the straight, and then you had Mulsanne Corner. The brakes weren't really up to that kind of punishment, and if you got brutal you could probably destroy them in 10 laps. So I'd back off soon after the hump before Mulsanne, let the car slow down on the over-run to about 150, and then brake. Parkes was right behind me, even though he was six laps down, and when he was in my slipstream I could still pull away at maybe 2-3mph. Then I'd do my early back-off, and of course he's all over me, flashing his lights, trying to goad me into killing my brakes. After four or five laps of this it started to get to me, so coming out of Arnage I pulled onto the grass verge and stopped. And he pulled over and stopped behind me. Here we were, running first and second at Le Mans, no problem with either car, sitting on the verge. After 15 seconds or so he got embarrassed and drove on. Once he was down the road I drove on too, and about seven laps later I passed him, but keeping to my rigid discipline of preserving the brakes." The Ford was still four laps ahead of the Ferrari when the flag fell at 4pm on Sunday.

"On the rostrum it was one of those moments: it felt so good to have won Le Mans at last, and they handed me this magnum of champagne. All the photographers were standing below with their expensive cameras, looking expectant, so I just put my thumb over the end, shook up the bottle, and sprayed it everywhere. Hank the Deuce [Henry Ford II] and his new bride were up there as well, and I got them in the firing line too." Gurney had initiated a routine for thousands of podia to come. On a shelf in his office, he still has that bottle.

Seven days later the American national anthem rang out over Spa. Dan missed the pre-race briefing, which told the drivers that the starting flag would fall any time after the 30-seconds board. When it did fall Dan, in the middle of the front row between the Lotus 49s of Jim Clark and Graham Hill, wasn't even in gear. He was eighth going up the hill into Eau Rouge. By lap two he was third, and by lap 21 the Eagle was in the lead. Setting a 148.85mph lap record around the old high-speed road circuit, he won by over a minute. He'd done it in his own car and with his own small team, on far too tight a budget, exactly one year on from their F1 debut. It was an extraordinary achievement. "Standing up there while the *The Star-Spangled Banner* was played was mighty high. I'll tell you something that addresses it a bit. In those days, flying back and forth over the Atlantic in heavy weather got a bit iffy sometimes. I used to say, 'Come on, aeroplane, don't go down, I haven't won a Grand Prix in an Eagle yet.' After Spa I'd say to the aeroplane, 'If you want to go down now, it's OK...'"

There was nearly another Eagle victory that year, in the German GP. Dan was always brilliant at the 'Ring, and with three laps to go he had a huge lead when a driveshaft universal joint broke. "That was one of the tough ones. Tim Wall [who'd followed Dan to Eagle from Brabham] said afterwards: 'It was my fault. For the 'Ring I like to grind more clearance on the UJs for full droop and full compression over the bumps, and I was so busy I didn't do one side.' I told him it wasn't his fault. Tim was a terrific guy."

Dan's versatility continued to shine. He drove his USAC Eagles to victory from Mosport to Sears Point, Brainerd to Riverside. For Can-Am he developed his own McLaren, so different from the works cars it was dubbed the McLeagle. AAR developed the Barracuda Trans-Am cars for Chrysler, and in NASCAR Dan made a speciality of the Riverside 500, winning it five times. "Those big stockers weighed nearly two tons, they'd run 160mph down the back straight, and they had drum brakes. If changing direction in an F1 car is like a water-bug darting across the surface of a pond, driving a NASCAR sedan on a road circuit is like trying to dock an aircraft carrier. But it isn't any easier or harder to win a race with a water-bug or an aircraft carrier. It's just different. In the end you still have four patches of rubber on the ground, and various ways of getting those patches to move around. It's like people used to say of oval racing: all you have to do is turn left. But you're up against the guys who are best in the world at turning left. A 100-yard sprint is pretty simple, until you come up against the best 100-yard sprinters. Each is a separate discipline, with good people applying creative thinking, and coming up with little increments."

At the end of 1968, Dan took the bitter decision to wind up the Eagle F1 programme, essentially because Goodyear's backing dried up. "Let's just say there were a lot of people trying to eat at the Goodyear trough, and some of them had more influence than others. The same old political thing, moves made when I wasn't at the table: maybe I have to blame myself for that. But it was a heart-rending choice to have to take." Nevertheless, the Indy programme continued apace. He was second in the 1968 500, using a stock-block engine: the winner, Bobby Unser, also drove an Eagle, with turbo Offy power. In 1969 he was second again. In 1970, his final 500, he was favourite to win but, in a fighting drive with a difficult car, he made 11 pitstops – and still finished third. After Bruce McLaren's tragic death that year he briefly partnered Denny Hulme at McLaren in F1 and in Can-Am too, winning the Mosport and St Jovite rounds. Then he hung up his helmet.

"I'd lost maybe half a per cent of my motivation, and unless you're 100 per cent as a driver you shouldn't be doing it. By 1970 I felt almost lonely on the grid, looking around and feeling who was missing. You'd see these bright-eyed youngsters who couldn't wait to roll the dice, but if you studied what caused the demise of this guy and that guy, you realised some of it couldn't have been foreseen and you'd have had a hard time avoiding it. That started to add up.

"I was always interested in safety. I was the first car racer with a full-face helmet: Bell developed that for motorcycle speedway, where the clods of dirt could really punish a rider's face. But I never sided with the group that began to say, 'We're not going there because it's too dangerous.' I always said, 'I'll be there', because that was racing, that was the way it was, that was what you were there to do. I loved circuits like the Nürburgring, Spa, the Targa Florio, Rouen. When I went to Europe in 1958 people were getting used up. I was there when Luigi Musso was killed at Reims, and then Peter Collins at the 'Ring. It wasn't as though you woke up one morning and said, 'Hey, this is dangerous.' Some drivers think, 'It can't happen to me', but I knew it could happen to me."

All American Racers remained energetically busy, and team and customer Eagles went on winning: the statistics show 78 victories and eight championships, including Indy again in

1973 and '75. There were Formula A and 5000 chassis, even an Eagle Formula Ford, and 18 generations of Indycars up to 1986. Then came the Champ Car and IMSA variants during a 15-year relationship with Toyota. The 1991/3 Toyota-powered GTP was the most successful Eagle ever, winning 17 straight races: some of its lap records still stand, more than 15 years later. In 2002 the Alligator was announced, fruit of Dan's lifelong passion for motorcycles. His long legs gave him the idea of a long-wheelbase design where the rider sits low between the engine and the rear wheel. "I ride my Alligator most Sundays with my sons. All five are talented riders and drivers." Youngest son Alex is a seriously quick professional racer: 2007 Rolex Daytona Prototype champion in Grand-Am with Jon Fogarty, he currently leads the 2009 series.

Our conversation ranges over many topics that stimulate Dan's sharp thinking: Boeing's experiments with BWBs, or blended-wing aircraft; the oil industry's effect on world politics; and race track design. "People laying out circuits never appreciate that every inch you move the spectators further back, you give them a corresponding reduction in enjoyment. You can keep them safe by putting them on the inside of a turn, and siting them higher up." And more stories, told in Dan's self-deprecating way: like persuading the authorities that running an F1 race around the streets of Long Beach was a good idea. Or turning down a drive in the Cannonball Run in a Ferrari Daytona in 1971, and then deciding hours before the start, 'Hell, let's do it' – and winning it. "It took us 35 hours from downtown Manhattan to Redondo Beach, California, and we only got one speeding ticket. Three lawyers in a Cadillac were second. They got seven tickets."

But that must do for your *amuse-bouche*. For the full tale you'll have to wait, like me, for the autobiography of one of the greatest drivers, and one of the nicest guys, in all of motor sport history.

Dan Gurney was talking to Simon in August 2009.

DAMON HILL

*The World Champion son of a
World Champion father*

Ten years on from that cold, grey afternoon in Japan when he became Britain's new World Champion, Damon Hill looks fit and relaxed. He smiles a lot, laughs at some of his more ironic racing memories, and can look back on the peaks of his career with quiet satisfaction. He's a family man now, absorbed by his life with wife Georgie and their four children, as well as various business interests and fund-raising work for the Down's Syndrome Association.

The dark, brooding eyes that I remember from the days when he was fighting his often lonely way up the motor racing ladder are calmer now. They're the eyes of someone who has come on a long journey – a journey that began when his World Champion father's light aircraft plunged into a golf course near Elstree on a foggy night in November 1975.

"He'd just retired and was running the Embassy Hill team. I'd started to go to races with him, and it was a lot of fun. It was a small team – in those days you could build an F1 car with four people, a few sheets of aluminium and some rivets. The team shuttle was a tiny Fiat 126. I remember in Barcelona going from the hotel to the track at Montjuich Park with about 10 people squeezed in.

"When he died, it was like having your head chopped off. I was just 15. I'm 46 now, the same age dad was, and Joshua is 15, like I was. I realise now how important that time is between a father and a son. You need that bit, from 15 to 20, to get yourself into the adult world. I sort of went into cold storage, I was left hunting around.

"Dad didn't want me to go into motor racing. He said I was too intelligent to be a racing driver; I proved him wrong there! When I was seven, I remember watching TV at home one afternoon and there was a newsflash saying Jim Clark had been killed. I had to tell my mum. He'd been dad's championship rival all those years, and by then they were team-mates, racing together. I'd grown up with all this, drivers who were mum and dad's friends coming to the house, and accidents happening in the background, and my little head going round thinking, 'what's going on here'? When Ayrton was killed 25 years later, a lot of F1 drivers were completely stunned that someone could die. I felt like saying, 'Didn't you know racing drivers can get killed?' I grew up knowing that.

"Dad's story was an inspiration – he'd come up from nothing: he was just a mechanic. But he wasn't an easy man. I was terrified of him. My becoming a driver was a way of standing up to him. Maybe if he'd lived and I'd got to 18 I would have been able to say, 'Dad, you're wrong'. But I had to establish myself beside him, and the only marker he left was as a racing driver. Now I feel I can say to him, 'Hey dad, I've been round Spa in the wet, I know what you're talking about'. It's a bonding."

We've met at an appropriate place for a British champion, the RAC's Country Club at Woodcote Park. Damon eats healthily – asparagus and artichoke soup, mushroom risotto, a glass of New Zealand red. I cast his mind back to his start in racing, on two wheels. There was no silver spoon to help him: after Graham's death the Hills' 25-room mansion at Shenley had to give way to a semi in St Albans, and Damon famously became a motorcycle messenger.

"I didn't have to become a despatch rider. I could have got a proper job. But I don't like people telling me what to do, that's my problem. And I went racing, bought my own 'bike, prepared it, did it all on my own. John Webb helped me, though – he knew my father's name was good for the gate. In 1984 I won just about everything I did, 40 races. One day my 'bike broke, the big end seized. I went up to John Webb in the Brands Hatch bar and said, 'I'm sorry, I can't race this weekend'. He got the barmaid to open the till, fished out £100 and gave it to me. He said, 'Go and find someone in the paddock who'll rent you a 'bike'. So I went to the paddock, rented some fellow's 'bike, and won on that too. I remember thinking, 'Bloody hell, it's not the 'bike, it must be me!'"

Today, most F1 drivers have been karting since the age of eight, but Damon had none of that. So did racing on two wheels develop his technique? "Of course. You try racing in the wet on a 'bike, aquaplaning through Paddock Bend. It gives you a very sensitive backside."

With John Webb's help Damon moved into Formula Ford, where he had a lot of success in 1985 before grinding through three seasons of F3 and three more in F3000. Always there were money problems, and repeatedly his career seemed to have hit the buffers. But he never gave up knocking on doors. In 1991 he netted a testing role for Williams, starting a relationship that was to endure for six years. In 1992 he got a race deal with the almost bankrupt Brabham team. After five failures to qualify, he finally started his first grand prix at Silverstone. It was two months before his 32nd birthday, dreadfully late to embark on an F1 career. Watching his uncompetitive and woefully underfunded BT60B-Judd finish in last place, four laps behind, we could hardly have guessed that a year later he would be a grand prix winner, and four years later he would be World Champion. So did he always believe in himself?

"No, I'm a massive doubter. A humongous doubter. But it's okay for me to doubt myself. If someone else doubts me, that's not allowed! I think life's a test. I'm not religious but I do believe that we have one life, just one chance to define ourselves. And I'm stubborn. I am quite obsessive when I get stuck into something. I've always found that, just when you think the way forward is impossible and the route is barred, something crops up, and you're ready for it because you're still looking for that little chink, that opening."

And something did crop up. Williams replaced Riccardo Patrese with Alain Prost for 1993. That put the nose of No1 driver Nigel Mansell seriously out of joint, and he left F1 for Indycars. Mika Häkkinen and Martin Brundle were both considered for the Williams No2 seat, but Patrick Head and Adrian Newey had been highly impressed by Damon's progress in the testing role, and Damon found himself with a one-year race contract. At once he rose to the challenge. He finished third in the Championship behind Prost and Senna, won three races on the trot and got on the podium 10 times.

"I have utter respect for Alain Prost. His style was effortless: he could be blindingly fast without ever seeming to do anything. He was charming, but I never learned a thing from him. And that's the right way to be. Why should he give me any help? Team-mates is a misnomer — you're not mates, you're racing each other. Of course, if you've agreed to team orders in your contract, then you have to live with that. I talked to Jean Todt about driving for Ferrari after I left Williams, and he said I'd have to drive to orders behind Schumacher. I said, 'Forget it. Unless I get equal position with Michael I'm not doing it'. Why would I sign my own death warrant?"

For 1994 Alain Prost retired, and Damon found himself alongside Ayrton Senna. "Ayrton was a powerful figure. He always walked into a place like he owned it. He was on a quest for what was right and what was wrong — although what was right was right for Ayrton, and what was wrong was wrong for Ayrton — but beyond that there was something else. He wasn't always totally admirable — I mean, knocking Prost off in the first corner in Suzuka in 1990 was a bit questionable! But he had an enormous amount of charisma and presence. There was an utter seriousness about him, an intensity.

"I never got close to Ayrton like, say, Gerhard [Berger] did. But I learned a lot just watching him in testing. He was very insistent on getting his message through: he would explain something over and over to the engineers until they'd got it. Because they couldn't be in the car with him, he had to be positive they really understood.

"I never went into this seeing myself as a number one driver. I thought, this is great, I'm team-mates with Alain Prost, and then, great, I'm team-mates with Ayrton Senna. And then Senna died, and suddenly I was thrown into the deep end. I had to raise my game. And I don't think I was prepared for that. It was horrible: his clothes still hanging up in the changing room, everyone in shock.

"I'm very confident I know what happened with Ayrton. A lot has been written about it, but there's no doubt in my mind. A number of factors made the car difficult to drive, the low tyre pressures after the slow safety car laps and so on, and he got into a tank-slapper over the bumps and the car got away from him. People don't want to accept that the great Ayrton Senna made a mistake, but even he made mistakes – he'd fallen off in Brazil two races before. This is not to detract from Ayrton in any way. He was a great driver and a great human being. But I've gone through it over and over; I've analysed it. It was just a tragic accident.

"At Imola we had to line up again, and we had to do the race. There was some question that Ayrton's power steering might have played a part in the accident, so they disconnected it on my car and I did the restart without it. On the grid we didn't know Ayrton was dead. Everyone said it was serious, but that's all they told us, so we just got on with the job." For the record, Damon had to pit for a new nosecone, restarted last, and stormed back up to sixth, setting the race's fastest lap on the way.

"After that everybody was reeling under the shock of losing Ayrton. I wanted to say, 'Hey, I'll do my best'. But remember I was a test driver two seasons ago – I'm not Ayrton Senna, OK? But I got stuck in, and we won in Barcelona four weeks later. It felt good to get a win in. I won at Silverstone, then Schumacher had his two-race ban and was disqualified at Spa, and I won three more. Then we had the wet race at Suzuka."

In the view of most who saw it, including me, the 1994 Japanese Grand Prix was Damon's greatest drive. Because of a red flag it was run in two parts, with the winner declared on aggregate. In treacherously wet and difficult conditions, over nearly two full hours, Damon beat Schumacher in a straight fight by 3.3secs.

"It was the most intense race I ever did, no question," asserts Damon. "I had to win to stay in the frame for the title, and I just kind of ratcheted myself up. The whole race was mad: in the first few laps you couldn't see a damn thing, all I could see was Michael's rear light, and I thought if I lose sight of that I'm finished. After the restart I was racing an invisible man – I'd finished the first part seven seconds down on Michael, so it wasn't enough just to win: I had to beat him by at least that amount. I knew I had to push, but not allow him to push me into making a mistake. I was driving on a different level from how I'd ever driven before. It was an experience which lived with me for a very long time.

"I think what we're capable of mentally is way beyond what we think it is. If you're a racing driver you choose to put yourself in an unnatural situation. Most people don't want to put themselves under that stress: it makes sense to avoid it rather than pursue it. But if you do put yourself there, it can start to become sublime. In the cockpit there's a solitude: you're in a private world where you feel at home. You're focusing so hard on one thing that it's like a form of meditation, a peace which seems at odds with the apparent chaos of racing. All this leaping in the air on the podium which Michael introduced – before that, drivers used to clamber out of the car at the end of the race with a glazed look in their eyes. You go into a post-race conference and you're not really there yet. You can't just switch out of that incredibly intense mental state straight away. It used to take me two days to come down after a grand prix.

"But as a driver you can't really enjoy your achievements. You're completely forward-looking: those points are in the bag and straight away you're looking to the next race, the next points, onwards and upwards the whole time.

"So we came to the final round in Adelaide with me one point behind, and Michael took me out. Typically, my first impulse was to blame myself. I thought, 'That was a crap overtaking manoeuvre, Damon'. There was an open door, and I went through it, and across he came, Boom! I didn't know his car had gone off the road, I didn't know it was damaged. But if you watch the replays there's no question it was deliberate. Lots of drivers would have done the same. You never know − I might have done it myself..."

Although Damon was second in the championship again in 1995, with four more victories and nine podiums, it was not a happy year. "It was one of those awful years when everything went wrong. I took a lot on myself, started to get into a downward spiral. I got negative press, and it all seemed to pile in on me. You're up and you're down with Fleet Street, and the misery of my year made a good story. It did get to me. At Suzuka the championship was lost, everything was crap, I was making mistakes and I ended up in the gravel at Spoon Curve. I remember getting changed in one of those little cabins behind the Suzuka pits, everybody falling over everybody else's flight bags, and Frank and Patrick were there. I literally didn't know whether I should be laughing or crying − until then I'd never realised the real meaning of that expression. And then two weeks later, in Adelaide, I took pole, won the race, lapped the field. Everyone else either broke or fell off and I just sailed serenely on. It was daft."

In 1996, of course, Damon became World Champion with eight wins, culminating in another emotional victory in Japan. "I realised this was my last chance − I was 35, and everybody else was 10 years younger than me. Michael had gone to Ferrari, and fortunately his car was a pile of junk at the time. The real challenge that year was sorting out [team-mate] Jacques Villeneuve.

"I really enjoyed my time with him. Whatever happened he was just Jacques. He never made excuses, never apologised for anything. He has a powerful sense of justice: he despises a lack of conviction or integrity in anyone. Testing at Estoril he said, 'Do you think you can overtake around the outside of the last corner?' The engineers said, 'Grow up, that's not possible'. And he did it in the race — he passed Michael round the outside of the last corner."

Predictably, Schuey didn't see the funny side. "After the race Michael went up to him and said, 'I don't think you should be doing that, it's not really safe'. Jacques was delighted, he laughed and laughed. It was priceless."

Midway through that championship season Damon arrived at Hockenheim to find the paddock full of rumours that Williams would fire him at the end of the season, rumours that he refused to believe but which turned out to be true. Did he feel shafted by Williams?

"Shafted is an emotive term. You learn that motor racing's no different from the real world. You think you're fantastic because you can drive an F1 car, but they're not overly impressed by just another racing driver. They've been around too long. You start to recognise that there's more to this than just driving. I really loved racing for Williams. I loved Patrick, I loved Frank, I loved all the guys I worked with. I had some tough times, but they gave me the most fantastic opportunity. I got to drive some of the most amazing racing cars ever made.

"So I went to Arrows. It wasn't a front-running team, but there were a nice bunch of people, there. And it was the only team that would give me a one-year deal. I nearly went to McLaren alongside Mika Häkkinen, but Ron Dennis would only pay me on a results basis, and that was completely unacceptable. I was World Champion, they were going to make marketing capital out of having me in the team, with number one on the car. Ron would never admit that, because he's had more world champions than hot dinners, but their whole attitude pissed me off. I don't think I would have been happy there."

High spot of the Arrows year was the extraordinary Hungarian Grand Prix, when Damon qualified third, passed Schumacher's Ferrari on lap 11 to lead, and stayed ahead until the 77th and final lap, when the car was crippled by a hydraulic problem. Heartbreak, perchance?

"Not at all. It was just one of those fantastic twists of fate. Goodyear got it wrong: it turned up with some tyres that turned out to be like chewing gum, and my Bridgestones were terrific: the car felt fantastic. People hate the Hungaroring, but I love it. It's like a giant go-kart track. With the Arrows it was work, work, work the whole way round − a hard race − and I was enjoying myself. When I passed Michael I thought, 'If it all stops now I don't mind, I've had a fantastic run'. But it carried on until the last lap! Then it went onto tickover. My first thought was, 'How can I stop Jacques getting past'? I was going down the back straight saying to myself, 'Wider, be wider...' and he went past me on the grass flat out. The car should have died, but it didn't and we were second. That was entertaining."

Were his last two seasons at Jordan entertaining? "No. It was a nightmare. It was very, very difficult: a delusional team. Eddie's focus was on the deals, on the business side, and he was distracted. Things needed to change and they did change − Mike Gascoyne came in to replace Gary Anderson on the technical side − and we managed to win a grand prix. But after that I'd had enough. I'd say something to galvanise reaction from Honda and I was in breach of contract because I was saying something negative. It worked, they pulled their fingers out, but all I got was, 'You've upset the workforce; you've demoralised them'. Well, what about me? I had to drive the thing. That's how F1 has become; the drivers are under contract and they're not allowed to say 'Boo'. It was all getting litigious and ghastly and I wanted to finish at the British Grand Prix in

1999, but contractually it was impossible. I saw Eddie the other day, and I said, 'I can see it from your point of view now; you had to get on with the business. But I did win your first GP.' "

Today Damon is President of the BRDC, which he sees as an ambassadorial role. "Silverstone is a high-profile £30 million business, and the commercial side of it should be run by professionals. I want it to be run profitably and in the best way, and the club needs to become what it is: an institution for people who are part of motorsport in this country to congregate and enjoy that part of their lives.

"Formula 1 has detached itself from its roots. It appeals to corporate clients, people with only a passing interest in the sport who like to come into the Paddock Club and be seen at the event. The BRDC has a responsibility to the core of the sport, the people who genuinely love it. But you have to move with the times, and recognise that Formula 1 is the pinnacle, and far and away the most visible and fiercely competitive end of the sport. If retaining the British Grand Prix puts the assets of the club in jeopardy then it's not a viable proposition, and there's nothing we can do about it. But clearly the best answer is if we can retain the grand prix and, under that umbrella, other levels of the sport can flourish as well."

We've talked for more than two hours, and Damon glances at his watch. He has to go: time for his daughter's netball practice. After 19 hard years of racing on two wheels and four, 116 grands prix, 20 pole positions, 22 wins, 360 points and a world championship, he has proved a point to himself, to the world, and to his father's memory. Now, with other priorities, he's moved on.

Damon Hill was talking to Simon in October 2006.

CHRISTIAN HORNER

Winning – and having fun
doing it

In the business world, management is all. The best managers earn the biggest salaries; companies with good profit growth are said to be well-managed. Management is studied at universities and business schools, and on countless courses. Bookshops' shelves are stuffed with textbooks claiming to help the reader become an effective manager. Management, they say, is what lies between success and mediocrity.

Christian Horner heads up today's most successful Formula 1 team, managing 550 staff and budgets running into hundreds of millions. Yet he has benefited from neither university nor business school, and I very much doubt if he's ever read a management textbook. When I ask him what a manager actually does to make his racing team win, he finds the question difficult to answer.

But if anyone knows, he should. He has run Red Bull Racing for seven seasons. He came in at 31 years of age, with no previous F1 experience, just after energy drink billionaire Dietrich Mateschitz had bought the ailing Jaguar team. Despite having the might of Ford behind it, Jaguar's F1 record was feeble. In five seasons the team had a succession of high-profile managers, including Bobby Rahal and Niki Lauda, but never won a race. In 102 F1 starts it achieved a couple of third-place podiums – and 74 retirements. Its best placing in the constructors' championship was seventh.

Christian's first four years at Red Bull were tough, but his single-minded vision never wavered, nor did the belief and backing he received from Mateschitz. In year five his team won six Grands Prix and 10 podiums, and finished second in the drivers' and constructors' championships. Year six brought real glory: World Champion driver, World Champion constructor, 10 victories and 11 podiums, defeating the might of Ferrari and McLaren in a closely-fought season. And in 2011, year seven of Christian's reign, it has been near-domination. As these pages went to press the last two rounds were still to be fought, but Red Bull already had both championship titles done and dusted. In 17 Grands Prix Sebastian Vettel had started from pole 13 times, taken 11 victories, and only been off the podium once. Mark Webber had added nine further podiums to that tally.

Key to this extraordinary success was the arrival at Red Bull's Milton Keynes base at the end of 2005 of Adrian Newey as chief technical officer. Christian's management skills were crucial in achieving this coup, for he had to persuade Adrian that he'd be happier at Red Bull than he'd been at McLaren; and he had to persuade Mateschitz to foot the bill for the world's highest-paid racing car designer.

Like most people who are very busy but very well-organised, Christian proves surprisingly easy to pin down. He agrees to fit in lunch between flying in from Korea — another win, another constructors' championship — and jetting east again to India and the next win. As I arrive in Red Bull's gleaming, trophy-lined reception area, hidden speakers are quietly playing Queen's *We Are the Champions*. Christian and I start our chat in his airy office, lit by standard lamps fashioned from stainless steel exhaust manifolds. Then a company driver whisks us to a pleasant gastro-pub, The Birch at Woburn.

Christian was born in Leamington Spa in 1973, one of three brothers. Motor racing wasn't in the family, but car manufacture was: his grandfather was purchasing manager for the old Standard Motor Company in Coventry, and then set up an agency with Christian's father for component suppliers to the big factories in the Midlands. "As a kid I pestered my parents for a kart, just to drive around the garden, and my mother found one in the local paper for £25. In time I managed to get something better, and ended up racing in a category called Junior Booster. In 1991 Renault offered scholarships to help kids move up from karts to Formula Renault, and I won one. Part of the deal was a free engine – so it's ironic that Red Bull is now with Renault in F1! Things went quite well for me in FR, I won a championship round and got some poles, and F3 teams started calling. So for 1993 I did F3 Class B with Roly Vincini's P1 Engineering. I had five wins, and finished second in the series.

"I persuaded my parents to let me take a year out after my A-levels to see if I could make a career in racing. My side of the deal was that I'd apply for a university place as a fallback if it didn't work out. I chose somewhere at random and filled in the forms, but I never had any intention of going. I don't even remember which university it was.

"For 1994 I moved to Fortec doing F3 Class A. I was still focused on my goal of making it to Formula 1, but at the end of that year I had no money left. I was determined to stay in racing, so I banged on a lot of doors and hustled together enough for a drive with Alan Docking alongside Warren Hughes and Gonzalo Rodríguez. And for 1995 I set my sights on moving up to Formula 3000. But of course I didn't have the budget to go to a decent team and buy myself a seat. Finally I decided that if I could buy and run an F3000 car myself, at least at the end of the season I might still have the car left and something to show for it. It was a bit brave, but I thought I'd give it a go.

"I sold everything I had, borrowed as much as I could from the bank, from my father – who helped me on condition that I paid him back at some point – and from everywhere else I could think of. That got me a chassis. I leased two engines, persuaded Roly Vincini to be my race engineer, and based the car in a shed behind Roly's house in Norfolk. I called us Arden International. I was team manager, money hunter, secretary, cook and bottle-washer, did all the paperwork and the hassle. As mechanic we had a part-time lad who worked at the local Thresher's off-licence. He's with McLaren now.

"We needed a trailer, and for some reason I decided the best deal was one I found for sale in Austria. I took a cheap flight to Graz to look at it. The owner, a guy I'd never heard of called Dr Marko, drove a hard bargain, but I said I'd buy it if he delivered it to Calais for me to pick up. When I told my father I'd given the cash to a complete stranger in Austria on a handshake, and I hadn't even got the trailer yet, he thought I was mad. But Dr Marko's handshake was good, and the trailer duly turned up at Calais. By now I'd found out he was the ex-F1 driver Helmut Marko, and he was running two F3000 cars for Juan Pablo Montoya and Craig Lowndes, so I soon got to know him better.

"Our tiny little team operated on a wing and a prayer. We didn't have a single spare part. If I'd had a shunt it would have been, 'Do we pay the wages, or do we buy the bits to mend the car?' I was the only guy running around paying the bills, so if I'd been in hospital with a broken leg it would have ground to a halt. I was tenacious, and I did get in the points in the last race of the season at Jerez. But my trouble was I thought too much about the consequences – I knew I simply had to end the season with the car intact – so I couldn't help building in a subconscious safety margin. In any case, I was a long way from being really special, and I was on the grid with people like Montoya, Ricardo Zonta and Tom Kristensen. But I really worked out how to deal with motor racing, not just from inside the cockpit, but with organisers, suppliers, travel companies, sponsors if I could find them. In 1998, to share the overheads, the Belgian driver Kurt Mollekens came under the Arden umbrella. Kurt was quick, and actually led the F3000 championship at one point, but he had a big accident at Hockenheim and his campaign rather fell apart.

"Before the end of 1998 I made my big decision to stop driving. I'd loved all the racing I'd done, but I was honest enough to recognise that I was simply not at the same level as the best guys. I'd learned a lot, and motor racing was all that I knew. I felt there was an opportunity to build Arden into a team that was a viable business. Money was still the problem: I ended up borrowing again, from banks, from my dad, leveraging everything I possibly could to come up with the budget to run a two-car team.

"Then David Richards called. Prodrive had been working in touring cars with the Russian oil company Lukoil and the boss's son, Viktor Maslov, wanted to go racing in F3000. David asked how much it would cost for Prodrive to become a 50/50 shareholder in Arden. At that point Arden consisted of an entry ticket for two cars, a leased truck and a few bits of old pit equipment. I made up a number that seemed totally ridiculous, David was happy with that, and I moved the team into the Prodrive premises in Banbury. For 1999 we ran Marc Goossens and Maslov.

"That season was a bit of a disaster, so I bought back the half-share from Prodrive, paid David rent for the workshop space, and put Darren Manning in our number one car. But to move the team to the next level in 2002 I knew I had to take the risk of moving away from the Lukoil funding, saying goodbye to Viktor, and taking on two really quick drivers. The Czech Tomáš Enge was a proven F3000 race winner, and the Swede Björn Wirdheim looked a very promising rookie. Suddenly we were winning − four victories for Tomáš, one for Björn − and after a season-long battle Tomáš beat Sébastien Bourdais to the title by four points. We also won the team title.

"But unfortunately it turned out Tomáš had been enjoying himself outside the cockpit as well. In Hungary, scene of one of his victories, he was selected for the standard random drug test. And he failed. It was marijuana − it wasn't as if he'd been putting something serious up his nose − but six weeks later he was summoned before the FIA World Council in Paris. He apologised, and all they did was give him a suspended 12-month ban and dock him the points for that race. But it was enough to lose him the title. More seriously, the test offers he'd had from BAR and Newman/Haas melted away at once. Tomáš was a good guy, and very fast. He's doing sports cars now.

"Meanwhile Björn was getting better and better. He won the F3000 title for us in 2003, and we were top team again with the American Townsend Bell as number two. Now Helmut Marko comes back into the story, because he'd sold his team and was running Red Bull Junior. He was looking after Vitantonio Liuzzi, who looked very strong. So I did a deal with Helmut to run him with Red Bull backing in 2004, the final year of F3000 before it was replaced by GP2. Helmut did a really aggressive deal — just like when I'd bought the trailer, seven years before — with a very cheap base line and good win bonuses. If Liuzzi hadn't done well Arden would have gone bust, but he won seven of 10 rounds and the championship, plus our Dutch number two Robert Doornbos had a win, and we were team champions again.

"After three winning seasons in F3000 it was time to raise my sights, and I started thinking how I could make a move somehow into F1. I'd got to know Bernie [Ecclestone] a bit, representing the F3000 teams when we needed to talk to him, and I asked him what he thought. He told me Eddie Jordan was keen to sell, so I went to see EJ. But his numbers were just ridiculous. I mentioned it to Helmut, and he said, 'That's interesting. Dietrich is thinking about changing Red Bull's F1 involvement.' At that point they owned a chunk of Sauber, and were sponsoring Christian Klien at Jaguar. So Helmut set up a meeting in Salzburg and I met Dietrich for the first time. It was all very amiable, he gave me plenty of time, and we seemed to get on well. His understanding of F1 was very acute. We had a chat about Jordan, but he said, 'That doesn't look interesting for us. We might have an opportunity with Jaguar, we're looking at that.' After that I heard nothing more for a while."

Ford had put Jaguar F1 up for sale on September 17 2004. On November 15 entries for the next year's F1 series had to be lodged with the FIA. Negotiations between Mateschitz and Ford were protracted, but in the early hours of Sunday November 14, with barely 24 hours to go before the FIA deadline, the deal was done. Six weeks later came the announcement that David

Coulthard, his nine-year relationship with McLaren at an end, had been signed as Red Bull's number one driver.

"I continued to talk to EJ, but that just became more and more frightening and improbable. I was also putting Arden's GP2 programme in place, and I'd signed Heikki Kovalainen and Nicolas Lapierre. Then, just before Christmas, Helmut asked me to fly to Salzburg and see Dietrich again. I detected he had a degree of frustration with the senior management he'd inherited from Jaguar, team principal Tony Purnell and managing director David Pitchforth. Very quickly he outlined his vision for Red Bull in F1, and he offered me the role of team principal. It was a huge thing for me, that he was prepared to put his faith in me to deliver that vision. Of course I said yes.

"My first day, January 7th, was quite interesting. Helmut Marko and Dany Bahar, who was a consultant to Dietrich then, flew into Heathrow, went to Milton Keynes, informed Tony Purnell and David Pitchforth that their services were no longer required, and asked them to leave the building. Then Helmut and Dany got all the staff together, announced that I was the new team principal, and departed for Heathrow. I found myself sitting at Purnell's desk with his half-opened post and his half-drunk cup of coffee thinking, 'Where on earth do I begin?'

"The workforce – it was about 450 people then – had long been subjected to revolving-door management, and now they were really confused. F1 is pretty insular, so I'm sure very few of them knew anything about F3000 or had even heard of Arden. They probably thought, who is this 31-year-old whippersnapper? Are these Austrians mad? And the first Grand Prix of the season in Australia was eight weeks away.

"The first thing I did was get the factory manager to take me round. I wanted to know what the facility consisted of, but most of all I wanted to meet the people, sit down with all the senior managers, and try to understand what was in place. Straight away I could see that there were pockets of real skill within the team. But also there was a serious lack of confidence after all the constant changes going back to the Stewart days, and a lack of technical direction and co-ordination. On the shop floor there was genuine quality, but a poor infrastructure. No one seemed to be clear what the real goals were. I spent the first few weeks learning how the team operated, identifying the strengths and weaknesses. And then we had to go and do some racing. We had to be in Melbourne.

"Early on that January I met David Coulthard for a quiet meal, here in this very pub. I had known him since karting, and I was absolutely delighted he'd been signed, because he was a winner, and he was bringing us 11 seasons of experience with two top teams. I could draw so much out of DC in terms of bench-marking, telling us how things compared with what he'd been used to at McLaren. He was already fairly dismayed by what he'd seen at Milton Keynes, but I really wanted to get the best out of him, because when he left McLaren people thought his career was pretty much at an end. He'd been written off. I wanted to regenerate his self-belief. As it turned out, he was a crucial factor in our first year. In our first race, even: he qualified fifth in Melbourne, was second for a long time, and after his second stop finished a brilliant fourth. And Christian Klien in the other car finished seventh. It was a real morale-boosting start: after that race we were lying third in the constructors' championship.

"Our goal for that first season was to concentrate on the basics, make sure we finished races, and score more points than the nine Jaguar got the previous year. In fact we scored 34. David was in the points in six of his first eight races. As well as that, the Red Bull recipe for having a good time had arrived in the paddock. That came from Dietrich. Inside the stiff, corporate environment that F1 had become, he wanted to display the core values of Red Bull, wanted his team to be non-conformist. The Energy Station, which arrived at the first European race of the year, was his idea."

This was the immense three-storey Red Bull motorhome and hospitality centre, which needed a gang of 25 people to erect and dismantle it and 11 trucks to take it from race to race.

It thrummed with loud music all weekend and, unlike most Formula 1 motorhomes, it had an open-door policy, so you didn't need a hen's-teeth pass to get in.

"Dietrich wanted to inject fun, give good access to the drivers, and allow them to say what they liked without PR-speak limitations. Even DC grew designer stubble and stopped talking corporate-speak. Dietrich wanted the team to be successful, but in a Red Bull way: because it's no good having fun at the back of the grid. You need to be winners. In that we were every bit as serious as any other team."

What signalled to the F1 world just how serious came with the shock news in November 2005 that Adrian Newey was leaving McLaren after eight years to become Red Bull's chief technical officer. "That first time in the Imola paddock we were next to the silent grey McLaren motorhome – I'm not sure what Ron Dennis made of our loud music – but I found Adrian outside, looking up at the Energy Station. He was curious, and he'd come to have a look. I'd never had a conversation with him before, but in my mind he was absolutely the best in the business. I took him in, showed him around and gave him a drink. He couldn't help but see the contrast between McLaren's way and our way.

"At Monaco we had the Energy Station floating on the harbour, we had a *Star Wars* thing going, and Adrian was inquisitive. So he came on board to see what we were doing. I confided to David, who of course had worked most of his time at McLaren with Adrian and knew him very well, that I'd like to have a crack at getting him to join us. David said, 'Here are his phone numbers. Let's see if we can sort out dinner.' So in July David and I had dinner with Adrian and his wife at the Bluebird in the King's Road. David exuded enthusiasm about Red Bull and the team, but we didn't talk about the prospect of Adrian joining, we just had an enjoyable, relaxed evening, and he and I really hit it off. I could sense that he was frustrated at McLaren. They hadn't treated him particularly well, and it didn't seem like there was any magic between him and Ron. And his contract was about to expire.

"I told Dietrich I thought we had a chance of getting him — although I didn't tell him at that stage how big an investment I thought it would be! Dietrich said at once, 'Let's see if we can make it happen.' So in October we flew Adrian to Salzburg, helicoptered him into the mountains for a casual lunch with Dietrich, and then we showed him something of what Red Bull is like. Among other things, we stuck him in our Alpha Jet fighter and he went inverted over Kitzbühel at 500ft.

"That evening I broached the subject: 'Adrian, we'd love to have you. Do you want to come?' He stated a figure which caught my attention, because it was about 70 per cent higher than I'd warned Dietrich we might have to pay. I called Dietrich, he went quiet for a few seconds, then he said, 'Let's go for it.' That's the great thing about Red Bull. It's his company, it belongs just to him and one other person in Thailand. No board meetings, no shareholders' approvals, just an instant decision. By Sunday evening Adrian and I had shaken hands, and he flew home to deliver the message to Ron.

"Adrian started with us in February 2006. That year's car, the RB2, was already set, of course. For the new 2.4-litre V8 regulations we'd switched from Cosworth to the customer Ferrari engine. It was a difficult year: the engines were unreliable and overheated, and they bore little relation to Adrian's design philosophy. We had a meeting with Jean Todt in Bahrain before the first race, and Adrian asked what the development programme was for the engine. Jean made it clear that we were just customers, there would be certain upgrades during the year, but we shouldn't expect anything else. That was something new for Adrian, and even before that first race he was telling me it wouldn't do. Fortunately at the end of the season we were able to swap engine deals with Toro Rosso, which Dietrich had also bought, and that gave us our relationship with Renault.

"At Williams and McLaren Adrian had been in established teams with an established infrastructure, and he'd just had to bring his creativity and technical direction. We had unstructured departments, an out-of-date wind tunnel, no CFD [computational fluid dynamics], no simulator. We had to start from scratch, get the right people, the right equipment. Coming from the bottom actually appealed to Adrian, but I think even he underestimated the scale of what there was to achieve.

"Meanwhile I was making other key appointments. Rob Marshall joined as chief designer: he came from Renault, as did team manager Jonathan Wheatley and chief mechanic Kenny Handkammer. Peter Prodromou, head of aerodynamics, had worked under Adrian at McLaren. Paul Monaghan had been at Renault and then Jordan, he's now our head of car engineering, and Mark Ellis runs vehicle dynamics. Ciaron Pilbeam, son of race car designer Mike Pilbeam, came from BAR and is Webber's race engineer. Guillaume 'Rocky' Rocquelin was at Newman/Haas. I'd wanted him at Arden in my F3000 days, but I couldn't afford him then. He's now Vettel's race engineer.

"Adrian forced a change of culture on us, because the way he works is completely different. We weren't prepared for the amount of detail he gets involved in. For starters, he still uses a drawing board. I had to do a deal with Martin Whitmarsh and make a payment to charity to get McLaren to release his beloved board, which had followed him there from Williams and is now in his office at Red Bull. In F1 nowadays a technical director is usually a technical manager, someone who chairs meetings and agrees philosophy and strategic direction, but isn't involved in the actual architecture of the car. Adrian draws the surfaces of the car himself and then passes that over to the aerodynamicists and designers. He stimulates and encourages them, they feed off him, and he feeds off them. You'll see him perched on the edge of somebody's desk, looking at a component or a piece of bodywork. He is a total perfectionist: he has a very nice manner, but he's utterly uncompromising. But just because something isn't his idea, he's not afraid to say, 'Your idea looks stronger, let's pursue that.'"

Adrian's first car for Red Bull, the 2007 RB3, coincided with Webber's arrival in the team and the switch to Renault engines.

The learning curve was steep: there were 14 retirements that year and just one podium. In '08 the team slipped to seventh in the constructors' championship. For '09 Vettel moved across from Toro Rosso, and DC hung up his helmet and moved into a team consultancy role. And with the RB5 the team really started to come good.

"For 2009 F1 had possibly the biggest regulation changes in 20 years: new front wing, narrower rear wing, losing a lot of aero appendages and cleaning the cars up. And back to slick tyres. The double-diffuser debate lost us some time [during the design stage Newey had considered and rejected it, believing it would be declared illegal] but once we'd introduced that our car was very strong." Vettel and Webber ended up with six wins between them, second and fourth in the drivers' table, and the team beat McLaren to second in the constructors'. Then came 2010. After a glorious battle down to the wire, Red Bull took the drivers' and constructors' titles. And now we've had the back-to-back repeats in 2011. For those who like statistics, Red Bull has won 23 of the past 39 Grands Prix.

Clearly Vettel is as much of a key ingredient as Newey. "He's been part of the Red Bull family since he was a 12-year-old karter. His car control is phenomenal, so he has no inhibitions about the car being 'on the nose', being loose at the entry or exit of a corner, which might unnerve other drivers. His ability to carry that off has been accentuated by the Pirelli tyre. It's all down to the set-up: Mark drives the car in a classic style, whereas Sebastian may be happy to wind on more front wing to chase front-end performance and just deal with a looser rear.

"In 2010 he had a tough year. He was publicly criticised for some of his actions, and unreliability cost him three wins. But he never gave up, and it all came right for him in Abu Dhabi. Once the championship was on his CV that pressure was gone, replaced with a new confidence, and he's stepped up a level this year. Based on 2011, you have to say Sebastian is currently the best driver in the world. He works harder on his own performance than any other driver in the pitlane. He'll be in the paddock later than anyone on Friday and Saturday night, even if he has pole, trawling through his data and Mark's, soaking up information like a sponge. He has the speed, the racecraft, the intelligence and the technical sympathy to understand what the car is doing and what it requires. He can create strategic options and opportunities by the way he drives the car.

"One of his stand-out races for me this year was Monaco. It must be the hardest thing to be leading a race and know we'd made a mistake and he had the wrong set of tyres on the car. He thought it through: if he kept pushing he would run out of rubber, so he purposely slowed to back up the others and make the tyres last. He had the confidence to dictate that race. The other stand-out was Barcelona, when he had all sorts of KERS issues. When your KERS fails it alters the brake bias significantly. He had Lewis Hamilton breathing down his neck in probably a quicker car. He dealt with Lewis, he dealt with the brake bias, he didn't make a mistake, didn't flat-spot a tyre, didn't give Lewis any opportunity by running deep into a corner. That was hugely impressive for me.

"It helps that he is a very nice young man. He's a wise head on young shoulders, but he has a sense of fun, and he's humble. He just sees himself as one of the team. He doesn't have a manager, he's a shrewd guy who does his own deals. He and his girlfriend live in Switzerland, but he doesn't bring her to the races, he protects her from the media. He's got a thing about statistics, likes to tot up the wins, the poles, the fastest laps, the percentages. I'm always giving him grief about fastest laps. He'll be leading comfortably into the last lap, nothing to be gained by taking any risks, and on the timing screens the first sector goes purple [indicating fastest of the day]. Rocky's telling him to take it easy, stroke it home. Second sector goes purple. As he takes the flag, the third sector goes purple. So he's got fastest lap. He's doing all his celebrating on the slowing-down lap, and he comes on the radio: 'Did I get fastest lap?' Rocky says, 'No, you missed it by a tenth.' 'I can't believe that,' he says, 'that can't be right.' So then Rocky says, 'Yes, you did get fastest lap. And you're a bloody idiot.'"

How does Webber deal with being team-mates with the man who, according to his team principal, is the best in the world? "That's a tremendously difficult thing for any sportsman, and Mark deals with it admirably – in a similar way, probably, to how Jenson Button has dealt with Lewis. Mark is world-class, over a lap and over a Grand Prix, but he knows that to beat Sebastian he's sometimes got to take a slightly different approach. Last season he was quite wily with that. This year it's been more difficult for him, certainly in the first part of the season when he had to adapt to the new tyre. We've signed Mark again for 2012: he's tremendously fit and he absolutely still has the mental hunger. But we've both decided that, now he's 35, we'll take it one year at a time. As for Sebastian, he's tied up for a minimum of three more seasons.

"Adrian very much has an input into driver choice, he's involved in all major decisions. Dietrich will have the final say on the big things – choice of driver, engine, strategic investment – but Adrian and I run the business day-to-day. We're now to all intents and purposes Renault's works team in F1. Adrian has won seven of his eight constructors' championships using Renault power, and he has a key input into the architecture of the new engine."

FOTA rules now restrict the number of car-involved personnel travelling to each Grand Prix to 47, although trainers, marketing people and others swell that number to 75. But Red Bull's bonus scheme means that every one of the 550 staff, from designers to office cleaners, share equally in the team's success. "For winning the constructors' championship in 2010, every employee got £10,000, and it'll be the same this year. That was something Dietrich insisted on." So the constructors' title alone will be adding £5.5 million to Red Bull's wage bill. "But then, we've clocked up over 100,000 hours of unpaid overtime this year.

That's the commitment of a workforce that wants to see our cars running at the front, people who are proud of what they do. You've only got to walk around the factory and the offices to feel the vibe here. It's tremendously stimulating. It epitomises the cultural change we've gone through in seven years."

In the business world, success is measured when the annual, or half-yearly, or maybe quarterly results are published. In F1 the whole world can see graphically, on a billion TV sets, whether you're doing a good job or not – every couple of weeks. It's the most public measurement possible of whether a team is well managed. "Yes, at every race you get measured again. And what happens on the track is effectively measuring every area of the organisation – not just the race team but R&D, design, production, logistics, planning. F1 moves so fast now. The timing to get a component from Adrian's drawing board through all the processes and onto the car is unbelievably tight, and at every stage there's a deadline to hit. At Jaguar I think they had three update packages a year. We'll be looking to introduce something significant at every race."

So, back to my first question: how has Christian's management of Red Bull raised it to the top of the Formula 1 ladder?

"My aim is always to try to get the best out of people. We've tried to create a culture in which people have the confidence to express themselves. Sometimes they need an arm around the shoulder, sometimes a push. But there's no point in employing a specialist and then trying to tell him or her how to do the job. So: hire the right people for each role. Give them clear objectives. Then empower them, put them in an environment where they can do whatever they do best really well. And have some fun doing it. That's what we intend to go on doing at Red Bull."

Christian Horner was talking to Simon in October 2011.

JACKY ICKX

Only the final link in
a long chain

Each month for the past six years it's been my privilege, on your behalf, to take a motor racing name to lunch. Then, on these pages, I've passed on to you the intimate details of our conversation. The 80 personalities so far have spanned six decades, and have ranged from the extrovert to the shy, from the proud to the modest. Without exception all have been remarkably open and honest. Beside a string of great drivers, including eight World Champions, other disciplines have been covered: team owner, designer, mechanic, circuit boss, Formula 1 doctor, Land Speed Record holder, FIA president. All have been happy to tell me about the achievements in their lives that have meant most to them.

But Jacky Ickx is different. As a working race reporter and broadcaster, I knew him quite well during the 20 years of his brilliant career in F1 and sports cars. He was an eight-time Grand Prix winner for Ferrari and Brabham, and twice runner-up in the World Championship. And he became the most successful endurance racer of all time, supremely fast in darkness and in rain, with six Le Mans victories and countless other sports car wins to his name. Above all I knew him to be an individualist: always friendly and courteous, but a man not afraid to speak his mind and stand by his principles, even when they separated him from the rest.

When I ask to take him to lunch, he is happy to accept, but insists – with surprising passion – that he is not interested in describing his own achievements. "I do not want to be talking all the time about me, myself, I. Motor sport is a selfish sport, but every victory is like an iceberg. The small part of the iceberg that is visible is your drive in the race, it receives all the glory. But under the waterline is the majority of the iceberg: the mechanics of course, but also the talents of the people back at the factory who designed and built the car. Most of the winning is done before the car even gets to the track: the driver is just there to finish the job. As a driver you may become famous, and nowadays you may also become very rich. But you are only the final link in a long chain of many people who live in the shade, who work hard to do their jobs right, and who get their satisfaction when the whole combined enterprise achieves what it was striving to do.

"I only have one regret, looking back on my time in motor racing. In those days I was a sort of monorail, I was always thinking about myself and about winning. That is what it is like when you are a racing driver: mentally you are not very grown-up. I respected the people who helped me, of course, and I always had the courtesy to say thank you to them. But I regret not being more aware of all the links in the chain. The victories were theirs, not mine; but I was not big enough intellectually to see it. Now I have grown up, I have more of a 180-degree vision. So that's why I will have lunch with you: to give myself a chance to acknowledge publicly what I owe."

As the Eurostar pulls into Bruxelles Midi station, Jacky is waiting for me beside his Audi A8. Rather than nominating a favourite restaurant, he insists on welcoming me to his home in the centre of the city, a superb period town house with high walls hung with African art — but not a single racing picture or trophy — and a lush walled garden. There his tall and beautiful wife, the Burundi-born singer Khadja Nin, serves a superb meal combining cuisines from Africa and the Far East: rice with spices, endives in sugar, chicken with coconut, beans with onion and garlic, mango and raw mint.

"My time in cars was a different life. When I am shown pictures of me in races, I hardly recognise myself." But little by little I persuade Jacky to delve into his memories of his racing days, although much of what follows comes from what I witnessed at the time, because either he has forgotten many of his great races, or prefers not to talk about them.

Despite being born into a car-centric household — his father was the Belgian motoring journalist Jacques Ickx — as a child Jacky had no interest in racing. "Aged 10 I was taken to Spa for the 1955 Belgian Grand Prix, and saw Fangio and Moss in their W196 Mercedes. But it didn't excite me at all. At school my results were always poor: I liked to sit at the back of the class, near the window and the warm radiator. My parents had no idea what to do with me. When I was 15, with my school results a disaster and my teachers saying I was good for nothing, my father bought me a 50cc Puch motorcycle. It was pure destiny. At last I discovered something I wasn't bad at.

"By the time I was 16 I was doing trials and the results began to come" — he was rapidly crowned European Champion in his class — "and then I was offered rides by works teams. I suppose I am one of the few Belgians to have done the Scottish Six Days Trial. On two wheels on those steep, slippery surfaces I learned a lot of lessons about balance, which probably helped me in wet-weather racing later. I moved into circuit racing on Kreidler and Zundapp — all nine-speed gearboxes and 20,000rpm — and then I was lent cars to race: a BMW 700 coupé, then a Cortina." Having won the Belgian Touring Car Championship, Jacky began to attract attention outside his home country, in particular from Ford, which led to outings in works Cortinas and the ex-Alan Mann Mustang. At the 1964 European Touring Car round in Budapest Ken Tyrrell, running the works Mini-Coopers, noticed the speed of a Lotus-Cortina driven on the wheel-waving limit by a teenager with a wide smile.

He summoned Jacky to Goodwood for a test in an F3 Cooper. Jacky crashed the car, but beyond the minor damage Ken saw in the youngster remarkable natural talent, and a true racer's spirit. So he ran him in an F3 Matra in 1966 at Monaco, and then at Silverstone in July. Most of the day's top Formula 3 names were there: Irwin, Gethin, Oliver, Bell, Nunn, Beckwith, Lucas, Crichton-Stuart. Having practised out of session Jacky started at the back of the 30-car grid, and in pouring rain he sliced through the field, passing cars right and left, to finish an astonishing third. It was many people's first sight of Ickx in the wet: he doesn't recall this race, but I certainly do.

But Jacky holds the memory of Ken Tyrrell and his wife Norah in great affection and respect. "So many people helped me in my racing, but Ken and Norah were, without doubt, the most important. One of my memories is going to a test at Oulton Park in a van from Ken's timber yard with the car in the back, singing Beatles songs, *We all Live in a Yellow Submarine,* and Ken was singing too." Rapidly promoted to Formula 2 in the Matra-BRM alongside Jackie Stewart, Jacky ran in the F2 section of the German Grand Prix. His 1-litre car qualified quicker than two of the F1 entries, and 8sec faster than the next quickest F2 runner, although his race only lasted one lap. Three weeks earlier the still-unknown youngster had his first race at Brands Hatch in the sports car race supporting the British Grand Prix, in a 6-litre McLaren-Chevy owned by Alan Brown. He qualified it on the front row alongside Richard Attwood's Lola T70 and Chris Amon's McLaren, spun, but fought back to finish fifth.

In 1967, in the now 1600cc F2, Jacky did a full season for Tyrrell's Matra team alongside Stewart. He was a sensation, taking the European Trophy — effectively the F2 championship, but excluding graded drivers — and winning at Crystal Palace, Zandvoort and Vallelunga. Still only 22, he showed he could race competitively against Clark, Stewart, Rindt, Surtees and the rest. But the race that really put Jacky at the top of many F1 team managers' shopping lists was the German GP. Once again F2 cars were admitted to make up the numbers. In practice Jacky dumbfounded everybody with an 8min 14sec lap in the little Matra, which for a long time was fastest of all. Eventually the F1 cars of Jim Clark and Denny Hulme (just) went quicker, but he remained third-fastest qualifier, although he had to start with the other F2 cars at the back. At the end of the first lap he was 12th; at the end of lap three he was fifth — having set a new outright lap record. On lap five he came through in fourth place, ahead of Amon's Ferrari and Surtees' Honda. Amon did get by him again later, and both Hulme and then Gurney took a bit off his lap record, but Ickx was still in fifth place when, with three laps to go, a ball-joint broke on his front suspension.

Typically, Jacky is self-deprecating about that drive. "It was funny because a lot of people had still never heard of me. And with my name, it was like I was called Monsieur X, a mystery man. But you have to remember, at that time the Nürburgring was very difficult in a Formula 1 car. There were 17 different places each lap where we used to get off the ground. So a properly set-up F2 car had an easier time. Also I had twice done the Nürburgring 84 Hours, in a Mustang and then in a Lotus-Cortina, both times with only one co-driver. So I really did know every centimetre of the track. Jo Bonnier, who was head of the Grand Prix Drivers' Association, said I must not be allowed to start from the front row, because I would get in everybody's way and it would be dangerous. That did me a good turn, made it look better because coming up from the back I was overtaking all these F1 cars in my little Matra." Jacky passed Bonnier's Cooper-Maserati on the first lap.

His first race in a proper F1 car came a month later, at Monza. "I think Ken suggested me to Roy Salvadori, who was running the Cooper-Maserati team. Jochen Rindt was the number one driver there, and he was very helpful to me while I learned the car." In the race Jochen, in the lighter T86, was fourth; Jacky, in the unwieldy old T81B, was sixth, scoring a championship point in his first true F1 drive. By now he knew where he was going for 1968.

Jackie Stewart, anxious to move on from BRM, had been approached by Ferrari, and after two meetings with Enzo believed a deal was done for the '68 season. According to

Jackie's 1970 book *World Champion,* "Ferrari was just what I was looking for. Next thing I heard was the drive had been offered to Jacky Ickx because I had asked for too much money." At the same time Ken Tyrrell was setting up his own F1 operation to run the DFV-powered Matras, so Stewart duly signed for him. Ken would have liked Ickx as Stewart's number two, but Matra wanted a French driver in the team, so Johnny Servoz-Gavin was signed.

"If life had decided differently, I would have loved to stay with Ken. Matra had all that aircraft and missile technology, the Ford DFV was the best engine. But [Ferrari team manager] Franco Lini was sent to the August F2 race at Enna in Sicily to speak to me, took me to Modena to meet Enzo Ferrari, and I signed. You can imagine how I felt, at 22 years old." It was barely two years since Ickx had been racing a Cortina in Belgian clubbies. "I was still living at home. When I went off to a race my mother would say, 'Jacky, be careful, don't drive too fast.'

"I drove for the Scuderia for five of the next six seasons. For me they were great, great years. You hear many former Ferrari drivers making mixed comments about their time there, but I was well-treated at Maranello. Yes, there were arguments sometimes, like in any team, but I always felt I had the same cars and opportunities as my team-mates. Enzo Ferrari himself was careful not to get too close to his drivers. I think he was protecting himself, because it must have been very painful for him down the years to lose talented people from his F1 team: Ascari, Castellotti, Musso, de Portago, Collins, von Trips, Bandini − it is a sad list. It may surprise you, but to me he was a very sensitive man, tender even. I think I did have a special relationship with him − I am one of very few drivers who left Ferrari, and was asked back."

During 1967 Jacky had also begun a fruitful relationship with John Wyer's JW Automotive sports car team. In the Spa 1000Kms in JW's updated GT40, the Mirage, he demonstrated not only his knowledge of the circuit but also his speed in dreadful weather, driving almost single-handed to win in heavy rain. He won the Montlhéry 1000Kms with Paul Hawkins, again in the wet, and then the Kyalami Nine Hours with Brian Redman. The following season Jacky's JW GT40 won three rounds of what was effectively the World Sports Car Championship, with Redman at Brands Hatch and Spa and with his countryman Lucien Bianchi at Watkins Glen. Spa was almost flooded from the start, and at the end of the first lap Ickx's lead over the rest was 39 seconds...

Meanwhile his first full F1 season had been going superbly. At Spa he qualified on the front row and, despite a misfire, put it on the podium. He was fourth at Zandvoort. Then at Rouen, in only his fifth Ferrari Grand Prix, it rained heavily and he came into his own. On a waterlogged track his speed was sensational, and he led virtually from start to finish, to score Ferrari's first Grand Prix victory since Monza 1966. More podiums at Brands Hatch and Monza left him lying second in the Championship, three points behind Graham Hill with three races to go.

But during Friday's practice for the Canadian GP his throttle jammed open just before a fast right-hander. The car flew a long way before destroying itself against St Jovite's fences, and his injuries included a broken leg and facial wounds. He was back for the final round in Mexico with a metal brace on his leg, but ignition trouble stopped him, and he slipped to fourth in the championship. "But I never thought about the championship, or about the points. It was the races that mattered. Like Stirling Moss, I just wanted to win each race."

It was a surprise when Jacky left Ferrari to join Jack Brabham's F1 team for 1969, but this allowed him to continue with his JW sports car contract. Stewart dominated F1 that year with the Matra, while at first the Goodyear tyres used by the Brabhams lacked the dry-weather speed of their Dunlop and Firestone rivals. But after third at Clermont and second at Silverstone, Jacky put his BT26 on pole at the 'Ring. At the end of the first lap he was only fourth, but then began one of the drives of his life – in the dry this time – as he climbed past first Rindt and then an on-form Jo Siffert in Rob Walker's 49, winding in Stewart relentlessly and taking an extraordinary 21.4sec off Stewart's own lap record. On lap seven the Brabham passed the Matra going into the South Curve, pulling away to win by almost a minute.

The following month Jacky won the Canadian GP after a controversial incident when, battling with Stewart as they lapped a backmarker, the two cars touched and Stewart retired with a broken wheel. After the race Ickx apologised, publicly and to Stewart personally. The season ended with Stewart champion, and Ickx runner-up. In those days Jackie Stewart was vociferous in his efforts to improve motor-racing safety, but Ickx created much controversy by resigning from the GPDA, saying its threats of boycotts and strikes were uncivilised.

"Jackie and I meet often now, we are good friends. Now we can call ourselves survivors, and any of the disagreements we had 40 years ago look ridiculous. But I have to say that, for a while, we disliked each other deeply. I was not against the idea of improving motor-racing safety: that would have been foolish. My problem was with Jackie's methods. I was conservative; I accepted the risks without argument or discussion. You have a steering wheel in your hands, you are happy. You win, you are even happier. Can you imagine, back then, stopping a race because the conditions were too wet? No driver would think of such a thing for a single moment, it was part of the job. And the job's not meant to be easy. If you win without difficulty, you win without glory.

"But, of course, the dangers were constant at that time. For those of us who did survive it was not a matter of talent, because many talented people didn't make it. It was a matter of luck. We lost Courage, McLaren and Rindt in '70, Giunti, Rodríguez and Siffert in '71. It didn't change my attitude to racing at all, but often when I shut my front door leaving home for a Grand Prix it went through my mind that maybe I would not be back to open that door again after the weekend. I'm sure it was the same for every driver. In the car there was no room to think about having a mechanical failure, but the thought was buried in your mind somewhere. We were still in the era of straw bales, and the FIA was not taking care of making things better. Jackie was the first to focus on safety, with Jochen Rindt as well: the two of them worked on it together. But Jochen did not survive. Jackie is the man who changed racing, and for that a whole generation of drivers must be grateful."

At Le Mans Jacky was prepared to make his own demonstration: no boycott, no ultimatum, just a statement that would affect only his race. Almost all racing drivers were now wearing seat belts, but the 24 Hours still started as it had done since the 1920s, the cars lined up in echelon on one side of the road and the drivers running across to jump in, start up and drive off. Most drivers would struggle into their belts at speed during the first lap: some didn't wear them at all for their first stint. Jacky felt this was stupid, so when the flag fell and everybody else sprinted across the road he walked deliberately across to his car, got in, did up his safety harness, and then departed dead last. "In fact I did have to run the last few metres to my car, or I would have been run over! A lot of people were upset with me, because that start was a great Le Mans tradition."

And there was a dreadful accident on that first lap, when John Woolfe lost control of his Porsche 917 in the old high-speed kink at White House. In the closely packed mayhem just after the start, several cars were involved. Chris Amon was lucky to escape unhurt from his burning Ferrari after it hit the Porsche's dislodged, and full, fuel tank. Woolfe died in the accident.

After four hours Ickx's JW GT40, shared with Jackie Oliver, had climbed from the back of the field to seventh place. By dawn on Sunday morning it was third, and by 11am it was in the lead. But in the closing stages it was caught by Hans Herrmann's Porsche, and a flat-out wheel-to-wheel battle ensued, Ickx forced to go 1000rpm above his conservative 6000rpm rev limit as he tried to calculate how to manage the final lap. He decided to let the Porsche lead out of Tertre Rouge, so he could slipstream past on the Mulsanne Straight and stay in front to the flag. It worked, and he crossed the line a few lengths ahead of the Porsche in the closest finish in Le Mans history. He admits now: "It would not have looked good if I had lost the race by the amount I used up in my demonstration at the start. But fortunately, like all the best stories, it had a nice ending." And the next year the traditional Le Mans start was gone.

For 1970 Jacky was back with Ferrari, to conduct both the 312B F1 car and the big 512S in sports car races. In the season's second Grand Prix at Jarama, on the opening lap, Jackie Oliver's BRM lost its brakes and T-boned Ickx's Ferrari, rupturing its full fuel tanks. Both cars were engulfed in fire: Oliver got himself out, but Ickx could not. His life was saved by the prompt action of a Spanish policeman, who went into the fire and dragged him out of the wreck. "That man from the *Guardia Civil* beat out the flames in my overalls with his hands, and he got burned too. Later I spent months looking for him to thank him, but I could never find him. I was burned on the face, hands, back, legs. When I turned up for the Monaco Grand Prix three weeks later I was a horrible sight, all strapped up and covered in grease. Burns are the worst thing. But you recover. It didn't affect me at all."

In fact, Jacky went on to have another great Grand Prix season, with three victories, four poles and four fastest laps. But Rindt's string of five victories put the Austrian well ahead in the championship, until the dreadful tragedy of his death at Monza. By winning two weeks later in Canada, Jacky was now second in the table with two races to go. If he were to win at Watkins Glen and Mexico City it would prevent Rindt from being posthumous World Champion. "That was absolutely not what I wanted. Winning the title like that would have been no pleasure." He must almost have been relieved when, running second to Stewart at Watkins Glen, a ruptured fuel pipe put him out. That left Rindt's total unbeatable, even though Ickx did win the final round in Mexico.

Jacky's best race in 1971 was the Dutch Grand Prix, when he fought and won a torrid battle with Pedro Rodríguez's BRM, and lapped the rest of the field. It rained almost throughout, and a March blew its engine and clanked on for half a lap, covering the track with oil: yet another example of Jacky's genius in slippery conditions. I suggest that he must have welcomed rain, because it gave him a clear advantage. "No, no, you are totally wrong. I hated the rain, because the dangers were multiplied. But maybe it disturbed other drivers more. If everybody believes you are good in wet conditions, perhaps they give up more easily, they let you go."

The 1972 German GP was vintage Ickx, starting from pole, leading from start to finish, and taking another 6.5sec off the Nürburgring lap record. But the rest of the season, despite three more GP poles, was ruined by unreliability: he retired from the lead at Brands and Monza, and from second place at Nivelles and Clermont. Things got worse at Ferrari in 1973, and the bulky B3 was both heavy and uncompetitive. After qualifying a depressing 20th at Silverstone, Jacky agreed a release from his contract with Enzo Ferrari. He had one-off drives for McLaren (finishing a strong third at the 'Ring) and Frank Williams − with one more Ferrari ride at Monza − before signing for Team Lotus for the '74 season alongside Ronnie Peterson.

It was not a happy time at Lotus either, Jacky swapping between the unpredictable 76 and the now elderly 72, although he does remember fondly his victory in the 1974 Race of Champions at Brands Hatch. Once again it was a win in heavy rain, and it included in the closing laps a famous overtaking manoeuvre on Niki Lauda's Ferrari, around the outside of Paddock Bend. "At Lotus Colin Chapman was a legend, but I cannot say I was close to him, because Ronnie was really the number one. But Colin loved very much that Race of Champions win. I made one attempt to pass Niki at Paddock and luckily he did not see me, so that got in my mind how it could work on the next lap. If he had seen me maybe he could have stopped me coming around him. But in rain you are quite busy at Paddock Bend".

By mid-season in 1975 Jacky had left Team Lotus, and the rest of his F1 career, with Frank Williams and then Morris Nunn's little Ensign team, brought no joy. In the 1976 US GP at Watkins Glen his Ensign charged the barriers head-on and caught fire. Jacky escaped with fractures to both ankles and burns. "The car was cut in two. They decided to take me to hospital in Elmira, but on the way they had to stop at a gas station to put petrol in the ambulance. We were in the amateur days then."

Over the next two years he did isolated races for Ensign, but his F1 days seemed over. Then in 1979, while he was driving for Porsche in sports cars and for Carl Haas in America — winning the Can-Am title in a LolaT333CS — Ligier driver Patrick Depailler was injured in a hang-gliding accident. So he was drafted in alongside Jacques Laffite. "I thought it might be an opportunity to make an F1 comeback. But I found I was usually three or four tenths slower than Jacques. There may have been reasons for that, but I felt inside myself no capacity to go any faster. It's never pleasant to say to yourself, 'I am not as good as I was before'. You try to find excuses, say you will have a better race tomorrow. But I have always been honest with myself. I understood I was never going back to the front of F1. When you know that, the decision is easy. You pick up something else where you can get the motivation. I was still winning sports car races, but in that type of racing, if you are in a good car with a good partner, there isn't the same pressure, nor the same level of opponents."

In sports car racing Jacky's record continued to be extraordinary. While at Ferrari he had won races in the jewel-like 312P, effectively a two-seater streamlined F1 car, which Jacky remembers as "a lovely toy, very easy to drive". In 1972 alone he won Daytona, Sebring, BOAC Brands, Monza, Zeltweg and Watkins Glen. In '75 he drove for all three top sports car teams, winning Spa for Matra, and also racing for Alfa and Mirage. By

1976 he had begun his long and highly successful relationship with Porsche, for whom he scored four of his six Le Mans victories and some two dozen other major wins over 10 seasons. During his career he scored nearly 50 victories in international endurance events.

"But that's something else that is not down to you, because you are nothing in sports car racing without a co-driver. Derek Bell, Jochen Mass, Mario Andretti, Brian Redman, Jackie Oliver − those five in particular, we shared the same goal, we did the same job. You relate so closely with your co-driver: he comes in during the night, jumps out, it needs only a few words − how is the track, what is the feeling with the car, pay attention to this little noise. In 1975 Derek and I did half of Le Mans with a broken chassis on the Mirage. On every corner there was a grinding from the back. We dealt with it together, and we won.

"And 1977, that was the most extraordinary Le Mans for Porsche. I was sharing a 936 with Henri Pescarolo, but after four hours the engine blew. The other 936, driven by Jürgen Barth and Hurley Haywood, lost a lot of time changing a fuel injector pump. They were 41st. I was put in that car as reserve driver, and we all three had to drive flat out for 20 hours." With Ickx doing the lion's share, the Porsche was back up to ninth place by 9pm, and by 3am it was third. By 10am on Sunday it was leading. "It was good to see the impact on the team as we climbed up the classification, place by place." Then in the final hour, dismay: the car came smoking into the pits with a burned piston. The mechanics disconnected the valve-gear on one cylinder and turned down the turbo boost, and at 3.50pm it chugged out for two final slow laps − to victory.

In 1985, in the Spa 1000Kms, Jacky was innocently involved in the accident that cost the life of the young German charger Stefan Bellof. As Ickx's factory Porsche led Bellof's Brun car up the hill into Eau Rouge, Bellof tried an impossible overtaking manoeuvre and they collided. Both cars were destroyed: Ickx escaped with light injuries, but Bellof was trapped in the wreckage for 20 minutes, and died shortly after. Jacky was deeply upset: "There are some things you never forget. Although you are completely innocent, you are still part of it, you cannot stop saying to yourself, 'If, if'. He was a charming boy, very promising, a rising star. Ken Tyrrell was promoting him, like he promoted me 20 years before. My decision to stop racing came naturally after that. If you are realistic you allow these things to push you towards a decision." He scored his final Porsche victory, sharing a 962C with Mass in the Selangor 800Kms in Malaysia. Then, just before his 41st birthday, he retired.

But he remained a racer. He'd been introduced to the Paris-Dakar desert race by the French actor Claude Brasseur in 1981, campaigning a Citroën CX until they crashed out, and he was entranced by the magnitude and challenge of the event. The next year he and Brasseur finished fifth in a Mercedes, and at the third attempt they won. He got Porsche interested and finished second for them in '86, and also did it for Lada, Peugeot and Citroën. Then he became involved in the organisation of the event, which due to unrest in Africa has moved to South America in recent years.

"If you ask me what is the most satisfying competition of my life, it isn't F1, it isn't Le Mans, it's the Paris-Dakar. It's the hardest, most complex race in the world. Flat out for nine hours at a stretch, 130mph on sand. And the sand is unpredictable, like the sea: you can't trust it to remain the same, because suddenly it will be different. A desert is a place where nobody lives. Nobody. If something goes wrong, you have to find a solution by yourself, out there in the silence. If you think you are important, out there, alone, you realise you are not. And in discovering the event, I discovered Africa. I saw different peoples, a different part of the planet." For Jacky it was the start of a love affair with the continent that continues to this day.

Jacky's daughter Vanina, now 36, has been racing for 15 seasons, and at Le Mans this year Jacky watched her finish a fine seventh, second petrol-powered car home, in the Kronos Lola-Aston. "I am proud of her. She is very brave, and drives a big fast car really well." They have done the Paris-Dakar together: in 2000 their Toyota finished 18th. "It was fantastic to do that event, father and daughter. After that you really know each other. But she navigated; I did the driving. I am not that brave...

"With the Grands Prix, all the endurance racing, the testing, and then the desert races too, spanning 32 years I have probably done more racing miles than almost anybody else. And I only had two bad accidents, at Jarama and Watkins Glen. I have been so fortunate. Now that I have grown out of my monorail vision of the world, what interests me is people, the human race. Khadja and I plan to spend more and more time in Mali, where we are having a house built on the Niger River, miles from anywhere. The local builders are wonderful, they work from dawn till dusk, and the workmanship is perfect. Not like on a racing car, nothing is straight, nothing is square, but everything is perfect.

"The article you are writing, I want it to be an expression of my thanks to all the people who helped me in my racing, who shared it with me. Ten years with Porsche, five years with Ferrari, all fantastic people. The father figures: Enzo Ferrari, Jack Brabham, John Wyer, Carl Haas, and of course Ken. And the people who worked with them, who were almost more important: David Yorke and John Horsman at JW, Ron Tauranac at Brabham, Peter Warr at Lotus, and all the people in the chain whose names I never knew. Even the spectators: I do not think they are always well-treated. They should not be like lemons, squeezed for their money to the last drop. Their hearts beat with the passion of racing, and without spectators there would have been no racing for me to do.

"It's all the other people in your life who help build your story. If you have been as fortunate as me, you cannot say Me, Myself, I."

Jacky Ickx was talking to Simon in July 2011.

ALAN JONES

Forging a winning way with
Frank and Patrick

Scroll down the roster of drivers who won a single World Championship – names like James Hunt and Jody Scheckter, Nigel Mansell and Damon Hill – and for each there's a different reason why they never took a second title. In the case of Alan Jones, it's probably down to the English weather. Between 1978 and 1981 Alan forged a tremendously strong working relationship with Frank Williams and Patrick Head. The three men, hardened racers all, were comfortable with each other, talked the same down-to-earth language, and wasted no time on sentiment or ceremony, and together they achieved one drivers' title and two constructors' titles. In 1982 a Williams driver won the World Championship again – but that was Keke Rosberg, and by then Alan was driving a tractor on his farm in Australia.

"Over the winter of 1981 Patrick came up with the six-wheeler [the Williams FW07E] and Frank said I had to go to Donington to test it. I'd bought the farm, we had our son Christian, and I'd really got the shits with England. I stayed at that bloody motel at Donington, and I had to boil the kettle in my room to unfreeze the lock to get in my car the next morning. I thought, 'This is exactly why I want to go home'. I tested the car, drove back to a cold, grey Heathrow and got on a Qantas jet. As soon as we burst through the clouds into the sunshine I thought, 'I'm not going to miss Formula 1.' But of course I did come back, twice. I've had more comebacks than Dame Nellie Melba."

Which is appropriate, because we're having lunch at Melba's, a swanky restaurant and nightclub just behind the gilded beach of Surfers Paradise, where Alan lives in a waterside property with his second wife Amanda and seven-year-old twins Zara and Jack. The weather is glorious, and Alan is wearing the Gold Coast uniform of shirt and shorts. He looks healthy and relaxed as he instructs the waiter to bring a plate of oysters and a filet mignon "medium on the inside, burnt to buggery on the outside".

Any discussion of Alan's career has to start with his father, for during the 1950s Stan Jones was one of Australia's top racers. "He was a colourful character. He had a string of very successful car dealerships, and he never took a back seat to anybody. Liked the whisky, liked the ladies. I was surrounded by racing cars since I was knee-high. When anybody asked little Alan what he was going to do when he grew up, I'd always say I was going to be a racing driver.

"Dad bought the famous Maybach Special, and he won the first New Zealand Grand Prix with it in 1954, against Wharton's V16 BRM and Whitehead's V12 Ferrari. That year he was leading the Australian GP on the old Southport road circuit. Going over the bridge, as the fuel load got lighter, the gap between the road and the wheels started getting wider. Finally something broke as he landed, and he went off into the trees. Huge accident. The Maybach was cut clean in two, and all he's done is cut his chin. Then he got a Maserati 250F from the factory – with a brand-new 300S engine as a spare. He won the 1959 Australian GP with that. He also had an F1 Cooper, and he even did the Monte Carlo Rally in a humpy Holden, in an all-Aussie effort with Lex Davison and Tony Gaze. They finished, too.

"My parents split up when I was 12, and Dad got custody of me. He was always a bloke who got what he wanted, by one means or another. We had a housekeeper to cook and clean, and I had a lot of days off school to go to the races with him. When I was 16 I started hillclimbing a Mini, and I began working in Dad's businesses.

"Then Dad went broke. The credit squeeze hit at a time when dealers had to carry huge stocks, because if someone wanted a blue one with red seats and you didn't have it you'd lose the deal to someone up the road. Until then I'd been a spoiled brat, a big-headed little bastard, and suddenly I had to learn some hard lessons about life. If Dad hadn't gone bust I don't think I'd have ended up much of a racing driver.

"I knew if I wanted to go motor racing properly I had to be in Europe. I arrived in London with £50 in my pocket, and my mate Brian McGuire and I ended up, of course, in Kangaroo Valley – Earls Court. I got a job in Selfridges, selling fireworks, but then we started to sell VW campers to poor unsuspecting Kiwis and Aussies. We'd park them in the Earls Court Road with a For Sale sign in the window, and by the time we got home the phone'd be ringing. It was money for old rope. We worked all sorts of tricks to source them. Sometimes we'd buy them for £150 and sell them a few hours later for £600. All we cared about was getting the money together to go racing."

They bought a Formula Ford, which Brian crashed, and then Alan got a twin-cam Lotus 41, which was wrecked in a testing accident at Brands Hatch. "The guy in front dived across the road to go into the pits, I swerved to avoid him and hit the bank. I was a bit crocked, had a broken foot, so they took me to a hospital which must have been bang up-to-date in the Boer War. The lady doctor started lecturing me about how motor racing endangered life. Then she got some scissors and was about to cut off my brand new overalls. I had a major blue with her about that. Later I found out they'd operated on my foot all wrong and I had to have it done again. I patched up the Lotus and sold it."

Next came a Brabham BT28 which, for 1971 and the new 1600cc F3, was updated to BT35 spec. With McGuire and New Zealander Alan McCully, Alan ran under the proud banner of the Australian International Racing Organisation, with cars and van smartly turned out in orange colours. "People thought AIRO was sponsored by the bloody Australian government. The paint looked good, but we had no money at all." What Alan did have was a good relationship with George Robinson of Vegantune, who lent him engines. "What I like about the Brits is they never worry if you're English, or Australian, or from Timbuctoo. They just base their support on whether they have faith in your ability. I owe George a lot."

A borrowed GRD and another Vegantune engine got Alan through 1972, and he and his new wife Beverley were now paying the bills by running a boarding house. "We rented a big house in Ealing, filled it with bunk beds bought from an Army surplus store, and put up Australians, New Zealanders and Canadians. Four rooms, four to a room, £11 a week with breakfast, it was a bloody gold-mine. I'd get up early and do the breakfasts, dish out the cornflakes and the bacon and egg, and everything had to be finished by 9am so I could piss off and spend the rest of the day hunting for a drive."

For 1973 Robinson recommended him to the Scottish industrialist Denys Dobbie, who had grand plans for DART, his Dobbie Automobile Racing Team. Initially it was an F2 for Dave Walker, a sports car for John Miles and an F3 GRD for Alan, and there were whispers about F1 in the future. The F2 and the sports car soon fizzled out, but Alan led the British F3 Championship until the final round, when his engine blew in practice and the spare turned out to be badly down on power. He lost the title to Tony Brise by two points. By now Dobbie had had enough, and Alan spent another difficult winter wondering where his next drive was coming from. Meanwhile his father had had a stroke. "We got him over from Australia and he lived with us in Ealing. He came around the races with me, leaning on his stick. Then he had another stroke and he had to go into care. It was very sad. He died in 1973, and he was only 51. I'd just won an F3 race at Silverstone, and we put the wreath in the coffin with him.

"Then I heard that a man called Mike Sullivan needed a driver for his Formula Atlantic March. I called him at once and he came on strong: new car, big transporter, the works. I was down there almost before he'd hung up the phone. When I got to his house I saw an old Nestlé van outside. That was the big transporter, and that's when I started to feel less excited. The car was two years old, and in its first race it overheated. But in the second, at Silverstone, I got lucky: all the people in front of me broke down or fell off, and I won. I gave Sullivan a list of things that needed doing before the next round at Oulton Park two weeks later, and when I got there nothing had been done. He'd just put the car back in the Nestlé van. So I refused to drive it, and I made sure everybody in the pits knew why.

"So Harry Stiller offered me a test. His Atlantic March really was a new one, and he had a good engine deal. But his driver, Bev Bond, had been complaining that the car had an understeer problem. I knew Robin Herd pretty well – I'd been doing some journeyman testing for March at Goodwood – and he came to the test. We dialled out the understeer, I got under the Formula Atlantic record, Bev Bond was promoted to team manager, and I had a drive for the season." There were lots of lap records but lots of retirements, although a pole-to-flag win in the British Grand Prix support race did his reputation no harm.

And in 1975 Alan got his foot in the F1 door at last. "Harry called and told me to go to some place called Easton Neston and have a seat fitting." Stiller had done a deal to run the original Hesketh 308 alongside James Hunt's works car. In his first outing, in the Silverstone International Trophy, Alan finished seventh, less than a minute behind Niki Lauda's winning Ferrari. His first Grand Prix was the dreadful Barcelona race, with the drivers' boycott of practice and Rolf Stommelen's crash in which four spectators died. "I remember everyone sitting around arguing about safety, and I wondered what I had got myself into. I'd gone to Spain to go racing, so I sided with the drivers who were saying, 'Let's get on with it and get out there'. Then came Monaco – they had 27 entrants going for 18 places on the grid, and when I scraped in 18th we felt like we'd won the bloody race. But in the race a wheel fell off."

After four GPs with the Hesketh, Harry Stiller moved to the USA for tax reasons. With Stommelen still injured, Graham Hill offered Alan a seat alongside Tony Brise for four races. His fifth place at the Nürburgring was the Hill GH1's best-ever result. "Having been World Champion, Graham felt he knew better than his drivers how to set up the car. He was stubborn and inflexible. A great ambassador for motor racing, but a wretched man to work for." Then Stommelen returned and Alan slid backwards into Formula 5000, driving John Macdonald's V6 March to two victories and five fastest laps. He was determined to get back into F1, but the future looked bleak. The inevitable midnight phone call from Louis Stanley promised the world at BRM, but: "I just didn't believe him. However desperate you are, there are some cars you don't want to drive, and some people you don't want to drive for.

"Then John Surtees gave me a run at Goodwood – which I knew well after all those March sessions – and he offered me a drive on the spot. He was off to South Africa testing, and asked me to go. At Heathrow he waved a piece of paper at me. It was a two-year contract, and he said, 'Sign this, or you're not coming.' I said, 'Hold on, John, we're in the departure lounge. I'd quite like the chance to read it through.' He said, 'I'm not paying all this money to get you down there unless you sign.' I skimmed through it and we started to argue about it all. The airline staff were chasing us because we were keeping the Jumbo waiting. So I signed.

"We were at Kyalami for a week and I think I did six laps, because the uprights kept breaking. Then came the Race of Champions at Brands Hatch. There was uproar because BBC TV were refusing to televise the meeting, all because our Surtees had the terrible word Durex written in big letters across the nose." The broadcaster didn't want the name of a contraceptive to appear on screen, but cynics were saying it wouldn't be a problem, because a Surtees was unlikely to be anywhere near the front, so the cameras wouldn't show it anyway. "And when I got to Brands there was no sign of my car. It transpired they were still finishing it in the transporter on the way to the track.

"Well, for the race it was cold and slippery. At the start Scheckter pissed off into the distance – I think Tyrrell ran lots of toe-in to get some false heat into the tyres – but on lap two he threw it into the bank, and I'd just passed Niki Lauda's Ferrari, so I was in the lead. I held off James Hunt's McLaren for about half the race, and by the end I was still second, so that was good. But two weeks later we were at Long Beach, where it was warm and dry, and we were nowhere.

"John would always go through this time-wasting ritual in practice, trying endless small adjustments. He'd fiddle with the car, I'd do some laps, tell John what I thought the car needed, he'd fiddle some more, I'd do some more laps, and by the end of practice we'd just manage, with luck, to get the car back to where it was when we'd started. John said to me once, 'The reason why the car isn't quick enough is because the chassis is too good, it's not putting enough heat into the tyres.' So I said, 'Well, John, why don't you just fuck it up a little?' Basically it was a good car, and we scored fourth and fifth place points on occasion, but it was a frustrating season. The two most difficult men I've ever driven for have been ex-World Champions. At the end of the first year of my two-year contract I said to myself, 'If the only way I can do F1 is with Surtees, I'm not doing it.'

"I did the Tasman races in Teddy Yip's F5000 Lola – I won the Australian GP, 18 years after Dad, but I'd jumped the start so they demoted me to fourth – and then Teddy said, 'Come and try Indycar racing on the ovals.' We went to Ontario with a McLaren M16, and I've never worn overalls for so long and done so little driving. We had to wait three days for the wind to drop before they let us out. It seemed every time an aeroplane flew by and cast a shadow over the track they'd stop running. I didn't like it, I didn't like the ovals, it was weird.

"Then Tom Pryce was killed at Kyalami, and Jackie Oliver came on the phone. 'What are you up to, Alan?' 'Nothing much.' 'Come and drive for Shadow.' 'Well, trouble is I've got this contract with Surtees.' 'Let me handle that,' said Jackie. I don't know what happened, but he did handle it, and I became a Shadow driver for 1977. Don Nichols was a bit different – anybody who wears a black hat and a black cape is a bit different – but Alan Rees was a good team manager, he made things happen. We had a podium at Monza and a couple of fourths. And I won the Austrian GP."

On a damp and slippery Österreichring Alan started 14th, and carved his way up to eighth by lap nine, fourth by lap 12 and second by lap 16. It was an inspired drive, and when Hunt's McLaren retired with 10 laps to go he took Shadow's only GP win. "It was a big surprise to everybody, including the organisers, who didn't have the Australian National Anthem ready. Some drunk played *Happy Birthday To You* on the trumpet instead. I didn't mind a bit."

The joy of his victory was tainted a couple of weeks later when his old friend Brian McGuire was killed racing a two-year-old Williams FW04 in the British Aurora Championship. A pin came out of the brake linkage at Brands Hatch and he hit a marshals' post. "I used to say to Brian, 'Look, mate, when these cars were new they were taken back to the factory after every race, stripped down to nothing and rebuilt. You can't just put them through a car wash.' I always worry when I watch people racing F1 cars from my period. Most are properly prepared, but there's a few people who buy them and don't give them the attention they need. You could get killed in them when they were new, and since then the barriers haven't got any softer."

The Austrian win was a big turning point in Alan's career. "Because I was going well in a Shadow, people were saying, 'Look at Jonesy, he's doing well in that old shit-box, isn't he?' At the end of the season Frank Williams rang me and said he was interested, but then I got a summons: come over to Maranello and meet the old man.

"First off, Luca di Montezemolo said to me, 'When you meet Mr Ferrari he will ask you why you want to drive for Ferrari. Make sure you have your answer ready.' I should have thought it was pretty obvious why I wanted to drive for Ferrari. Piero Lardi showed me round the facility, which was amazing especially for those days – the foundry, the test track, everything – and then I was taken to Mr Ferrari's villa. They ushered me into the presence of this white-faced figure with dark glasses, and my first thought was, 'He's dead. They've propped him up and they've got a recording of his voice coming from behind a curtain.' He asked me why I wanted to drive for Ferrari and I must have given the right answer, because they gave me a contract, and I signed it. Part of the deal was I had to live in Modena, which was no drama for me. Then they said, 'We want a North American driver because it helps our road car sales in the USA, so we're trying to sign Mr Andretti. If we don't sign him, you are a Ferrari driver for 1978.' That seemed pretty straightforward.

"Two weeks later I read in the comics that Mario Andretti had signed for Lotus, so I thought, 'How good's this – I'm a Ferrari driver.' I called Maranello and said, 'When do you want me?' 'We don't,' they said. 'We've signed a North American – Gilles Villeneuve.' So I hung up, dialled Frank's number, and said, 'Frank, I've been giving a lot of thought to your offer...'

"By signing Villeneuve, Ferrari had done me the biggest favour of my life. I met Frank; typically he went all clandestine on me, and we had a secret tryst in a lay-by just off the M1. Then I went to the factory, saw the FW06, and met Patrick Head for the first time. I was unbelievably impressed with Patrick. Compared to what I'd come to expect in Formula 1, he just seemed so down-to-earth. It was a one-car team, and I was a bit worried that the 06 wasn't ground-effect, but what I did like were the five letters painted on it, SAUDI, because that meant it was properly funded. What I didn't realise was that, although the signage was on the car, the deal wasn't done yet. I've always reckoned the first two GPs of 1978 were done on Frank's credit card.

"By the time we got to the fourth round, at Long Beach, the young princes and a lot of the top Saudis were there. I was up the backside of Reutemann's Ferrari and pushing him hard for the lead. The nose wing started to collapse, but I didn't notice any difference. But then a misfire set in. Reutemann spun later, so we would have won that one. The 06 was a clever little car, and it should have won a race, but the team was on a steep learning curve. The nearest we got was second at Watkins Glen."

It was a busy year, for as well as the F1 programme, Alan also won the Can-Am Championship with a Carl Haas Lola. "I'd do F1 one weekend, then go testing for Frank in the week, then fly to America for the next weekend's CanAm. But Carl had a good set-up, and it was pretty much C&C – cruise and collect. The boss of CityCorp couldn't believe I commuted from England for each race, and he said to Carl, 'This boy has to fly Concorde.' 'Good idea,' says Carl, 'if you want to pay for it.' So he did.

"The Concorde lounge at Heathrow gave you free international calls, so I'd camp outside the door waiting for it to open like it was a Harrods sale, to get all my phone calls done on the house." Still lurking inside this jet-setting F1 driver was the struggling hustler who'd cooked breakfast for his tenants in the Ealing boarding house.

Alan's rugged personality fitted the Williams team like a glove. "Patrick and I had a fantastic relationship. We understood each other so well that he could almost double-guess me. If I wanted an adjustment on the grid after doing the warm-up lap, he'd know precisely what I wanted almost before I asked for it. Frank was more involved in the business side, doing the deals. During debriefs in the motorhome Patrick would take me through everything, and then all of a sudden Frank would pipe up, 'Driver comfort OK?' Every debrief he said it. Finally one day I said, 'Shit no, Frank, I'm not too comfortable.' It made his day! Frank is the best bloke I ever drove for, because he was such a great motivator. He could make you walk over glass. He was, and still is, a bloody racer. I cannot in all honesty fathom how he and Patrick still go to the races they go to, year in and year out. It's been nearly 40 years for Frank now..."

For 1979 Clay Regazzoni joined as Williams' number two, and Head came up with FW07, with full ground effects. "It was a bit late coming, so we did the first four rounds with 06. When I first got into 07 I did five laps and came in and said to Patrick, 'Now I know why Andretti and Lotus have been winning all those races.' The grip going into corners, the commitment you could make, was just unbelievable compared to what I'd been used to. We led Zolder until the electrics failed, and then at Silverstone we had pole, murdered the lap record, and led all the way until the water pump sprung a leak. Regazzoni was running behind me, so he scored Williams' first win. But I won four of the next five GPs – Hockenheim, Österreichring, Zandvoort and Montréal."

This string of late-season victories promoted Alan to third in the 1979 World Championship behind Scheckter and Villeneuve, with more wins than either of them. And in 1980 the job got done. After a stirring battle with Brabham and Nelson Piquet, Alan was World Champion, with five victories, and Williams was champion constructor. His team-mate was now Carlos Reutemann. "All the stories that Reutemann and I hated each other are bullshit. He was no different from any of my team-mates. I never said to any of them, 'Come round for a barbie,' because I had to race against them, and I wasn't going to give them anything.

"But the last thing Frank wanted was his two drivers having each other off, and if you own the bloody team you call the tune. So he wrote into Carlos' contract that if we were more than 10 seconds ahead of everybody else, and we were separated by less than two seconds, I would win. Carlos read the contract, and he signed it, and I didn't see anyone holding a .45 to his temple. In fact it only ever arose on one occasion, at Rio in 1981. It was pissing down, and we took off into the distance with Carlos ahead of me. I thought, if I stay within 2sec of him he's got to let me through. It's getting closer and closer to the end of the race, the pit signal goes out JONES-REUT, and I think, 'What's going on here?'

"Then I thought, 'I know what he's going to do, he's going to play Mr Obvious and move across for me on the last lap where everybody can see.' So I carried on sitting behind him. But he just kept going and won the race. I got out of my car and went to the podium, which wasn't in the main body of the pits, and after standing in the rain for what seemed like a long time with nothing happening I went back to the paddock. This was interpreted as me getting the shits with Carlos and storming off, but that's not what happened. The next round was in Argentina, home ground for Carlos, and in Buenos Aires I had taxi drivers giving me the finger. Even the bloody marshals at the track were giving me the finger. People were blowing it up into something it wasn't, but the team orders scenario never came up again." But Frank Williams, annoyed that Carlos had ignored the agreement, only paid him second-place money for Rio.

Among his other contemporaries, Alan singles out Ronnie Peterson. "I always got on well with Ronnie. Everybody knows about his fantastic car control, but he was so naturally gifted that he had no idea why he was quick. He couldn't analyse it. That's why he was no good as a test driver: give him a problem and he'd just drive around it. With Gilles Villeneuve you always had a fight on your hands. He was very tough to drive against, but he was always fair. Mind you, when he had that puncture at Zandvoort in 1979, and just kept on racing with a back wheel hanging on by a brake line, he behaved like a dickhead. I wouldn't want to be the guy following when the brake line snaps and his wheel comes flying into my cockpit."

Alan arrived at Monza in 1981 with a broken finger on his gear-change hand, the legacy of an altercation with two thugs in a London street after a traffic incident (in which you assume Alan gave as good as he got). That weekend he quietly told the team, to Frank's dismay, that he wanted to retire, and then he climbed through the field to finish second. In the final round at Las Vegas the outgoing World Champion led from start to finish to score his 12th GP victory, then turned his back on F1 and dug in on his farm north of Melbourne.

"We had 2200 acres, breeding Simmental cattle and Charollais sheep, and it was a full-on operation. I was sick of the travel and I thought, 'Great, I'm never going to see another airport again.' Pironi had his accident at Hockenheim in the August, and when Ferrari came on the phone I didn't take the call. It was stupidity on my part, I was just being bloody-minded, and I really regret it now. They gave the drive to Andretti, and he took pole for them at Monza. He's never paid for a plate of spaghetti since.

"I was cutting the 100-acre paddock by the main house, sitting on this tractor for bloody hours, and a plane went over high in the sky and I caught myself thinking, 'Jeez, I wonder where that's going?' Then I fell off a horse and broke my femur, and while I was laid up Jackie Oliver came on the phone and said, 'It's all happening at Arrows, we've got a major new sponsor, come back and drive.'

"So I got my femur pinned, flew to the States and did the Long Beach race. I had to bash the side of the monocoque with a hammer to clear my bad leg." He qualified mid-grid and ran eighth, but eventually retired when the cockpit chafing the pins in his leg made it too painful to continue. He was third in the Race of Champions two weeks later, but "the mysterious billionaire sponsor was showing no signs of appearing, there weren't the funds to go testing and develop the car, so in the end I just said, 'No.'

"Back home a friend who was Australia's Porsche distributor got me racing a 935, and then in 1985 I got a call from Charlie

Crichton-Stuart, who'd been a good mate when he was working with Frank Williams. He was full of a new F1 deal that was going to be wider than Cinemascope and brighter than Technicolor. He said, 'I've been told to sign you. They told me to offer you X, but if I have to I can go to X plus Y. So why don't I just offer you that?'

"What was going on was Beatrice, the eighth-largest company in America, had decided to go F1. Carl Haas was putting it together, and it sounded good enough to get my overalls back on. Goodyear, Lola, exclusive use of a new Ford V6 turbo engine, smart new factory, all the kit. And lots of money. All the ingredients to bake the cake, but they couldn't turn the oven on."

So why didn't it work? "Well, it's debatable how good the chassis was, but the engine was shit. Beautiful little engine, beautifully put together, but no horsepower. The Hondas had electronically variable turbo boost, but we had to do it manually, with two plastic things coming out of the dash. You could only adjust the boost on constant revs on the straight, so you'd do one bank on one lap and then you'd have to wait another lap before you could do the other bank. They were coming up with all this bullshit, F1 was going to see American muscle at its best, but we were 20kph slower down the straight than the Ferraris. Teddy Mayer was the team manager, and in my opinion he was hopeless. Other people will disagree with that, but Teddy didn't have a good way about him. There's ways to get the best out of drivers, and he found out how not to get the best out of me." Alan did 20 Grands Prix for Beatrice. The tally was 15 retirements, one non-start – and just four points. The Beatrice episode paid well, but brought no joy.

"So I came home and went touring car racing. Australian touring cars are pretty serious, 600bhp and under-tyred, and very competitive. I really enjoyed that. My last race was Bathurst about five years ago. Then the Masters: loved the idea, loved the car, but at Kyalami in practice for the first race I rooted my neck. I've had a dickey neck for a while and when it seizes up it affects everything, even my vision. I wasn't kidding myself, I was nowhere near as quick as I should have been. So I turned into a bloody expert and did the commentary with Murray Walker. That was fun. Now I'm involved with the Australian A1GP team: 10 rounds, and I go to every one. I love getting to the track early in the morning, discussing pitstop strategy and which way to go on set-up. I enjoy helping the drivers [currently John Martin], we go through the data and I'll offer advice, but no way do I tell them what to do. I don't want to do a Surtees and try to get back in the cockpit with them."

Alan's son Christian went via karting to Formula Ford, and in 2004 he won the Asian F3 Championship. He was Australia's A1 driver in 2005, and has raced in the Porsche Supercup. "And this very morning, in the swimming pool at home, seven-year-old Jack said, 'You know, Dad, I might be a racing driver when I grow up.'" Stan would be pleased to know that the Jones genes are all present and correct.

Alan Jones was talking to Simon in December 2007.

NIGEL MANSELL

Whatever else, an out-and-out
racer

Surely no World Champion has provoked greater extremes of adulation and criticism than Nigel Mansell. From his earliest days in Formula 1 he was the darling of the British crowds: when he scored his first Grand Prix victory at Brands Hatch in 1985, and then went on to win his home Grand Prix four more times, the scenes of unbridled joy from the spectator banks were unprecedented. When he raced for Ferrari the Italian *tifosi* loved him too, and their name for him, *Il Leone,* was tribute as much to his lion-hearted courage as to his nationality.

Yet for much of his career he was castigated by some sections of the media. They wrote that he was difficult and paranoid with team managers and with team-mates, and prone to exaggerate the effect of painful injuries – accusations which Nigel robustly denied then, and denies now.

But, love him or loathe him, there was never any dispute about Mansell's out-and-out speed as a racer. Nor his sheer bravery in the cockpit. And his climb up the motor racing ladder from humble beginnings bore witness to extraordinary determination and dogged self-belief. His Formula 1 career spanned 15 years, and during eight of those years he scored 30 victories. No sooner had he clinched the World Championship in 1992 than, unable to agree terms with his F1 team, he decamped to America – and won the Indycar Championship at his first attempt. He returned to F1, and scored a 31st win for Williams. Then, with a brief and uncomfortable seat at McLaren, a great career ended on an unhappy note.

Today Nigel is very busy, overseeing the racing careers of his sons Leo and Greg, and even getting back in the cockpit himself at the recent *Autosport* 1000Kms at Silverstone. He has sold his Devonshire golf club and leisure complex, but he's now president of UK Youth, a charitable organisation which works to develop the skills and potential of 750,000 young people, supporting some 7000 youth clubs and 40,000 youth workers. When we met for lunch on the 28th floor of the London Hilton he was on a flying visit from his home in Jersey – he still uses his own private jet – to the House of Lords to raise youth issues about which he feels passionate. "Nothing is more important than young people. To incarcerate one child for 12 months costs £138,000. So whatever government is in power, you just have to do the numbers: if you can stop young people getting into trouble, and equip them with the skills and the ability to enjoy a constructive life, it's got to be the best investment of all."

The trademark moustache is long gone but Nigel, 56 now, looks as fit as he did when he was racing. His lunch is austere: plain roast chicken, no sauce, a few steamed vegetables and a Coke. He is relaxed, amiable and comfortable with himself, a far cry from the angry racer I remember in so many edgy press conferences. He is still bemused by the way some of the specialist press portrayed him at the height of his career, but in those days his huge determination and will to win was strangely overlaid with a thin-skinned sensitivity, and also an ever-present belief that he was on his own, fighting a lone battle for the common man against the motor racing establishment. And, not far below the surface, that belief is still there. When referring to himself he mixes his pronouns, as he always did, but there is no mistaking the fervour of his views:

"When I look back I say to myself, with what we were up against, we were so lucky and fortunate that we accomplished what we did. Because you realise the forces that were against you, the manufacturers, the sponsors, the politics, the governing body, the other competitors, seven or eight World Champions racing together – to have achieved what we achieved in that era of competitiveness... if the World Championship had gone on race wins, I would have won the title three times. When the big interests decide they want to do something in a different way, it doesn't matter who you are, if your face doesn't fit then it doesn't fit. That's why motor sport is one of the toughest sports in the world, because there are so many outside factors. If you play golf or tennis or you're an athlete it's up to you. You've got to have the right training and medical back-up, but ultimately you do it yourself. In motor racing you're involved with hundreds of people, millions of pounds, big organisations, big business, all with their own agendas."

And Nigel always seemed to have more than his fair share of dramas – team conflicts, contractual battles, accidents and injuries. "I was motivated by adversity, because I lived with it all the time. I don't think there'll ever be another driver who will make it into Formula 1 without any financial backing and resources. I got to F1 with nothing. I mean, nothing. What I brought to the table was commitment. I could dig deeper than probably any of my contemporaries, because of where I'd come from. Where we came from and where we've ended up is an extraordinary story. Lewis [Hamilton] was picked up by the age of eight. He's been chosen, and that's great for him."

Nigel started in karts, winning several titles in his teens, despite suffering a serious head injury when his steering broke at Morecambe. His first racing car, a second-hand Formula Ford, was bought with the help of his wife Rosanne, who sold her own road car to fund it. They were married when Nigel was 21, and she has always been his strongest supporter. Despite indifferent equipment, results started to come, and in 1977 he was able to borrow a new Crosslé. He gave up his job at Lucas Aerospace to race full-time – and three weeks later broke his neck at Brands Hatch. Wearing a neck brace, he was back in the cockpit seven weeks later. He came to the final round of the Brush Fusegear FF Championship at Silverstone needing to win the race and set fastest lap to take the title, and he did just that.

Formula 3 had to come next, but despite working nights as an office cleaner, with Rosanne doing overtime as a British Gas demonstrator, Nigel had no funds to make the move. So they sold their house, which raised £6000, and he took the money to March. That gave him a works drive – for half a dozen races: then the money was gone. "March promised the earth, but it was the worst money we ever spent." But for 1979 Dave Price hired him for the Unipart-backed team of Dolomite-powered F3 Marches. Journalist Peter Windsor and Team Lotus assistant manager Peter Collins had noted his speed, and at the British GP meeting they persuaded Colin Chapman to watch him in the F3 race. Soon afterwards, notwithstanding a cartwheeling accident at Oulton Park which injured his back, he was invited to a Lotus F1 test at Paul Ricard.

The other drivers being tried were Elio de Angelis, Eddie Cheever, Jan Lammers and Stephen South. Nigel spun the car on his second lap, but fortunately kept the engine running and settled down to turn in consistently fast laps. De Angelis was hired as number two to Mario Andretti – and Nigel was offered a testing contract. The following August Lotus ran a third car at the Austrian GP and, at the ripe old age of 27, he finally got his first F1 race. He did it in considerable discomfort after fuel was sloshed over him when the car was topped up on the grid, but he raced well until the engine blew. He did the Dutch GP too, crashing when the brakes failed. But he'd impressed Chapman enough to be hired as Elio's number two for 1981. He did it for virtually nothing – his retainer was £25,000, but he had to pay his own travel and hotel expenses – but in May, after he had finished on the podium in Belgium and qualified third for Monaco, Chapman doubled his retainer. And at the end of that season Team Lotus signed him for three years. The deal made him a millionaire, four short years after he and Rosanne, penniless, had sold their house to fund an abortive F3 drive.

Nigel is unstinting in his praise of the Lotus boss. "Colin believed in me, he saw something in me that he liked, not just as a driver but as an individual. We had a fantastic relationship, he was like a father to me. So when he died at the end of 1982 it was absolutely dreadful. Part of me died with him." At the start of that year Peter Warr had returned to Team Lotus as team manager, and almost from the start he and Nigel took a strong dislike to each other. And, after Chapman's death, Warr was in charge. "I wish he'd tried to be himself and not tried to emulate Colin. He probably did some good things, he kept the team going, but he was vindictive and nasty. He wanted me out for 1984, but my contract was too strong for him. But he did manage to halve my salary."

Biggest disappointment was when Nigel led the Monaco Grand Prix in the rain, only to lose the car going up the hill to Casino Square and clout the barriers. It was after this that Warr made his ill-advised comment, seized on with delight by the press, that "Mansell will never win a Grand Prix as long as I've got a hole in my arse". Badly demoralised by his Monaco error, Nigel bounced back with pole position in the burning heat of the Dallas street circuit, leading for half the race and holding second place to Keke Rosberg's Williams when his transmission failed with half a lap to go. He jumped out and pushed, collapsing with heat exhaustion just as he got the car to the line. "I was so angry, I just kept pushing. Then the lights went out and I woke up in hospital, on a drip in a bed packed with ice."

By mid-season, with Ayrton Senna's move to Lotus an open secret, Nigel heard he was on Frank Williams' shortlist. But in late August, when Frank refused to give him an answer, Nigel told Frank to take his name off the list. After the difficult atmosphere at Lotus he was prepared to walk away from motor racing if he couldn't drive in a team where he felt appreciated. That had the desired effect, and a few days later he was signed by Williams as Rosberg's team-mate for 1985. It was the start of a very fruitful relationship.

By the end of that season the FW10B-Honda was a formidable racing car, and at the European Grand Prix at Brands Hatch in October, Nigel's 75th Grand Prix, he went past Senna's Lotus to score his first Grand Prix victory. Two weeks later he won the South African race at Kyalami, from pole position. Brands provided many people with their first sight of Mansell-mania, as the British crowd went mad for their hero. Why did the fans love him so much?

"I think it's because you can't con the fans. I was honest. When I got into a racing car I wrung its neck. Whether I was leading or in 18th place, I gave 110 per cent, gave it the full money, and the fans loved that. They could identify with it. You have drivers, and you have racers. The driver waits for things to happen, the racer makes them happen. Long before I was World Champion I was the 'People's Champion', and that's an accolade only the fans can give you."

For 1986 Nigel had a new team-mate in Nelson Piquet. As a double World Champion, Piquet's contract made him number one, with a far higher retainer than Nigel. Clearly each regarded the other as his closest rival, and Nigel's win at Brands, when he pressured Piquet into missing a gear, was a psychological turning point. As the cars went to the final round in Adelaide Mansell, with five wins, was leading the table by four points: all he had to do was finish in the top three to be World Champion. He started from pole and, with 19 laps to go, he was in a comfortable third place when, at full chat in sixth, the left rear tyre exploded. Having got so near to his life's ambition, he was gutted. "It was pretty depressing. But the welcome I got when I flew home, you'd think I'd won the title 10 times over. You can't buy that."

In 1987 Mansell took eight pole positions, led 12 of the 16 rounds, and won six Grands Prix. His victory over Piquet in the British GP at Silverstone was a classic. The plan was to run without a tyre change, but one of Nigel's front wheels lost a balance weight, giving him a severe vibration. Just after half distance he dived into the pits. He rejoined with 30 laps to go, almost half a minute behind leader Piquet. With his adoring British crowd whooping and willing him on, he turned in a relentlessly brilliant drive to chase Piquet down. With three laps to go he was on his tail, and at 190mph on the Hangar Straight he sold Nelson a perfect dummy. As Stowe rushed up he jinked to the left, Nelson jinked left to block him, and at once Nigel was diving for the right, deep and late into Stowe, and was pulling away to win. On the slowing-down lap his Williams ran out of petrol, and he was engulfed by his public.

But in Hungary a wheel fell off with six laps to go and he lost certain victory. At Monza and Estoril Nigel believed that, for political reasons, Honda was giving Piquet better engines than him: at season's end both Honda and Piquet were leaving Williams for Lotus. He won in Mexico, but a practice crash in Japan injured his back and he missed the last two rounds. At season's end he'd won twice as many races as Nelson, but Nelson was champion.

"I knew three different Nelsons. The youngster coming up through the junior formulae, when we raced in F3 together; the one whom a lot of people disliked; and occasionally the human one. He's got all the ingredients to be a great person, it's just that he chooses not to be. He'd lower his standards to attack people in a very cruel way. He did it to his fellow countryman Ayrton Senna [whom he accused of being gay], he's done it to me, my wife and my children. He did that to try to destabilise me, because he couldn't beat me on the track. All it did was make me stronger, more determined to beat him. After I passed him at Silverstone in 1987 he didn't speak to me for ages."

Williams could only replace the Honda turbo with the normally-aspirated Judd, and Mansell had a frustrating 1988. At Silverstone he qualified 11th but, remarkably, climbed up to second, setting fastest lap among the turbos on a high-speed track. Ferrari was after him – the Scuderia had first approached him in 1986 – and in the summer of '88 he signed a highly

Having been a great F1 racer for Ferrari, Porsche, Brabham and his own Eagle team, and won Le Mans, Dan Gurney guided his All-American Racers outfit to be a major force in US racing. (LAT)

Gurney's finest hour was winning the 1967 Belgian Grand Prix at Spa in his own Eagle-Weslake. (LAT)

Damon Hill remains motor racing's only F1 World Champion son of a World Champion father. (LAT)

Hill receives Michael Schumacher's congratulations after beating him in a straight fight in the treacherously wet 1994 Japanese Grand Prix at Suzuka – one of his finest victories. (LAT)

Since taking over at the helm of Red Bull Racing in 2005, Christian Horner has made it the most successful team in Formula 1. (James Mitchell)

Directing operations at the pit wall, Horner is flanked by his team personnel during a Grand Prix. (Red Bull Racing/Getty Images)

Jacky Ickx was winning Grands Prix for Ferrari at 23, and became renowned for his speed in the rain. But it is as an endurance racer that he found his greatest successes. (LAT)

The closest Le Mans finish in history came in 1969, when Ickx's Ford GT40 passed Hans Herrmann's Porsche on the final lap to score the first of the Belgian's six victories in the 24-hour classic. (LAT)

Alan Jones' tough, uncompromising approach to his racing fitted in perfectly with Frank Williams' team, with which he won the World Championship in 1980. (LAT)

First win of five in Jones' championship year came in the opening round in Buenos Aires. (LAT)

Nigel Mansell looking glum in 1991, when he fought a season-long battle for the World Championship with Ayrton Senna. His title was to come the following year. (LAT)

Mansell was almost invincible in 1992, scoring nine wins and winning the World Championship by a huge margin. His favourite victory was in front of his adoring home crowd at Silverstone. (LAT)

Gordon Murray was the technical powerhouse behind Brabham and then
McLaren, and probably the greatest Formula 1 innovator in his day. He
now directs his own design company. (James Mitchell)

Murray confers with Niki Lauda in the Interlagos pitlane before the
1979 Brazilian Grand Prix. The car is the Brabham-Alfa Romeo BT48.
(sutton-images.com)

Roger Penske, serious-faced, before the Penske PC4's single Grand Prix victory in Austria in 1976. Winning driver John Watson is in the cockpit. (LAT)

Penske's relationship with engineer/racer Mark Donohue produced a string of victories, including dominating the 1973 CanAm Series with this Porsche 917/30. (LAT)

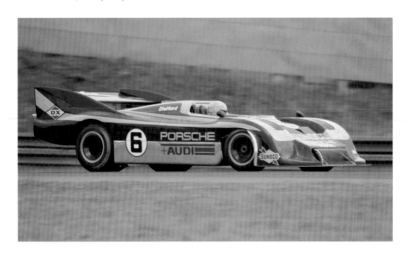

lucrative two-year contract, with an option for a third year. "I was the last driver to be signed personally by Enzo Ferrari. He died a few weeks after I met with him. I was the last driver to have dinner with him. I cherish that."

Nigel won his first GP for Ferrari, in Brazil. His other 1989 victory was in Hungary, and it was another Mansell classic. He started 12th, and by lap 53 he was second. Five laps later he was on the gearbox of Senna's McLaren as they came up to lap Stefan Johansson's Onyx.

Mansell and Senna had quite a bit of history. They'd collided in Adelaide in 1985, and in Rio in '86, and again at Spa in '87, after which Nigel went to the Lotus pits, grabbed Senna by the overalls and pushed him up against the wall. "Ayrton tried to intimidate other drivers. We weren't too dissimilar except in how we achieved it. But Ayrton and I were born to compete with each other. Some of the best overtaking manoeuvres in the history books, Ayrton and I share them. It took years, but eventually the penny dropped with Ayrton. He realised I was the only driver in the paddock he couldn't intimidate. When his red and white car came up behind anybody else they'd virtually cave in, but when he came up behind me, and equally when I came up behind him, it was different. Eventually there was mutual respect between us and we could race together, hammer and tongs, with an unspoken agreement that we wouldn't try to kill one another – although it was pretty tenuous at times. But he hated it when I passed him in Hungary, boxed him in against Johansson and won the race."

Alain Prost, wearing the World Champion's No 1, became Nigel's team-mate at Ferrari in 1990. In Nigel's view, Prost worked on the Ferrari and Fiat management to persuade them that they were more likely to win the title if they threw their weight behind one driver, and that driver should be Prost. "I was brought up to compete with fair play, I wasn't any good at politics. Ayrton was a ferocious competitor, but he had a lot more fair play in him than Piquet or Prost, those two were very political animals. They were prepared to do whatever it took, and they were very successful because of that." By mid-year Mansell was very unhappy at Ferrari. Things came to a head at Silverstone, when he discovered that "his" chassis, which he'd put on pole for the French GP, had passed to Prost at Prost's request. Even so, he took pole, and was leading when his gearbox failed. Prost won the race. Afterwards, Nigel astonished the world by announcing that he was retiring.

"People said it was a spur of the moment decision because I was upset after my car broke. Others said it was just a ploy as part of the driver negotiation market. Neither of those is true. It was a genuine decision. Rosanne and I had talked it through before Silverstone, and we'd decided we were being manipulated. I was nearly 37, I'd had a good career, been team-mate to three World Champions, won 15 Grands Prix. I knew I wasn't going to drive for Ferrari any more, and I didn't want to drive for a lesser team. I felt I wouldn't have another opportunity to win the World Championship, so I decided not to play any more."

Before Silverstone, Nigel had talked to Frank Williams about going back to Didcot, but Frank had told him he was expecting to get Senna for 1991. Later it turned out that Senna had only been talking to Williams as part of his negotiation process with McLaren and, when McLaren confirmed that it was keeping Senna, Frank approached Nigel. Nigel demanded undisputed number one status, plus various assurances from Renault that he would be fully backed in his efforts to win the title. "Frank said my demands were impossible. I said, 'Fine, I'm happy, I'm retiring.'" In September he put his Ferrari on pole for the Portuguese GP, and went past Senna's McLaren to win. Prost, battling with Senna for the title, finished a disgruntled third, and launched a furious attack on Ferrari's lack of team tactics. A month later, his demands fully met, Mansell signed for Williams.

In 1991 he fought a stirring battle with Senna for the title, winning five races and leading four more. "There were a few indiscretions by certain people, and when you're leading a race and you come out of the pits on three wheels it doesn't help" – referring to the Portuguese GP, when his right rear wheel came off immediately after a pitstop. In the chaotic final round in Adelaide, a lap before the race was stopped due to torrential rain, he hit a wall and, as he thought then, bruised his left foot. "When I got back to my home in Clearwater, Florida, I had it looked at and they told me I'd splintered the bones in two toes. They told me if I had an operation the recovery period would be two months. Well, I couldn't do that, I wanted to train for the new season. So we made a Kevlar insert for my shoe, and I walked on the side of my foot without putting any pressure on the damaged toes. I never told anybody, I didn't tell the press, and I got shit because at the end of the races I looked ghastly, or tired. The truth is I drove for a whole year with a busted foot. Some journalists chose to interpret my limp as play-acting. Pretty laughable – but I don't think any of them have ever driven a Formula 1 car flat out for two hours, with or without a broken foot. And when they're gone they won't be remembered, but I will be. Anyway, as soon as I had won the title I went to the hospital and had it done, and I attended all the awards parties on crutches."

That 1992 season, with the active-suspension FW14B, had been one of pretty total domination. Nigel won the first five races on the trot. Then came Monaco, where he led until, with eight laps to go, he had to stop for tyres, rejoining to finish second a few feet behind Senna's McLaren. In Canada, trying to take the lead from Senna, he went off. Then he won the next three races, including his home Grand Prix once again, which he led from start to finish. By the Hungarian Grand Prix in mid-August, his life's ambition was realised: he was World Champion.

An ingredient in his success was a strong working relationship with his engineer at Williams, David Brown. "David and I complemented each other and respected each other, we ended up like brothers. If a driver tells an engineer, 'Do this and it'll go faster,' and it does, he respects him because it makes him look good. David is pure and solid, a fantastic guy. I'd drive any car he engineered. He's working in the USA now."

Even before he'd clinched the title Nigel learned, to his dismay, that Prost was about to return from a year away from Formula 1 – to become his team-mate again. Nevertheless he agreed terms with Frank Williams in Hungary for 1993, as joint number one with Prost. But four days after his glory day in Budapest, the goalposts moved. Senna had come into the equation, offering to drive for Williams "for nothing". This merely sowed confusion, for Prost had already got a clause in his contract allowing him to veto Senna as a team-mate. Still Williams and Mansell could not agree, and things came to a head at Monza. On race morning Mansell called a press conference. Just as he was about to speak, an emissary from Williams arrived and whispered in his ear. Nigel says now that the whispered message was total capitulation, agreement to all the original terms. But by now he felt he no longer had the support he would need to defend his title in '93. He'd had enough, and he read out a statement announcing his retirement from F1.

"Looking back now, to be fair it wasn't just Frank. The engine manufacturer was French, the fuel company was French, there were other factors. But winning the World Championship was the culmination of all I had worked for, all I'd dreamed about since I was seven years old. Then to have the rug pulled from under me, and not to have the opportunity to defend my title, that was very hard to bear. All these years later, even understanding the politics a lot more now than I did then, it shouldn't have happened."

In fact Nigel had already met Carl Haas in London, a week before Monza, and agreed a provisional deal for a seat in the Newman-Haas Indycar team. After Monza he signed a firm contract. He won the Portuguese GP, retired in Japan – having waved Riccardo Patrese past to win, and take second place in the championship – and then in his final race in Australia he tangled with Senna one more time, and they both went off. The new World Champion complained to the stewards, who decided there was no case to answer. Two months later, Nigel had his first test in an Indycar, and in March came his first race, at Surfers Paradise. He started from pole, and won.

"Adapting to Indycar, plenty was different. The car was 50 per cent heavier, had less downforce, no active suspension, no carbon brakes, and a manual gearchange. But the most difficult thing to get used to was that I wasn't defending my World Championship. It wasn't my chosen path, I was in foreign territory. But having Paul Newman on the team was marvellous. He was a wonderful man, motivating, inspirational, and a lot of fun."

Nigel's first oval race came at Phoenix two weeks after Surfers Paradise. In practice, taking Turn 1 at 187mph, he spun backwards into the wall, sustaining concussion and back injuries. A fortnight later, with painkillers injected into his back, he finished third at Long Beach. Then he won on the ovals at Milwaukee, Michigan, New Hampshire and Nazareth, tying up the championship by mid-September. For one week, until Prost clinched the F1 title in Estoril, Nigel was simultaneously World Champion and Indycar Champion.

The first oval race he actually started was the Indianapolis 500, and he was leading when it was yellow-flagged late in the race. His inexperience with Indycar ways meant that, when the race went green, Emerson Fittipaldi and Arie Luyendyk jumped him and he finished a disappointed third. "I was walking away with it, and they put a full-course yellow out. They didn't want me to win. How can you put a full-course yellow out when nothing's happened? All that happened was that Lyn St James came into the wrong pit. There was no accident, no debris. It was politics again."

Things didn't go so well for Nigel in Indycar in 1994, when the Penske chassis had the legs of the Lola. Meanwhile Bernie Ecclestone was working behind the scenes to buy him out of his Indycar contract and get him back into F1. Senna's tragic death came in May at Imola, and David Coulthard replaced him as Damon Hill's team-mate at Williams. But the French Grand Prix in July didn't clash with an Indycar round and, helped by Renault money, Coulthard was stood down and Nigel was back with Williams as Hill's number two. Damon took pole, with Nigel alongside less than a tenth slower. He was running third behind Michael Schumacher and Hill when the oil pump drive broke. At the end of the season he did three more GPs, the last of which was the finale in Australia, when Schumacher resolved the championship by taking Hill off. "I put it on pole, but I was told not to interfere with the race. So I deliberately made a bad start and just sat behind them. I could read what was going to happen, it was just a matter of where and when. I'm a huge supporter of Damon, and I'd have told him to hang back and he could have had him, but he was a bit impatient unfortunately. They had their coming together, and I won the race."

Nigel had agreed to do those four races for Williams on the basis that he returned to the team full-time in 1995, with a hefty penalty payout if the team didn't take him. But in the end Williams opted for David Coulthard. So, with the Williams door closed, he signed for McLaren in its new partnership with Mercedes. His fee was said at the time to be $10 million – on top of the Williams payout. Early testing was disastrous: the car had handling problems, and Nigel was very uncomfortable in the tight cockpit. For the first two rounds he was replaced by Mark Blundell, while a modified monocoque was produced. It was ready for Imola, where Nigel qualified ninth and finished 10th after tangles with Morbidelli and Irvine. Two weeks later at Imola he qualified 10th, but the car's handling was not to his liking and, after a trip across the gravel, he retired. Nine days later an announcement from McLaren confirmed that, by mutual agreement, their relationship was at an end.

Nigel is still reticent about the affair. When I asked him about Bernie Ecclestone's involvement in his F1 return, he said: "I'm not permitted to talk about that. Let's just say that, among all the power brokers, I was a small pawn in a big game. It was great to come back to F1, but not in the way it happened. There was a lot of politics behind it, and one day the truth will come out. I would have loved to have been driving for Williams for a full season in 1995. I'd have liked to win more World Championships, and I think I was able to do it. But I had to watch the car I should have been driving, knowing full well I could have won the title in it, while working with a team that had promised me a lot and then I couldn't even get into the car. It wasn't Ron's fault, it wasn't my fault, the engineers built a car that Mika Häkkinen couldn't get into, let alone me.

"I still had contracts that bound me until 1997 and prevented me from driving anything else. I'm a simple person – all I ever wanted to do was drive a racing car fast. Then the lawyers show you that even when you think you've agreed something, that's not exactly what was meant. I don't regret not having a manager, because I don't think he would have been able to do anything differently. When they can buy out three years of contracts in America from under your feet, and you turn up to do your job and your lawyers tell you that anybody can be put on gardening leave if they're paid in full, and you can't do anything about it – well, it's not the way to finish."

Today, 14 years on, and with both Leo and Greg in the sport, what are his views about racing now? "When I was racing there was a healthy respect between drivers, or if not for the drivers then for the circuits we drove on, because if you were to do some of the things that drivers do today you could end up crippled, or lose your life. And there were horrific accidents, and people did lose their lives. Since then the evolution of the racing car, with crushable structures to dissipate energy, big run-off areas, gravel traps that actually work instead of the ghastly catch-fencing we had, all that means drivers are coming through from the lower formulae who think they are bulletproof. They think they can't get hurt, and they over-stretch their ability and they cause accidents. The officials should come down very hard on the drivers that cause those accidents, but sadly they don't.

"There's a number of drivers in F1 now, with power steering and driver aids, who wouldn't have been able to do F1 in my day. We used to go haring into the first corner, 26 cars each with 55 gallons of fuel on board, but now you haven't got the same weight or the tyre degradation to deal with. Before refuelling, the strategy was more important, when to push hard and when not to. So there was more difference of pace, and more overtaking, whereas now there are short sprints between stops, and the differences are very small. Banning refuelling is a great step in the right direction, and it's long overdue."

Despite his strong views, this is a more mellow Nigel Mansell than I remember from his time at the top of Formula 1. He is comfortable in the knowledge that, whatever his critics said about him, he was the greatest British racing driver of his era. He knows the people who mattered most to him – his fans – will never forget him. They'll remember him not just for the statistics, his 31 wins, his 482 points and his world title. They'll remember his move on Piquet at Silverstone in 1987, his dive past Senna at Budapest, and a score of other special moments. Some of us may remember the difficult, truculent Nigel; but perhaps it's better just to remember Nigel the racer.

Nigel Mansell was talking to Simon in September 2009.

GORDON MURRAY

Genius, innovation and
hot-bath ideas

A genius, according to the Oxford Dictionary, is someone "possessing exceptional intellectual or creative power". It's an overused word, but that definition describes Gordon Murray perfectly. We know him for his achievements in the world of Formula 1, but his brain is equally adroit exploring oenology, or architecture, or rock music. He is at his happiest when he faces an apparently insoluble problem, so he can examine it logically from every angle, and come up with an inventive solution. This constant cranial activity is hidden beneath an extraordinarily calm, laid-back exterior. Gordon talks fluently, but quietly, and his speech is as logical as his thought processes. I have seen some notes he kept of meetings during the early planning of the McLaren F1 road car: they are detailed, ordered, logical and extremely neat. Yet he was scribbling them down during the meeting itself as the ideas emerged, not writing them up afterwards. Confront him with any topic, whether within or outside his personal experience, and he will consider for a moment, and then deliver a view which is often surprising, but always ordered, incisive and intelligent. He really does seem to possess a mind unlike most of the rest of us.

During his 17 seasons as a top Formula 1 designer his cars won 56 Grands Prix, five World Drivers' Championships and three Constructors' Championships. In 1990 he turned away from F1 without regret, since when a stream of unique automotive designs has flowed from his pencil. Now he heads up his own design company, and is well into the development of a revolutionary city car which, he says, is a complete rethink of every single aspect of the automobile.

We're eating in one of Surrey's very few Michelin-starred restaurants, Drake's in Ripley. Gordon has been there before, when Ron Dennis threw a birthday party for his wife Lisa a year or so back, and chooses scallops and John Dory. He prefers to drink red wine and, after careful discussion with the sommelier, selects a Rioja.

Gordon was born in Durban, South Africa in 1946. His father worked for a Peugeot dealer as a mechanic, and prepared local racers' cars in his spare time. "Nobody in South Africa had any money to go racing, so it was a very fertile ground for people with imagination. My dad helped people build up specials out of production car parts, tuning their engines, making their bodies. Every weekend we were off racing somewhere. There was a round-the-houses track in Durban, plus the Roy Hesketh Circuit in Pietermaritzburg, and lots of hillclimbs just on bits of country road. We'd go to Speedway every week, too. All I ever wanted to do was be a racing driver. I had no interest in car design at all. It was just that I couldn't afford to buy a car, so I had to build one.

"But I was very into engines. I designed a twin-cam racing engine when I was 17. I thought South Africa needed its own Coventry Climax, so I drew one. When I was 19 I did a day-release sandwich course in engineering, and for the thesis we had to design a 3hp stationary engine. I drew a self-igniting rotary with only three moving parts. It would have been no good for a car – very high revs, very low torque – but it would have been just right for third-world countries to drive their pumps and that sort of stuff. I've still got all the drawings. I'll get around to prototyping it one day."

Gordon also still has all his student notebooks. In one of them is an inventive sketch of a futuristic rear-engined road car, with a centrally-seated driver and two passengers sitting each side of and slightly behind him. The McLaren F1 road car was still more than 20 years away.

"The car I built to race was called by my initials, IGM. I bought a crashed Ford Anglia 105E for £60 to get the block and the head, but I made my own pistons, camshaft, inlet and exhaust manifolds. I made a gas-flowing device to get the head and the manifolds to breathe, and it gave really good power. I made the chassis – it was a cycle-winged sports racer, like a clubmen's car. I was quite successful, and was National Champion in my class. One of the best-known South African hillclimbs was Burman Drive, which had been going since pre-war days. I won the last one, so they let me keep the winner's trophy, inscribed with all the names of the past winners going back to 1936. I've still got that too.

"After a couple of seasons winning in South Africa it became a bit unsatisfying, because I was competitive in a rubbish home-made car. I thought I should move to England because it was the centre of the universe for my two loves, racing and music. I'd been into music since I was 10, when I first heard Little Richard; that day my life changed for ever. I wanted to race, but I had to get a job, so I wrote to Colin Chapman. He not only replied to my letter, he offered me a job. In December 1969 I arrived in England in the middle of a bitterly cold winter, and I hadn't even bothered to bring a jumper. I went up to Norwich by coach, and when I got there I found Lotus were laying people off and there was nothing for me. For several months I lived on the floor of a bed-sitter in Hendon, cold and jobless. I didn't have the money to live, let alone race."

Then one day he wandered into the Brabham factory. It was still run by Jack Brabham and Ron Tauranac then, and coincidentally Tauranac was interviewing that day for a vacancy in the drawing office. He mistook Gordon for one of the formal applicants, and gave him the job. As well as doing detail work on the F1 car of the day and on the customer F2 and F3 cars, Gordon drew a simple road car in his spare time. This used Mini subframes and a sporty Moke-like body, and four were built in a shed on the edge of Heathrow Airport. One served as Gordon's sole road car for two years. Soon a chance meeting with Alain de Cadenet led to Gordon designing the Duckhams Le Mans car. "It was the first real racing car I'd designed, and I did it in four months, during the night. I was doing a 14-hour day at Brabham, finishing work at 10pm, going home and working on the Le Mans car until three in the morning, and then back at work at 8am."

At the end of 1971 Gordon was about to move on when he heard Brabham was changing hands, so he decided to hang around and see what the new owner was like. This was Bernie Ecclestone, who on his first visit to the New Haw factory found Gordon's tall frame squeezed into a corner of the drawing office. Bernie said later: "Tauranac told me I should get rid of him and keep everybody else. So I kept Gordon and got rid of everybody else." After a difficult season for Brabham in 1972, Gordon was called into his office. "Bernie said, 'I want a completely new Formula 1 car, and you're doing it.' I had a clean sheet of paper to do what I wanted. Bernie's a go-for-it type of guy, and maybe that's what he saw in me, I don't know. He left me on my own to run things, but he was always totally supportive. When I went out on a limb, like with the fan car or the surface radiators, he actually liked all that."

That first car, the BT42, with its monocoque triangular in section, was designed and built in four months. It would have won its first Grand Prix, at Barcelona with Carlos Reutemann, but for a split rubber driveshaft boot with seven laps to go. It was smaller and more compact than its rivals, and it looked sharp and elegant at a time when most racing cars were workmanlike but intrinsically ugly. "I'm unusual for an engineer in that I went to art school when I was 13. I still do a bit of drawing and painting, and I love styling. I couldn't bring myself to make an ugly car. Before wind tunnels, shaping a car was all practical – wool tufts and intelligent guesses. Even with basic wind tunnel work there were a lot of areas on the car that made absolutely no difference to performance. The bit leading up to the cockpit could be virtually any shape you liked, as long as the bubble you looked through didn't buffet the driver's helmet. So why not make it look nice? And it went deeper than that, because you were trying to sell an image to sponsors, an awareness of what they'd get with Brabham. Most engineers are not sympathetic to artistic stuff at all, they couldn't draw something pretty if you put a gun to their head. But I like elegantly simple engineering too. Talk to the mechanics, they'll tell you my Brabhams and McLarens were always simple cars." They were also innovative: Brabham were the first to use carbonfibre in their construction, initially to make the cockpit safer, and the first to use carbon brakes.

Until 1972 Gordon had clung to his ambition of racing himself, and he chose the 750 Formula not just because it was cheap, but also because it allowed car designers so much freedom. "You had to use two 2-inch tubes as the main chassis members, echoing the old Austin 7 chassis frame, so I designed the IMG T2 as a lay-down aluminium monocoque and just let these two tubes lie there to cover the rule. I came up with pull-rod suspension for it, and I used that on my second F1 car, the BT44. Now everybody's got it in F1, of course. I was doing the IMG with a mechanic at Brabham called Ian Hilton, but he was killed in a car smash on a level crossing. A Shadow mechanic wanted to take it on and I gave him all the drawings, but by now I was too busy and it never got built. That was the end of my racing career."

The BT44 would have won its first race, too, except that a fuelling error in Argentina made Reutemann stutter to a halt two laps from the end. But there were three victories that year, and two more in 1975 with the BT44B. Then, in a major deal by Ecclestone, Cosworth power was replaced by Alfa Romeo's flat 12 for 1976. The Italian engines were heavy and thirsty, and the BT45 never won a race, although in BT45B form in 1977 John Watson had several strong drives, culminating in a near win at Dijon. For 1978 the BT46 included another Murray innovation, surface radiators – thin panels disposed along the sides of the monocoque to reduce frontal area – but these proved unable to cool the engine. Gordon's solution to that was sensational: the BT46B fan car.

This had a conventional radiator mounted horizontally over the engine, cooled by a gearbox-driven fan at the back of the car. The engine bay was shrouded and sealed by flexible skirts running on the track, so that not only was the radiator fed with cooling air but also the car was sucked down onto the ground, giving hitherto undreamed-of levels of downforce. Two BT46Bs appeared unannounced for the Swedish GP at Anderstorp in June and, to the consternation of every other team, Niki Lauda ran away with the race.

"The car was legal as the rules stood then. Article 3.7 said: 'Any device whose primary function is to have an aerodynamic influence on the performance of the car has to be firmly fixed to the sprung part of the car.' So I had to ensure that more than half of the air was cooling the radiator. After the race the CSI sealed the car in the truck at Anderstorp, and then came to the factory with an anemometer . They got us to run the engine, and measured the flow of air through the fan and through the radiator. They found that 60 per cent of the air was for cooling and 40 per cent was for downforce. Not its primary function, you see. So the CSI wrote to us and said, 'The car is legal, but it's using a loophole in the regulations. In next year's rules we'll close that loophole, but you can use it for the rest of the season.'

"But Bernie – I didn't understand this at the time – had his eyes on much bigger things. He was working on getting his foothold in the Formula One Constructors' Association and launching himself towards what he's doing now. He reckoned the uproar was in danger of collapsing FOCA completely. So he asked me – to be fair, he didn't dictate – he asked me to fit normal radiators to the car. I was obviously very pissed off, but I agreed."

The last Brabham-Alfa was the ground-effect BT48. The team was back with Cosworth engines for the 1980 BT49, which the rapidly maturing Nelson Piquet drove to three victories and second place in the World Championship. In 1981, with the BT49C, Piquet was World Champion.

"Basically Bernie left me to run things, he trusted me. We employed a fraction of the personnel of the big teams like McLaren and Williams. We were giant-killers. I did the design work, I did the hire and fire, oversaw production, oversaw parts supply, the test programme, the wind tunnel work. I did all the strategy at the races. Stupidly I refused to have a race engineer. Other teams had an engineer per car plus a T-car guy, and a technical director. I did it all myself. God knows how many hours a week I was working. But I only ever need to sleep four hours a night, and I feel good on that."

In 1982 came Bernie's deal with BMW, for which Gordon designed the BT50. Initially there were many reliability problems with the hugely powerful turbocharged four-cylinder, but this became the vehicle for one of the great Murray innovations. Mid-race refuelling stops are so much part of today's Formula 1 scene that is hard to remember the intrigue and scepticism surrounding Brabham's wheeze to run lighter fuel and softer tyres and set up a refuelling rig in the pits. Making it happen involved a series of strategic and design headaches which were meat and drink to Gordon.

"It started as a hot bath idea. I used to have a lot of good ideas after a hot bath. Recently a medical guy I met on holiday explained to me that there's a physical reason for this, there's a channel in your spine that opens up in the heat and increases the blood supply to the brain. I knew how much the tyres used to go off. And I'd learned from running the cars light in qualifying that the weight of one litre of fuel cost around one hundredth of a second in lap times. So I lay in the bath doing the maths.

"The clever thing wasn't having the idea, it was developing all the stuff that went into it. That's the bit I love. Throw me a series of connected problems and I've got to find a way to make everything work together. In this case it was how do you change the tyres quickly, how do you put the fuel in quickly, how do you avoid losing pace going back out on cold tyres. We videoed the mechanics changing tyres, analysed it frame by frame, and I redesigned the hubs, bearing carriers, threads, nuts and wheel guns, with a device to retain the nuts. And I put titanium on-board air jacks on the car. Now they can use simple lever jacks because they have so many mechanics on a pitstop, I think it's 19 these days, but we only had eight mechanics working on a stop. Tyre warmers didn't exist then, so I made an oven, a big thing like the Tardis, with temperature probes and hot air circulating through four tyres. Then we did the fuel kit. Nowadays it's all the same for all the teams, and it all has to be done at atmospheric pressure so it's pretty slow. But there were no rules about it then. So I designed a twin-barrel fuel system running at 4 bar. The damper barrel fed the fuel barrel and the fuel barrel fed the car, and we could push in 35 gallons in 3.5 seconds. Which is like an explosion, believe me.

"With the refuelling we had one guy on one side of the car opening the breather, one on the other putting in the fuel. Big heavy hoses over their shoulders. If the breather's not on when the fuel guy opens the pressure, the car disintegrates. Four bar inside a carbon and aluminium monocoque, you wouldn't find the pieces. So I designed all sorts of little mechanical interlocks inside the tank and it all got really complicated, castellations and cams and Geneva mechanisms. And I looked at it and thought, on a racing car it's going to vibrate, one day it's going to fail to work and the car's going to explode. No more Brabham, no more pitlane, maybe no more F1. I studied the videos again, and I realised that during a stop the breather guy and the fuel guy would be facing each other each side of the roll hoop with their noses about four inches apart. So I scrapped the interlocks and I got the two of them together and I said to the breather guy, 'When you approach the car with your hose, you're looking down to where you've got to lock the hose on, so don't look up until it's on.' And I said to the fuel guy, 'Don't turn on the fuel until he looks up at you and you see the whites of his eyes four inches away.' So that's what they did, and it worked.

"Then we found that when the car came in from being on full power and was stationary for eight seconds, the turbo was so hot that its bearings melted, just seized solid. We looked at water jackets, we looked at another radiator, and then I suddenly remembered the air jacks. The jack man plugged in an air line fed by an enormous air bottle, and it only took a bit of that air to jack the car up. So we took a tube off the jack line and made a shroud around the turbo, and when the car was jacked up it blew cold air over the turbo bearings. That fixed it.

"All this stuff was designed and developed in three months, with a tiny team of people. We hired Donington for a secret test, guards on the fences, and we needed to beat 20 seconds for slowing down, doing the stop, and accelerating away. We did it in 19. Then I worked out a simple mathematical equation for each circuit. You filled in the circuit characteristics and it gave you the optimum moment to stop for fuel."

Unrelated turbo problems meant that the strategy only really came into play late in the season, with Piquet and Patrese between them winning the last three Grands Prix of the year. "For 1983 I was sure that all the other teams would copy us, but we arrived in Brazil for Round 1 and nobody had half-tank cars. Nobody had done the maths. I said to Bernie, 'We've got away with it!'" Piquet was World Champion again that year – and then refuelling stops were banned.

Somehow Gordon found time in the 1980s to put together a rock band. "I play guitar and drums, both very badly. Our lead guitarist was the only one who could sing. One day he said he was just going out to the pub, and he never came back. But we had various people float in and out, sometimes we'd have a jam session that would last a weekend. Leo Sayer sang with us for a bit, and George Harrison played with us one night. We had a lot of fun."

In 1986, after 17 years with Brabham, Gordon decided to leave. "Brabham was sliding downhill. Bernie's priorities were more and more with FOCA, and he let Nelson go over what I believe was a small amount of money. It had been a strong relationship with Nelson, he'd been with us for seven years, won two championships. The tyre contract was running out, the sponsorship deals were running out, the engine contract was running out, and to cap it all we just couldn't get the BT55 to work. We couldn't get the engine to scavenge." The BT55 was the revolutionary, ultra-low 1986 car, with the engine lying on its side. "Then Elio de Angelis was killed in a testing accident at Paul Ricard. I was disenchanted with all the travel, and the general direction that F1 was going in, and I didn't see it as an on-going challenge any more. I decided I should try something new.

"Then Ron Dennis came chasing after me, because John Barnard was leaving McLaren. So I said to him, 'I'll come on board on one condition: three more years of Formula 1, and then that's it. That'll be 20 years in F1, and that's enough.' And he agreed to that.

"McLaren was different because so much of what I'd had to do at Brabham, from talking to sponsors to dealing with staff issues, was taken care of. Which was great, because I could concentrate on structuring the engineering. I made a lot of big changes. When I got to McLaren I found they had no process whatever. I introduced post-race analysis, failure reports, all the stuff they didn't have and badly needed. I ran the team technically, did the strategy at races, everything I loved to do. Ron just let me get on with it. When I arrived in October 1986 the 1987 car was already done. I did the 1988 car (MP4/4 with Honda V6 turbo), the 1989 car (MP4/4B with Honda V12) and the 1990 car (MP4/5 with Honda V12). All of them won the World Championship."

In fact the McLaren domination of Formula 1 during the Murray years was just about total, earning both the Drivers' and Constructors' titles three years on the trot. In 1988 the red and white cars of Senna and Prost won 15 of 16 rounds, only missing victory at Monza when Senna was put off the track by a back-marker. But Gordon held Ron to his three-year promise. "The days of real technical innovation in F1, with big steps forward overnight, were rapidly disappearing, because of the increasing levels of regulation. Young engineers joining F1 now don't know any different, and for them it's probably great, but it didn't appeal to me as much as the earlier times, when it was more sports and engineering-driven. Now it was just all business."

So Gordon left F1, but he didn't leave McLaren. Since 1988 he'd been talking to Ron and McLaren directors Creighton Brown and

Mansour Ojjeh about taking another clean sheet of paper and building the ultimate road car. McLaren Cars Ltd was formed in early 1989.

"Ron had the foresight to realise in the 1980s that McLaren was little more than an F1 team. He was determined to expand it. I'd wanted to do a road sports car since I was about 15, a proper Ferrari-beater. And there may have been an element of keeping me on board: Ron wouldn't have wanted me to go to another F1 team.

"I don't think a car like the McLaren F1 will ever happen again, not because the design capabilities aren't there, but because the process by which it happened wouldn't be allowed again. Very seldom in history has one person been given the responsibility of everything to do with one car – laying out the building including the furniture and the carpets, employing every single staff member, designing everything about the car down to the fitted luggage and the hi-fi, developing the car, putting it into production, even writing the owner's handbook. The McLaren F1 was able to be one man's vision, uncompromised.

"Apart from the Mercedes SLR, I can put my hand on my heart and say I've designed everything in all my cars. But what I'm not good at doing, and what we needed a lot of, are those wonderful quick illustrations where chrome looks like chrome and rubber looks like rubber, and there are reflections in the glass. I also needed someone to do the clay models. So I asked Peter Stevens, a top car designer in his own right, if he could recommend an RCA graduate who could do that for us. He wanted to know what I was doing, so I told him. And he said, 'I want that job.' I said he'd have to work for me and he said, 'Fine.' He didn't impose anything on me at all.

"Because of F1 commitments, I only really started towards the end of 1989. The whole programme was 43 months. We decided to launch it before we started development testing, because we wanted to get the impact of the three-seat arrangement, the big V12, and the weight – this was a car that was 50 per cent lighter than its opposition, the world's first carbon-composite production road car. We did the launch at Monaco in 1992. That was fun because I designed the stage, decided on the music, oversaw the brochure and the invitations."

For many of us the McLaren F1 is simply the finest supercar of all time. But before its development was finished Gordon was already working on McLaren Cars Project 2, a two-plus-two 911-sized mid-engined sports car. It was presented to BMW and they accepted it, but almost simultaneously Ron Dennis concluded a five-year agreement with Mercedes-Benz. "It would have been a nice little car, but the Mercedes deal put the kybosh on that, and we had nothing else to do. So we went racing with the F1.

"I'd said from Day 1 that we shouldn't ever think about the F1 as a racing car because we'd compromise it. It had to be a road car that you could drive to the South of France with the air-conditioning on, good sound system, comfortable suspension with long wheel travel, no external wings." But, inevitably, there were customers who wanted to change that, and the GTR was the result. On its first visit to Le Mans in 1995 it won a historic victory.

"I loved that period. It gave me a huge boost. From being disillusioned with Formula 1, it took me back to why I liked racing in the first place. There was enough competition between Porsche, Ferrari and ourselves to make it really nail-biting. But there was interaction between the teams. You could go into the Ferrari pit and watch one of their pitstops. Lovely old-fashioned camaraderie, like F1 in the 1970s. Then Porsche made the GT1, a bit of a homologation special although they did make enough production cars just in time. So we said, if you want to do that we'll do that, and we made the long-tail. We made five long-tail road cars. And we won the GT category at Le Mans in 1997, and were second overall. But then Mercedes made their car and jumped the rules without making a road car. You were meant to make road cars and sell them, but they came in with all the money and the best drivers, and the whole GT concept went out of the window."

Project 3 was a city car, which Gordon worked on for a year, but the McLaren board decided not to do it. Project 4 was a two-seater F1 demonstration car, which followed the tandem-seat layout that Gordon had used in the Rocket, the tiny Yamaha-powered fun car he'd designed in six months of spare time for his friend Chris Craft. Project 5 was a rear-engined V8 supercar. "We presented it to Mercedes and they said: 'The good news is you've got the job, the bad news is we want one with a front engine.' That became the SLR. It wasn't really my sort of car, but for the company it was a big prestigious chunk of work. And it's still the world's only full ground-effect front-engined car, and it's probably the safest car of its type on the planet.

"Project 6 was a very radical Le Mans car, underfloor radiators, high nose. Wind tunnel tests showed it would have annihilated everything at the time on downforce, lift over drag. But Ron didn't want to get into building customer racing cars for sale. The SLR was Project 7, and Project 8 was the next rear-engined car which was put to Mercedes. It would have been a huge step forward in sports car design – just what Ferrari are talking about now, lighter weight, modular construction, better material usage. We could have done that four years ago. Unfortunately that's all been canned now.

"At Brabham, and then to start with at McLaren, I used to go around the company every morning and say hello to every single person. I knew their families, I knew their kids' names, where they went on holiday. When we started the F1 project we were 36 people. By the time we started production with the SLR we were 450. I was going down into the workshop and seeing people I didn't even know. I don't like big companies, I like small teams. So in December 2004 I left to run Gordon Murray Design. Since arriving in England 34 years before I'd only worked for two companies, and I decided if I was going to start all over again at the age of 58 it would have to be with a team of people I knew. Luckily I've got 16 of them, straight out of McLaren, all people I worked with. They were my team, they just moved from Woking to Shelford.

"It started with a project that Creighton Brown was putting together, a sports car to build in Brazil. Then tragically Creighton died of cancer in 2006. So I took a deep breath and I pulled the environmental car forward. It's a complete rethink on the motorcar, every single aspect of it: wheels, tyres, brakes, seating position, luggage, child seats, visibility, wipers, congestion, parking. And life cycle and CO2, that's the biggest one, from digging the ore out of the ground to burying the car at the end of its life. I want to see a two-thirds reduction in the CO2 damage we're doing now.

"But it has to have the style, the image. You can't sell a small car that's not iconic, like the original Mini was. When you see one I don't want you to say, 'What the hell's that?' I want you to say, 'I want one of those.' We've got to make sure that happens.

"We've got 14 variants on the board at the moment: inner-city taxi, delivery van, pick-up, flat-bed, emergency medical supplies, holiday resort buggy, post van. I've got a full-time researcher looking at car journeys, occupancy, what we use our car for. You don't sit in it like an ordinary car at all. There are six layouts built into the internal architecture, so today I'm taking the kids to school, flip, flip, tomorrow I'm taking somebody to the airport with big suitcases, flip, flip, then I'm on a commuter run with a briefcase and want more room and comfort, flip, flip. Funky ergonomics, high eye-line, good peripheral vision. It won't require sophisticated production techniques. The chassis is designed to fold flat, like an Ikea wardrobe, so you can get more in a container. I'm looking at making the chassis in India."

When Gordon first came to England his girl-friend Stella followed him a few months later, and they were married in 1970. In 1975 they bought a farmer's cottage in Surrey, and they live there still, although Gordon concedes that the house has grown considerably down the years. "We've now got one bedroom, but the bedroom is bigger. And we've got lots of barns and things." One of these houses a replica of an American drive-in movie theatre, complete with original 1959 Cadillac convertible to watch the film from, and pop-corn machines. They have a dramatic house on the north-west coast of Scotland, and two houses in France: "the one we go to 10 miles east of Bergerac, and the ruin that I'm going to do up one day." In his garage are a McLaren F1, of course, and an SLR and a Rocket. "Then I've got a 1957 Ford Thunderbird with porthole hardtop, very American Graffiti, and a 1968 Series 3 Lotus Elan, which is a proper car." His everyday car is a Smart Roadster: "It's great, does everything I need." He loves Fiat Cinquecentos, of the original 1960s variety. His current one was built up from scratch around a seam-welded shell with a 650cc engine. He's also had a fully-tweaked 695 Abarth, and another to which he fitted a high-revving Yamaha motorcycle engine and six-speed sequential gearbox. He disapproves of Fiat's new Cinquecento: "It's like the new Mini, brilliant marketing but crap packaging, so big and heavy. As a purist I would have liked to see BMW take the icon that the Mini brand stood for and make a real step forward. But I suppose it wouldn't have made them the money the new Mini makes." He also has several motorcycles, including a full-race 996 Ducati and a Honda 1300.

Gordon is 61 now, and his environmental car has got him every bit as fired up and motivated as he was when he first started in Formula 1. "Three mainstream manufacturers have approached us. I'm talking to the Americans at the moment, and I'm flying to Japan next week to talk to a couple there. Our company is all about design, prototyping, development, engineering support. We don't do production, but I'm planning to retain the rights to the design.

"I want to create a new world class of vehicle. We're in the best bit now, the problem solving. I just love it." And once the environmental car is off and running, the Murray brain will no doubt hunt down more stimulating problems: and then come up with more hot-bath ideas to solve them.

Gordon Murray was talking to Simon in October 2007.

ROGER PENSKE

How The Captain goes racing,
every single day

I'm always fascinated by what racing drivers do with themselves when they hang up their helmets. For some, their cockpit careers are the high-point of their lives: afterwards, the only way is down. Others shrug off their racing overalls and use the talents that made them good on the track to find success in other arenas. And one or two regard their motor racing merely as something they did in their youth, a rite of passage, from which they moved on to more important things.

By any measure, Roger Penske is an extraordinary human being. He is 73 now, a fit, tall-striding bundle of energy who controls hundreds of different companies worldwide and employs 36,500 people. You'll find him in the Forbes List of the World's 400 Richest, with a net worth of around $2 billion. He controls a mammoth truck leasing organisation which operates in four continents. He owns car dealerships – at the last count, 329 of them, spread across America and Europe. He manufactures diesel engines in Italy, truck mirrors in England and fluid level management systems in Michigan. He has factories producing electrical systems and truck parts from Puerto Rico to Poland. He is a director of General Electric, has been the chairman of the Detroit Superbowl, and is a former director of Gulfstream Aviation. When General Motors was going through its recent difficulties he made a bid for one of its divisions (although, once he'd had a close look at their accounts, he withdrew his offer). He has owned and developed race tracks across the USA, and his other interests range from logistics and IT to a ski resort in

Utah. He is also a philanthropist, and a driving force behind the regeneration of urban Detroit.

Yet motor racing still consumes him. He runs an incredibly successful Indycar team: 15 Indianapolis 500 victories, 12 national championships, 147 race wins and counting. He is a major player in NASCAR too, with a five-car Dodge team running in the two top series. And with this, as with all his myriad activities, he is totally hands-on. He gets involved, imposing everywhere his uncompromising standards of presentation, cleanliness and attention to detail, and motivating everybody from race drivers to truckies with an indomitable will to win. They all know he's a racer, and they respect him for it. They call him The Captain.

I've long wanted to understand what makes Penske tick. He seems to work seven days a week, 52 weeks a year, and because his interests are spread across continents he is constantly on the move. I offered to meet him at his choice of venue anywhere in the world, but he's not a man you can easily pin down to a lunch table. He has little interest in talking about his own racing career, because he doesn't have that sort of ego. What gets his attention is not the past, or even the present. His focus is constantly on the future: tomorrow's opportunity, tomorrow's race, tomorrow's deal. Talking about himself bores him. What he loves to talk about is his people, his key players, the rising stars among those 36,500 employees. It's the Penske people who matter, he says. They make the story.

Eventually he agrees to breakfast. Among the plethora of English businesses he now owns is the hallowed British Ferrari dealership on the Egham bypass, Maranello Concessionaires. Over a Sunday night his Gulfstream G450 executive jet is bringing him from Nantucket Island, where he has a house, to Farnborough. He's flying in to address a meeting of 800 of his UK managers in the ultra-modern glass tower beside the M4 Chiswick Flyover that is Audi West London – he owns that, too. But he also wants to see the results of his major investment in Maranello's parts and service operation, so he's calling in there first. He suggests we meet there.

Even though Roger jets in to the UK roughly once a month, at Maranello there is still the feeling of a royal visit, with everyone on tenterhooks waiting for the boss to arrive. The Egham showroom, with its gleaming line-up of new Ferraris and Maseratis, is as spotless as ever, but the floor has been polished a second time already this Monday morning. Promptly at 7.30am The Captain strides in, looking crisp and groomed despite his overnight flight. With him is his son Greg, who's involved in several of his operations. (One of Greg's responsibilities is Longo Toyota in Los Angeles, the largest single car dealership in the world. When the sun's shining, it sells a car every eight minutes.)

Roger's people skills are extraordinary: even the receptionist is greeted by name, as is every salesman on the floor. He has a pertinent comment for each, which shows he's aware of their roles – and their latest sales figures. Then a Maserati Quattroporte whisks us off to the after-sales facilities: spotless servicing bays, and a huge parts warehouse decked out floor to ceiling with rows of multi-storey racking. Roger, totally involved as usual, hustles me up a ladder to show me £6 million-worth of classic Ferrari spares going back to the 1950s: a row of hand-beaten Pininfarina wings in primer here, a shelf of downdraught Weber carburettors there. In both locations he greets staff like old friends, and seems to know everybody personally. Back at the showroom, I prevail upon him to pause for a coffee and a croissant.

"There was no automotive interest in my family. As a young man I guess I just liked cars. In high school I had a Norton motorcycle, and I started buying old wrecks, fixing them up, selling them on. I worked up to a fuel-injected Corvette, and in 1958 I started doing local SCCA races with that." By 1959 it was a Porsche RSK, and he was winning at national level. In 1960 he was class champion. The wins continued with a Birdcage Maserati and a Cooper Monaco, and in 1961 he was overall SCCA Champion. By now he'd talked some sponsorship out of chemical giant Dupont, promoting their Telar anti-freeze. "The SCCA didn't allow sponsors' names on the car, so I covered them up with adhesive tape. I arranged it so that the tape'd blow off after about three laps."

For the 1961 US GP at Watkins Glen, Penske organised a ride in an F1 Cooper-Climax. In exalted company among the works teams, he came home eighth. Walt Hansgen was less fortunate: he crashed his Cunningham-owned Cooper trying to avoid the spinning Lotus of Olivier Gendebien. Roger, who'd thought of a way to improve on his Cooper Monaco, approached Briggs in the paddock and bought the wreck, plus one of two special 2.7-litre engines that Coventry Climax had prepared for Cooper's Indianapolis foray with Jack Brabham that year. The bent chassis was straightened and, having read the sports car regulations carefully, Roger had a neat all-enveloping aluminium body made, retaining the central seating position. A token passenger seat was fitted between the left-hand wheels, with the fuel tank on the right and tiny headlights in the radiator intake. The car was painted red and christened the Zerex Special, after another Dupont antifreeze brand. "I think Dupont gave me $5000 for the season."

The beautifully-finished car was ready for the 1962 Riverside Grand Prix, a big-money race which attracted the likes of Jack Brabham, Bruce McLaren, Dan Gurney and Masten Gregory. The Zerex beat them all. A week later, at Laguna Seca, Roger did it again. Reports of the day noted that his take from the two events was $20,000 and a new Pontiac, plus the $700 he'd cleared at the Las Vegas tables between the two. Two weeks later, in Puerto Rico, the Zerex won once more.

At Riverside there'd been mutterings about the Zerex's centre-seat layout. "I just pointed out that, further down the grid, there was an old bob-tail Cooper with exactly the same layout. That seemed to settle it." However, the establishment wasn't happy about being beaten by what it felt was merely a wide-bodied F1 car, and at the end of the season centre seats in sports-car racing were banned. "So I changed it to side-by-side seating, moving the cockpit tubes wider. It wasn't very comfortable, but it worked. In 1963 we took it to Brands Hatch for the August Bank Holiday race, the Guards Trophy, and we won there." Now running in the blue colours of John Mecom's team, the Zerex also won at Marlboro, Cumberland and Nassau.

In early 1964, in search of more power, an alloy Oldsmobile V8 was readied, but before it could be fitted the Zerex was sold to Bruce McLaren. Bruce bought the Olds engine too, and after a couple of wins in Climax-powered form he debuted the now stiffened, V8-powered machine at the Mosport 200 in Canada, and won. The little Zerex was the seed-corn of a great motor-racing marque: the very first McLaren, the Olds-powered M1 prototype, followed three months later.

Roger was now seen as one of America's most promising rising stars. He'd had another F1 ride in the 1962 US GP, in a Lotus 24 V8. In John Mecom's Ferrari GTO he scored a couple of wins in Nassau and, with Augie Pabst, took the GT class and fourth overall at Sebring in 1963. At Le Mans Luigi Chinetti's North American Racing Team paired him with Pedro Rodríguez in a Ferrari 330LM: they were lying third when a blown engine sent Roger off the road. He raced another GTO in the Goodwood TT, splitting the Lightweight E-types of Salvadori and Sears in qualifying. That year he also did his one and only NASCAR race, a 250-miler on the Riverside road course in a Pontiac. He won it.

For 1964 he joined Jim Hall's Chaparral operation to drive one of the futuristic auto-transmission 2As. He usually played obedient second-string to Hall – the cars finished 1-2 at Watkins Glen and Meadowdale – and then, after Hall broke an arm in a big accident at Mosport, Roger took the 2A to victory at Laguna Seca. His last meeting as a driver was the Nassau Speed Week in December. He swept the board, winning the TT in Mecom's Corvette Gran Sport, and then both the Nassau Trophy and the Governor's Trophy in the Chaparral. In the latter he started on dry tyres, and when it rained he crashed. So he took over team-mate Hap Sharp's 2A, and brought it through to win.

But Roger has little interest in any of this. "Some people sit down and work out the chronology of all they've done in racing, but I've never had the time to do that. I'm about now, not then. I'm about how we go forward. But I can tell you why I retired from racing. For a while my goal had been to become a Chevy dealer, and in August 1963 I joined McKean Chevrolet in West Philadelphia. But General Motors were formally not involved in racing then, and their policy was, no racing drivers as dealers. They said they wouldn't give me a franchise if I was racing. So I had to make a decision: do I want to be a businessman, or do I want to be a racing driver? Well, I wanted to build a business. So in February 1965 I announced my retirement, and I bought the McKean dealership."

Barely a year later he was back in racing – but as an entrant. "Sun Oil's Vice-President of Marketing walked into the showroom, and we sold him a Corvette. And we persuaded him to give us $2500 towards running in the Daytona 24 Hours. That was the start of a long relationship with Sunoco." Roger got GM to release a Sting Ray with the still very new alloy-block 7-litre engine. At Daytona one of its drivers, George Wintersteen, ran into the back of a Morgan during the night and sustained severe front-end damage. It wiped out the headlights, so Roger taped torches to the front wings: they gave the drivers no illumination, but nothing in the rules said how powerful the headlights had to be. The radiator was leaking badly, so Roger found a Corvette owner in the car park, and persuaded him to sell the radiator off his car. After 24 hours the battered Corvette struggled home to win the GT class. The following month, immaculate again and now in Sunoco's dark blue colours, it won its class in the Sebring 12 Hours. For Roger Penske, entrant, it was an auspicious beginning.

At the Le Mans test weekend that April the great American racer Walt Hansgen was killed in a Ford GT Mk 2. At his funeral Roger talked to Hansgen's young protégé and Ford co-driver Mark Donohue. The two had first met in 1960, when Donohue was starting out in SCCA racing with an Elva Courier. Penske gave the newcomer a piece of advice, which Donohue quoted in his wonderful book, *The Unfair Advantage.* "He stressed that if we were going racing [in whatever category] we should only go first class." Roger – no doubt aware of Mark's talents as an engineer as well as a driver – made him an offer. It was the start of a close and deep working relationship that was to last the rest of Donohue's life.

Almost at once, the Penske/Donohue pairing became a towering force in American racing. They dominated the TransAm Series with a series of highly-developed Camaros, and later AMC Javelins, and the USRRC with Lolas and then a McLaren M6A. With the highly intelligent, deep-thinking Donohue developing the cars in the workshop as well as in the cockpit, the wins piled up. Always the Penske operation was the most immaculate in the paddock, every item polished, every detail considered. In Technical Excellence at Speed, Michael Argetsinger's flawlessly-crafted biography of Donohue, long-time team member Karl Kainhofer is quoted thus: "Roger is always two steps ahead of you, always trying to improve on what you think is perfect. But he'll also listen to you, and change things in a second if he thinks your idea is better."

For Roger, USRRC and TransAm titles weren't enough. In 1968 he took the hard-working Donohue into Indy racing. Sometimes Mark would do an Indy race and a TransAm race in different states on the same weekend, flying between the two. In his first Indianapolis 500, with a Lola-Offy, he qualified fourth and finished seventh, to be rookie of the year. In 1970 he was second. In 1971, now in a McLaren, he led, but the gearbox failed. In 1972 he won.

Penske tackled NASCAR too, with an AMC Matador, and Donohue won the 1973 Riverside 500, echoing Roger's Pontiac win at the same track ten years before. But the CanAm Series, apart from a couple of isolated wins for Mark, was still locked up by the orange works McLarens.

At Le Mans in 1971, where Donohue and David Hobbs were sharing Penske's Sunoco-blue Ferrari 512S (a car substantially redeveloped by Mark), Roger was quietly approached by Porsche.

Having dipped a toe in the CanAm pond with a Spyder 917, the Germans wanted to mount a serious assault. Mark spent weeks at Zuffenhausen, totally involved in the project, and the result was the extraordinary twin-turbocharged, flat-12 917/10K. It vanquished the McLarens and won the 1972 CanAm, but in George Follmer's hands, not in Donohue's: Mark was injured in a mammoth testing accident at Road Atlanta when the rear bodywork came away at over 150mph. On crutches, he continued to help direct the car's engineering, and was back in the cockpit before the season's end .

For 1973 Porsche and Penske produced the 917/30, one of the most fearsome racing cars of all time: 1100bhp – or up to 1500bhp if the driver turned up the boost – and 850kgs dry. (With the 88-gallon fuel tanks brimmed, that weight went up somewhat.) Acceleration was in the order of zero to 100mph in 3.8sec, and zero to 200mph in around 12sec. Later, Donohue's world closed circuit record at Talladega of 221.12mph showed that the straight-line maximum was over 250mph.

Donohue dominated the CanAm Series in this monster. Then, after winning three of the four Penske-promoted IROC Porsche RSR races, he announced his retirement. The relentless seven-days-a-week schedule of testing and racing in several series at once had left him exhausted. At 36, he was appointed President and General Manager of Penske Racing Enterprises. And Roger Penske announced that he had taken over the McRae workshops in Poole, Dorset, to build a Formula 1 car.

Roger's competitive spirit had long been nudging him towards F1. For the 1971 Canadian GP he'd arranged for Mark to drive the second McLaren alongside Denny Hulme. In the Mosport rain Mark finished a brilliant third in his first Grand Prix, never running lower than fourth despite a pitstop for fresh goggles. Now, in 1974, he had to grapple with life as a retired racing driver, and he found it far more difficult than Roger had done, nine years earlier. The F1 Penske was slated to make its debut in the Canadian GP in September. On August 29 all media and public were barred from Mosport, and the new car was tested by a driver in an unmarked helmet. On September 13 Donohue announced he was coming out of retirement to race in Formula 1.

The Geoff Ferris-designed Penske PC1, in the red, white and blue colours of First National City Travelers Checks, was of course immaculately turned out, but inevitably F1 was a steep learning curve. Mark's first points finish came in its ninth Grand Prix, fifth at Anderstorp. The car consistently lacked speed so, mid-season, Roger decreed a switch to a March 751 while an improved Penske was built. During the Sunday morning warm-up for the Austrian GP, in the fast uphill right after the pits, a left front tyre failed. The March leaped the guardrail and crashed heavily, and a metal bar supporting a hoarding hit Mark's helmet. He was concussed, but in the ambulance he was talking rationally. A few hours later he lapsed into a coma. He was flown by helicopter to Graz and had a four-hour operation to remove a blood clot from his brain. On Tuesday evening Mark Donohue died.

Over our breakfast, Roger is poker-faced when I ask him about Mark. It's clear that, 35 years on, he still feels the loss of his friend. "Today's medical facilities are so much better. Maybe today we could have done something, and saved him. Mark was totally dedicated to racing. He was a very fine engineer, and he had the technical ability to take things much further than I could, while I looked after the business side. In personality he was introverted, but we really communicated well. Plus I'd raced, so I understood the pressures a driver goes through. Our goal was to win Indy, which we did, and the CanAm, which we did. We were in F1 for one reason, because Mark wanted it."

It's a cruel irony that Penske's finest moment in Formula 1 came without Mark, and at the very same circuit. "It was one year on from when we lost him that we won the Austrian Grand Prix. Racing is like that. One day it's tragic, the next day you're thinking, Well, we won this one." In the much-improved PC4 John Watson was third at Paul Ricard and fourth at Brands Hatch. Then at the Österreichring Wattie led all but nine of the 54 laps to score a brilliant victory – after which, at Penske's insistence, he famously shaved off his beard.

At every level of the Penske organisation, Roger insists that people as well as machinery are smartly turned out – spotless pressed clothes, short haircuts, clean-shaven. "It's true, when John joined us there was a discussion about his beard. I wasn't too keen on it." So they did a deal: as soon as the Penske won a Grand Prix, John would shave his beard off. He was true to his word, and has been beardless ever since. According to Argetsinger, when David Hobbs was hired as Mark's co-driver in the Ferrari 512S, Roger suggested that David might want to visit a barber to attend to his English-length locks. "Not a chance", said Hobbs, and nothing more was said.

But a drive for Penske was always a feather in any driver's cap. "People can't buy rides with us", says Roger. "That shows weakness in a team. We hire the best drivers, and if we can't afford the best we won't be racing. That's always been our DNA. I say to my drivers, You got the ride, now run the way you need to run to win."

Following the Austrian victory Penske, with a singleton entry against two-car teams, was lying fourth in the Constructors' Championship. But at the end of the season Roger pulled the F1 plug, and the cars were sold to ATS. "We were doing F1, Indy, CanAm, TransAm, IROC. We had a full plate. It was time for me to make a business decision. We didn't have then the international footprint that we have today, so we said, Let's concentrate on US racing. Since then Bernie [Ecclestone] has talked to me a number of times about starting an American F1 team. But if you're in anything you've got to be able to go to the top, so that when people talk about the best teams they're talking about your team. The investment required just to get onto the grid, the capital needed to get properly into the technology, is huge. Look at US F1, they couldn't even get started. I have great regard for F1's top teams, Ferrari, McLaren and the rest, but I'm an American. We've got so much good racing in the US, and we need to win the NASCAR Championship and do things like that before we get back into F1.

"Bernie has done an outstanding job bringing F1 to where it is today. In every country it goes to, it's a tremendous event. But in the US we race 35 or 40 weekends a year, and the average NASCAR race has 100,000 spectators at every round. Real paying spectators, not like some F1 races in the Middle East with lots of guest tickets. There's got to be changes in F1, because of the technological costs. And they need to do something about the spectacle. The race starts, it all happens into the first corner, and after that... The guys in the stands, the guys who've paid, most of them aren't interested in the details of F-ducts or diffusers or carbon brakes. What they know is the red Ferrari, the blue Red Bull, the silver McLaren, the white Mercedes. And they know Fernando and Mark and Lewis and Michael. Build the drivers, make them the stars. That's what people understand."

Roger has been in Indycar, through USAC, Champ Car and IRL, for an incredible 43 seasons. He was a major chassis builder for many years, but the cars are now Italian Dallaras, using the Honda-badged Ilmor engine. And Ilmor is another Penske company. "Back in 1983 Mario [Ilien]and Paul [Morgan]came to my home with a hand-written business plan. I read it, and I said, Let's go. We started with the Chevy V8, Rick Mears won Indy for us with that, and we went from there. In the end we sold off the F1 side to Mercedes. The guts and feathers of the McLaren and Brawn engines came from Ilmor, so you could say we're involved, indirectly, in today's F1. We build the Indy motors in England at Brixworth, and Ilmor US does all the servicing. We lease the engines to the teams, so it's quite a good business for us. There are Chinese walls, the IRL guys control the engine numbers, and when you get your new engine you don't know what number you're getting. There's never been a complaint that the engines aren't all exactly the same."

Typically, Penske Indycar statistics – all those wins and titles – don't interest Roger much, but one season he singles out is 1994.

"We did the stock-block Mercedes engine in great secrecy, didn't announce it until two weeks before Indy. Buick had been doing pushrod engines for years without much success, but we sat on pole, won the race, led every lap but about three. The key Mercedes directors flew over, came into the garage in their business suits and ties, took them off and put on Penske Mercedes shirts. Then I knew we'd arrived. We won 12 of the 16 rounds that year."

His drivers today are the Brazilian Helio Castroneves and Australians Ryan Briscoe and Will Power. This year's Indy 500 – although Castroneves started from pole, with Power second and Briscoe fourth – didn't go so well, but Power still leads the 2010 Indycar standings, with Castroneves fourth and Briscoe seventh. "Helio's got over that unfortunate court case [last year he was accused by the American authorities of tax evasion]. They made it into a witch-hunt, but he was completely exonerated of everything, and he won his third Indy a few months later. Briscoe is super, he had the championship all but won last year. In Japan he was nearly a lap ahead of the field, then he had that accident in the pitlane, knocked the front suspension off. Lost him the championship right there. Will is a great young driver, very committed. At Sears Point a guy spun and Will T-boned him. It broke his back, but he came back and won the first two rounds of the season, nearly won three in a row."

After his initial forays into NASCAR, Roger withdrew from that series in 1980. But he couldn't ignore such a fundamental part of American racing, and in 1991 he was back, first with Pontiac, then Ford and now with Dodge. There have been many wins and many great moments, like Penske's 1-2 in the 2008 Daytona 500 with Ryan Newman and Kurt Busch, but the NASCAR Cup title is a goal that Roger still has to score. This year the Dodge Chargers are raced by Busch, Brad Keselowski and Sam Hornish Jr, with Justin Allgeier in the Nationwide series. In May Busch won the season's longest race, the Coca Cola 600 at Charlotte.

"We build our NASCAR cars top to bottom, we build the chassis, we hang the bodies, we get block castings from Dodge and we build our engines. NASCAR's reach is a lot bigger than Indycar, apart from the Indy 500. The fan base is just gigantic, there are TV shows every night, you've never seen such passion for the favourite drivers. And cars: there are Ford fans, Chevy fans, Dodge fans, Toyota fans. You've got a level playing field, and it's the tightest racing I've ever seen. It's tough, too. Look at [Juan-Pablo] Montoya. Good as he is, he's now in his fourth year and it's been a long transition for him. We've brought Sam Hornish over from open-wheelers, and he's struggled to get to where he wants to go. Under the France family, NASCAR has been consistently strong for so long. In Indycar we had the split with Champcar and IRL but, now it's come back together, we've got better fields than we ever had. There's 12 or 14 cars that can win every race, and it's the same in NASCAR. I'm not sure that's true of Formula 1."

One programme that Roger mentions with pride is his three-season ALMS campaign for Porsche in 2006-8. The Penske-run 9R6 Porsche RS Spyders won the LMP2 title all three years, and also outright victories, notably the 2008 Sebring 12 Hours. "That was one of our best wins in recent years, beating the LMP1 Audi R10s that won Le Mans. It was good to be working with Porsche again. Wolfgang Dürheimer, their R&D boss, he's a very competitive, highly motivated guy. If Porsche ever decides to do Le Mans again, we'd love to be part of that. I'm not someone who collects old race cars for old times' sake, but I do have that Sebring-winning Porsche, in 100-point condition."

Roger has also been a circuit owner. "We started with Michigan, which we bought in 1972. Then we bought Rockingham in North Carolina, we did a joint venture with Homestead in Florida, and in 1997 we built California Speedway in Fontana. But we've sold them now, to the France family. Since then we've done Belle Isle, that's something I wanted to do for the City of Detroit. We have a great circuit there, a semi-permanent road course. Because the economy in the area has been a mess we haven't run there in the last two years, but we have all the pieces, the fencing, the barriers, and I see it as a place where we can run a really big event."

The state of down-town Detroit after the financial crisis concerns him deeply. "The city is shrinking. It used to be two million people, now its 900,000. Three-quarters of the city's kids never graduate from high school. I'm head of the Downtown Detroit Partnership, pulling the private equity people together to recreate the downtown area. It's safer now, we've got a great new mayor, we're working on charter schools, we've got a new medical group to reinvigorate the hospitals, and I think we're really making a difference. When I was a kid I was sent to Culver Military Academy in the summer, that's where I learned to be tidy and neat. We're taking inner-city kids and putting them through the same school. All the success, all the winning in the world, doesn't mean a thing if you can't put something back. After the Haiti earthquake, through all our companies, very quickly we shipped a million dollars' worth of heavy-duty trucks in there to help move food."

I suggest to Roger that the huge investment in money and energy that he still pours into motor sport has to be for one of three reasons: because it's lucrative, because it's good promotion for his other businesses, or because he just loves it. "Lucrative no, because we run a zero-based operation in racing. Everything we make we put back in, in equipment, in people. I guess you'd have to say the primary reason is, I love it. I'm a busy guy, I'm never going to run out of things to do, but racing is my golf game, my fishing trip, my skiing holiday. I do play golf, I do ski, but what I love is being personally involved in racing, sitting on the pit wall. That said, we try to use racing as a common thread in everything we do. It creates momentum. You can't put a price on the value of how racing builds your brand. It ties in with everything we're trying to do: execution, team-work, quality, reliability, integrity. Those are all ingredients you need to win, in racing, and in business. Look at Ron Dennis, look at Bernie: they've succeeded in business because they understand racing.

"Racing's a model for any business: you've got to motivate, you've got to think ahead, you've got to manage it through the down periods, and you've got to develop your people. That's a key lesson: everybody matters. The guy who drives the truck is as important as the guy in the pitstop changing the right front, or the guy in the cockpit steering the car. A race team is a flat organisation. That's how I like all my businesses to be. "

In recent years Roger's investment in Europe has grown enormously. Having bought several major dealer groups, including Sytner, he now has 139 dealership locations in the UK. He's our largest retailer of BMW, Audi, Porsche, Bentley, Lexus, Ferrari and Maserati. In Germany, too, he now owns major dealerships for Porsche, Audi, Toyota, BMW, Lamborghini and Ferrari. Of course, at the age of 73, he could retire, switch off, relax. "Why would I want to do that? I still like to win – and winning for me might equally be a race on a Sunday, or a big order in one of our businesses on a Monday, or persuading a bright talent that I've been trying to hire to join us on a Tuesday. I'm not going to stop until I can't do it any more. I couldn't sit at home or go to the golf course every day. I have a commitment to all the people who work with us, our human capital. That sets a bar for me to reach for.

"What keeps you young is mental effort, and risk. Risk keeps you on the ball. No risk, no reward – whether it's a judgement call on the track, or a financial risk in a business. If you're a racer you've got to be able to take risks, because there's always someone coming up from behind."

So the man who hung up his helmet 45 years ago is still racing. Once a racer, always a racer. Roger Penske's businesses are everywhere: if you live in the UK, Germany or the US, you might find yourself buying a car from him soon. And even if you don't, next time you take a black cab in London, you'll probably be Penske-powered. You see, the company that makes their diesel engines... The Captain owns that, too.

Roger Penske was talking to Simon in June 2010.

JO RAMIREZ

For 40 seasons, confidant
of champions

The problem is, lunch isn't long enough. Over 40 seasons, this man has been friend and confidant to a succession of F1 heroes, helped them celebrate their victories and, too often, mourned their loss. He was inside Ferrari when it was Enzo's fiefdom, with Tyrrell when Ken's little team won drivers' and constructors' titles, with McLaren during the height of its championship glories. When Ford took on Ferrari at Le Mans, when Dan Gurney won at Spa with the Eagle, when Siffert and Rodríguez jousted in the mighty Porsche 917s, he was on the team. Down the long years this modest man has made more friends in motor racing than anyone and, it seems, fewer enemies.

Yet Jo Ramirez thinks of himself merely as a link in the chain, grateful for the good fortune that has allowed him to earn his living from the sport he loves. He has lived in Italy, the USA, Spain and England; but Jo is Mexican. That's why we're lunching off chimichanga in Covent Garden's best Mexican restaurant, Café Pacifico.

Jo was born in the suburbs of Mexico City in 1941, one of 10 children. Around the local kart tracks he befriended a boy his age who, helped by a hugely wealthy father, had already made his name in karting and motorcycle racing. Still too young to drive on public roads, this lad Ricardo had a Porsche Spyder, and his elder brother Pedro had an XK120. Both the Rodríguez brothers were destined to burn bright, and die young.

"Ricardo raced the Porsche in the USA when he was only 16, and in 1960 he finished second at Le Mans, aged 18, in a NART

Ferrari. In 1961 the Scuderia put him in an F1 car for the Italian GP. His first F1 drive, in a Ferrari, in front of the Monza crowd! He qualified second, a tenth off von Trips, ahead of Phil Hill and Richie Ginther in the other works cars. It was fantastic: he was still only 19. The Lewis Hamilton of his day...

"For 1962 Ricardo had a works Ferrari drive in F1 and sports cars. I told him: I see nothing in Mexico, I just want to pack my bags and go to Italy. He didn't think I could do it. His first race that year was the Targa Florio. I was studying engineering at college, but I had a little night job, I'd saved $300. I gave up my studies – the hardest thing was to tell my father about that – and I got myself to New York and by boat to England. I hitch-hiked to Naples, and got the ferry to Sicily.

"Ricardo introduced me to everybody in the Ferrari team. Eugenio Dragoni was the team manager, very authoritarian: sometimes he grew too big for his shoes and got cut down by *Il Commendatore*. Mauro Forghieri was the technical director: he is still a good friend of mine. Ricardo was racing a rear-engine Ferrari 246 in the Targa with Willy Mairesse, but he had a GTO as a practice car and he took me round the circuit. I had never been on a race circuit before, and at first, as we say, I was wearing my balls as a bow tie. But his driving was so good I started to relax and enjoy it. He even let me drive for a lap, but we had to change over before the pits, so the Ferrari people did not find out." Just a pair of Mexican lads, enjoying themselves...

"As kids back in Mexico City we used to go out late at night in Ricardo's gold Oldsmobile down the Avenida Reforma, and he would teach me how to go round the roundabouts in the wet, faster and faster. He said he felt what the car was going to do, you know, through his arse and the tips of his fingers. As a racer he was just incredible in the rain, better I think even than his brother became later. They were very different. Ricardo was very extrovert. Pedro was two years older, quieter, he was the introvert. It all came naturally to Ricardo, but back then Pedro had to try harder to match his times in the same car, and it was usually Pedro that had the accidents."

Ricardo and Mairesse duly won the Targa at record speed. Back at Maranello Jo pleaded with Dragoni for a job, any job, at Ferrari. With no work permit, there was no job – but Dragoni offered food and accommodation at races in return for hard work. "I did everything nobody else wanted to do, cleaned the cars, cleaned the parts; they make a mess, I clean it up. Now I was in this world I'd dreamed about for so long." Ricardo and his young wife Sarita had a permanent suite in the Palace Hotel in Modena, and they let Jo bed down in a little side room.

First he had to learn Italian. "I bought myself a little transistor radio and I stuck it in my ear all day long, and I picked up the language quite quick." He scrounged lifts to the races with the drivers. "Giancarlo Baghetti took me to the Nürburgring for the 1000Kms in his Ferrari 250GT, and on the way he crashed into the back of a lorry, smashing a front wing. When we got to the Nürburgring it was raining. He offered me a lap, but I made an excuse and went round with Dan Gurney instead, who was there for Porsche. It was my first meeting with Dan: a brilliant driver, a brilliant man, and later for me a brilliant boss. He was the driver that Jim Clark always said he feared most.

"With Ricardo I met my hero, Fangio, and I told him about my ambitions for a proper job in racing. He took me to Maserati and introduced me to Giulio Alfieri, and I ended up with a job there. He was five times world champion, he didn't need to help me, but he did.

"For the non-championship Mexican GP, Ricardo fixed a drive in Rob Walker's Lotus 24. I had no money to go back to Mexico, of course, but I took Ricardo and Sarita to the airport. They were compulsive shoppers and they had a mass of stuff they couldn't take home. Ricardo gave me lots of clothes, and his spare helmet and overalls.

"On the Friday morning somebody at Maserati said they'd heard on the radio that Ricardo had had an accident. I didn't know what to do. I went back to the Palace Hotel and the girl on reception said there was a phone call for me from Mexico. As she passed me the phone she started crying. They all loved Ricardo at the hotel.

"It had been in the first practice session. Ricardo was fastest, and then John Surtees went quicker, so Ricardo went out to beat him. He went off on the outside of La Peraltada, the long right-hander at the end of the lap, hit the guardrail and was thrown out. When I heard that it was like my whole life was crushed."

Jo stayed at Maserati for the 1963 season, helping to run the monstrous Tipo 151 Le Mans car with which André Simon and Lucky Casner led Le Mans. Then his boss Gian Paolo Dallara was recruited by tractor magnate Ferruccio Lamborghini to set up a new factory. The goal was to make a road-going GT better than Ferrari.

"Gian Paolo took me with him. I was the second or third employee of Lamborghini. It was fantastic experience because I was involved in everything – building the engine, all the chassis, the suspension. I did a lot of the testing myself on the first prototype. But Modena wasn't the centre of the racing world any more. England was the place now. So I wrote letters to everybody I could think of: Chapman, Brabham, Broadley. Some answered, some didn't, but I packed up my Fiat 500, drove to England, and knocked on doors.

"One person who answered my letter was John Wyer, who was running the Ford GT40 programme at Slough. I said to him, 'I can't speak English yet, but I know how to work on racing cars. Just try me, you don't have to pay me, and if I'm any good you keep me.' I started the next day. My transistor went back on my ear, but now it was the BBC, any station with talking, even *The Archers*.

"John Wyer was a very imposing personality. He insisted on everything being tidy and clean. When he came into the workshop everybody went quiet, you could hear a fly walking on the wall. He spoke his gentleman's English very slow, and you had to get your words right when you talked to him. It was like Enzo Ferrari: I was afraid to stand close to Il Commendatore unless I knew what to say, in case I put my foot in it. He didn't say much: he listened behind his dark glasses.

"We took the GT40s to the Le Mans test weekend in April. Lucky Casner was there with the latest Maserati. In Modena Lucky and I had dinner often, to talk about everything, not just racing cars. He was my friend. At Le Mans we were laughing in the paddock, and a few minutes later the big Maserati went off into the trees at the end of the Mulsanne Straight and he didn't come back. That was difficult for me. You should not get involved outside your job with the drivers, because they come and they go. But sometimes they are such personalities, so you have to.

"A Canadian team, Comstock Racing, bought two GT40s and I was sent to look after them for a couple of months. At Sebring they overheated in practice, and I had to do something, so I changed the front bodywork to open out the air intakes of the GT40s. I thought, what would Wyer and Len Bailey say! But it worked. Both cars were going well when the quickest of the drivers, Bob McLean, crashed just after a refuelling stop. The car exploded like a bomb, with poor Bob trapped inside. It was the first time a driver died in a car I prepared. I had to collect the wreck, and his charred shoes were still inside. It was horrible. That kind of thing happened so much then."

When Dan Gurney was setting up the Eagle Formula 1 team he offered Jo a job, and he joined Anglo-American Racers in Rye in April 1966. At first they used the out-dated 2.7 four-cylinder Climax, but for 1967 the beautifully prepared blue and white cars had their glorious-sounding Weslake V12. With Richie Ginther in the second car they finished first and third in the Race of Champions at Brands Hatch, and then came Dan's historic victory in the Belgian GP at Spa.

"Most of the money for the Eagle F1 project came from Goodyear, and it was never enough. We really struggled. Dan was one of the greatest drivers I was ever lucky to work for. But when drivers become team bosses, they fancy themselves as engineers. Dan always had to fiddle with the car. At Spa, when the paddock was on that steep hill with rough ground, he was standing on the back of the truck and he said, 'That left front wheel, it's got too much toe-in.' 'No, Dan, we checked it in the garage, it's spot on.' 'It's not,' he said, 'add one turn.' He would ask for a change, then to prove he was right he would push himself even harder, so his lap times justified it. Then he would say, 'It's quicker than before, but it's not so easy to drive, so put it back to how it was.'

"But he is a fantastic man. When he won at Spa and we heard the US anthem, we were cheering and crying at the same time. We should have won the German GP too. We had a big lead with just over a lap to go when a driveshaft broke.

"The Eagle F1 thing stopped mainly for lack of finance. Dan couldn't keep up the two operations – Anglo-American Racers in Rye and All-American Racers in California – and he had more sponsorship in America, so Rye was closed down. It was very sad for all of us. Now, when I see an Eagle at Goodwood, I know it was the most beautiful grand prix car ever. It lifted the standards in F1.

"Dan offered me a job with the American operation, and my wife and I – I'd married Bea in 1967 – moved to California. We did Indy, Can-Am and Trans-Am. I loved Trans-Am with the Barracuda: Swede Savage was the driver, and Dan did some races too. I was mechanic and fabricator, and with the truckie we were five. The camaraderie between us and all the other teams was great.

"I loved my two years in America. My wife had a good job too, working for a real estate company, but she was homesick for England. So when John Wyer suggested I come back to help run the Gulf Porsche 917s I couldn't say no. The lead drivers were Pedro Rodríguez and Jo Siffert, and John put me with Siffert because he said one Mexican per car was enough. Siffert was a real racer, not much different from Pedro – except in the wet.

"One of the best races for me was Daytona. After 18 hours in the lead Pedro's car, shared with Jackie Oliver, came in stuck in fifth gear. You weren't allowed to change the gearbox, but you could change the bits inside. Everything was red hot, the gears almost welded to the main shaft, but with hammers, levers and a welding torch we got it apart and rebuilt the box. It took us 90 minutes. Then we sent Pedro out. First time round he put his thumb up, so we knew it was working. He drove flat out, passed everybody, caught the leading Ferrari in the closing stages, and won.

"Now he wasn't under the shadow of his younger brother, Pedro went better and better. He became probably the greatest wet weather driver of them all. At the Targa that year he took me round in a Porsche practice car, exactly 10 years after Ricardo had taken me round in a GTO, when I'd just arrived in Europe. After the lap Pedro said, 'How do I rate against Ricardo?' To wind him up, I said, 'Six out of 10.' 'Good', he said, 'I still have room for improvement.'

"At Le Mans JW always stayed at La Chartre sur le Loir. We worked on the cars in the garage beside the hotel, and drove them 25 miles on the public roads to the track each morning. Before the race we didn't have enough brake pads bedded in, so I said I'd bed in a set on my way in on Saturday morning. All the way I was accelerating hard in the traffic and then standing on the brakes, but when I got to the circuit and took them off they still looked new. I just wasn't driving hard enough. I tell you, in third gear a 917 is like an aeroplane. You have to drive one of those cars to realise why those guys earned so much money.

"Pedro loved England. He liked his old Bentley Continental, and he liked wearing his deerstalker hat. With the Porsches and F1 with BRM, he was usually racing every weekend, but after the French GP he had a weekend off. He and his lady, Glenda, had a new house in Bray, and they were due to come to dinner with Bea and me at our house in Maidenhead. But he rang me a couple of days before to postpone, because Herbie Müller had asked him to drive his Ferrari 512 in a race in Germany. It wasn't until I got to work on Monday morning that I heard what happened."

Pedro was leading when, for reasons that have never been explained, the big Ferrari hit the barriers and caught fire. It took several minutes to extricate him; he died on the way to hospital.

"In October I went to Brands to watch the end-of-season F1 race. Jo Siffert, who I'd worked with all season at JW, was on pole in the BRM, and I chatted to him on the grid. Half an hour later his BRM hit the bank and he was dead. With Pedro and Jo both gone, I didn't want to stay with JW.

"So for 1973 I joined Ken Tyrrell, and you couldn't work for a nicer team. F1 teams were so small in those days: we were less than 30 people including Jackie Stewart and François Cevert. It was like a family: Ken was the father, and Norah – we called her Mrs T – was the mother. It was three sheds, three cabins and a muddy yard, and they won the championship three times in five years. I was on Cevert's car.

"There was a wonderful relationship between Jackie and François. At Zandvoort the two Tyrrells were miles ahead of everybody, nose to tail, and Jackie missed a gear. François could have gone by, but he lifted off and waited for Jackie to sort it out. After the race Jackie said to him, 'You silly idiot, why didn't you pass me?' François said, 'I would like to beat you one day fair and square, not just because you make a little mistake.'

"That year Jackie clinched the championship at Monza. Then we went to North America for the last two races. At Mosport Cevert tangled with Scheckter's McLaren and hit the barriers very hard. I don't know how he got out of it, only bruised and with strained tendons in his legs. If he had broken a leg maybe he would be alive today, because at Watkins Glen during Saturday morning practice he had his fatal accident. Everything went silent, and when all the other cars came back to the pits he was missing. I tried to jump on a service vehicle that was setting off for the crash scene, but Jody Scheckter grabbed me and said, 'Don't go, there's nothing you can do.' The worst thing was having to go to his hotel room later and pack up his clothes and passport and stuff.

"François would have been a great successor to Jackie to lead the team. He was getting better and better every race. I don't think he would ever have left Ken: they had such a bond." Jo stayed with Tyrrell for 1974, working with Jody Scheckter and Patrick Depailler, but then moved to the new Fittipaldi Copersucar team as team manager.

"It was a step up in my career, and I felt if it didn't work out I could always go back and be a spanner again. But it was three very hard years. We had a lot of problems the first year, with Wilson Fittipaldi driving, but for the second year Emerson came over to us. He was twice World Champion, and it should have been better. But Emerson was very hard to deal with. He always wanted his own way, and he was not always right. It's strange how top drivers don't usually make good team bosses. Look at Prost: a great driver, a clever guy, but his F1 team was a failure."

In 1978, after the defection from the Shadow team that created Arrows, Shadow boss Don Nichols hired Jo to rebuild his team. There were only three employees left, and the opening round in Argentina was four weeks off. Jo set to, hiring mechanics, welders and fabricators: "I was as busy as a dog digging a hole in a marble floor." They got two cars to Buenos Aires for Clay Regazzoni and Hans Stuck, and both finished.

One of the hirings was a young lad called Nigel Stepney, who was desperate to get into F1. "He'd been working on the Broadspeed touring car team, a very bright guy, very quick, very hardworking, and a fantastic mechanic. My second year at Shadow our drivers were Elio de Angelis and Jan Lammers, and when Elio went to Lotus he asked Chapman to hire Nigel too."

From Shadow Jo went to ATS, and then Teddy Yip's Theodore team. Then in late 1983 Ron Dennis, whom Jo had known since Ron was a Cooper mechanic in the 1960s, offered him the job of McLaren's team co-ordinator. He was to stay for 18 years, and the roster of drivers he worked with in that time is impressive: Lauda, Watson, Rosberg, Johansson, Berger, Häkkinen, Brundle, Blundell, Magnussen, Mansell, Coulthard and Räikkönen. And, of course, Ayrton Senna and Alain Prost.

"When I joined McLaren it was Lauda and Prost. Alain was very professional, very down-to-earth. He would always go just as quick as he needed to go. If someone beat him to pole on 1min 24.38sec, he would go out and do 1min 24.34sec. I don't know how he could do that. Later, when Keke Rosberg was with us, after the race his cars would be finished, brakes, tyres, gears, everything chewed up. Alain's car would be perfect for another race.

"Niki had to cope with Alain coming into the team, just like Alonso has to cope with Hamilton now. Niki was very clever: he couldn't beat him in the car, so he beat him outside it, with the team, with the press, all the other things. Alain won seven GPs that year, Niki won five, but Niki got the title by half a point. But the next two years Alain was champion.

"When Ayrton arrived in 1988 Alain was very comfortable with that, received him with open arms. At first it worked pretty well. There was respect between them, they could have been good friends. But Ayrton was always so determined to beat Alain. He didn't care about anyone else. When he crashed at Monaco in 1988 he had built up a huge lead, but after Alain took second place he started to go faster and faster, breaking the lap record over and over. He didn't need to, because he was 46 seconds ahead, and Ron was desperately trying to slow him down. And then he crashed at Portier. He got out of the car, pushed past the marshals and disappeared.

"I couldn't find him for hours and hours. I kept calling his apartment in the Avenue Princesse Grace over and over, but his phone didn't answer. Finally his Brazilian housekeeper picked up. I'd been there for dinner with Ayrton two nights before, so I knew this lady, and I talked to her in Portuguese. She said, 'He is not here.' I said, 'I know he is there, it's Jo, he will talk to me.' In the end she passed the phone to Ayrton, and he was still crying.

He said, 'I touched the barrier at the apex and then went to the other side and hit hard. I am the biggest idiot in the world.'

"At Estoril Alain took pole and won the race. Ayrton led from the start, but at the end of the first lap Alain came out of the corner before the pits quicker and slipstreamed alongside. Then Ayrton pulled across on him and almost squeezed him against the pitwall. Alain was really mad at that. After the race he shouted across to Ayrton, 'If you want the championship so bad you are ready to kill for it, you can have it.'

"That year Ayrton won eight GPs, Alain won seven. In the end Alain had scored 105 points, Ayrton had 94, but on the dropping-points rule Ayrton was champion by three points. Then at Imola in 1989 they were both on the front row, with the Ferraris behind. Ayrton was the one who suggested they should not fight into the first corner and risk throwing the race away to Ferrari. So they agreed that whoever had the best start would stay ahead until they came out of Tosa, and then they would race. The race started, Ayrton led, took the ideal line into Tosa. Prost followed him and made no attempt to go up the inside. Then Gerhard Berger had his big accident, with the Ferrari on fire, so they stopped the race. I remember so clear before the restart, Ayrton said to Alain, 'Same routine, OK?' And Alain said, 'OK'. But this time Alain made the best start and went into Tosa first, looked in his mirrors, no worries, braked, took a wide line, and boom, Senna went by on the inside.

"Alain was just so mad about that, and afterwards they had it out in front of Ron. But Ayrton said, 'No, the agreement was not to pass under braking for Tosa, but I passed you before the braking point.' It was not true, but the thing with Ayrton, he would tell himself something over and over, and then he would believe it himself.

"Then Alain gave an interview to the French press and said Senna was a liar. After that they hardly spoke to each other, which made things difficult inside the team. After a while Alain tried to make it up, but Ayrton wouldn't hear of it. Ayrton became a little paranoid. At Hockenheim he had a slow tyre stop: the mechanic on the slow wheel normally worked on Alain's car, and Ayrton said he did it on purpose."

And then in Japan, with the championship battle going to the wire between the two McLaren drivers, came that notorious collision in the chicane six laps from the end. Alain went off to Ferrari for 1990, and they returned to Suzuka 12 months later with the battle for the title once again between the two of them.

"The McLaren and the Ferrari were side by side on the front row, and Ayrton said to me before the race, 'He better not get to the first corner before me, because I'm not going to slow down.' So you knew if Prost was in front there was going to be an accident. And that's what happened. I was gutted when I saw that. It wasn't until a year later that Senna admitted it was a deliberate thing, a payment for the year before.

"He was not an easy man. He was so intense. On the grid for his last race for McLaren, Australia 1993, he beckoned me over. I thought he wanted some help with his seat belts. He grabbed my hand very hard and said, 'I feel very strange doing this in a McLaren for the last time.' At that point Ferrari and McLaren were on 103 GP wins each since the beginning of F1, so if we won that day McLaren would become the most winning F1 team of all time. So I said to Ayrton, 'If you win this one for us, I will love you for ever.' And he gripped my hand harder and I could see tears in his eyes. I thought, 'Damn, I don't want to make him emotional when the race is about to start.' But no problem: he won the race.

"When Prost left Gerhard Berger replaced him, and Gerhard was very good for Ayrton. He wasn't a threat to him, and he made him laugh. Gerhard was terrible for practical jokes, and Ayrton learned to play a few jokes too. Over the winter Ayrton would disappear to Brazil, he'd say, 'I don't want to do any testing, call me when the car is ready.' At the end of the 1990 season Gerhard said, 'I will work very hard over the winter, I will get very fit, I will do all the testing, so I will be really sharp.' And then Ayrton turns up for the first race at Phoenix and straight away he's over two seconds a lap quicker than Gerhard. Gerhard was so demoralised he nearly wanted to leave the team. I told him, 'Don't worry, this guy is different, you won't go quicker than him. Just get as close to him as you can.' By the time Gerhard left us in 1992 to go to Ferrari he was burned out. He said to me, 'I love Ayrton, I go on holidays with him, but I can't keep driving in the same team when I haven't a hope in hell of beating him.'"

"Senna was very much aware of the dangers of motor racing. He never thought he could cause his own death – none of them do, do they? But the fear is always that something will happen that is not under their control. When he crashed at La Peraltada in practice for the 1991 Mexican Grand Prix, and was trapped in the car upside down, he was shaken. I took him back to his hotel, and he said to me, 'Today I saw it come close.' I tried to make a joke of it, so I told him the old Mexican saying, 'A bad weed never dies'...

"I used to arrange hire cars for the McLaren drivers, book their helicopters, all that. At Imola in 1994, although Ayrton was with Williams now, he came to me on Saturday and asked me if I'd mind booking a helicopter right after the race to get to Forli, where his plane was, so he could fly to Portugal. Roland Ratzenberger had been killed on that day, which had shocked everybody, and Ayrton was missing his girlfriend Adriane and wanted to get home as soon as possible. I said I was glad to do it: it showed that although we were in different teams now we were still friends. I went to see him on Sunday after the warm-up and told him where the helicopter would be and what name it was booked in.

"When the crash happened I just tried to carry on and do my work. He had been at the top for so long, your mind did not associate something happening to a man like that. The race was stopped, then restarted. After the race I kept doing the things I had to do, and Keke Rosberg came over and said, 'You heard the news?' I knew what he meant. I said, 'Don't tell me it's bad?' Keke said, 'It's bad.' It was a terrible day.

"That morning, in the pit lane, Prost was there for French TV, and he said to me, 'Guess what, I talked with Ayrton and we had a really nice friendly chat. It was like when we were first going to be driving together, no animosity either way.' I said, 'Good, maybe you are going to become friends.' A week later, Alain was one of the coffin bearers at Ayrton's funeral.

"Ayrton was an extraordinary man. He pushed the standard higher in all the things he touched. Everyone who worked with him learned something from him. He was such a precise guy in everything he did, the way he controlled his life. He probably could have become Prime Minister of Brazil. He wouldn't have just retired and spent his millions. He would have done something for his people.

"At McLaren Ron was always very intense about trophies. He believed they were team property. He had it written into drivers' contracts that they couldn't keep any trophies they won. But Ayrton insisted in his contract that he kept his trophies. So Ron got me to find out the maker of each trophy and get replicas made. Ayrton said to me, 'Make sure mine is the real one.' Ron said, 'Don't you ever give him the real one.' I told both of them they were getting the real one, and I'm not going to tell you now which I did!

"But Prost was never interested in trophies. His last win for McLaren was Monza 1989, when he'd already signed for Ferrari. The crowd of tifosi around the podium were shouting 'copa, copa,' so he dropped the cup down to them. They tore it to pieces, of course – one guy got the handle, one got the lid. Ron was furious. He thought Alain was saying I don't give a shit, I'm leaving McLaren, I'm going to Ferrari. Alain didn't mean it like that at all. He just thought it would be a nice gesture to the crowd.

"Mika Häkkinen was very uncomplicated. Sometimes he'd try impossible things because he was too naïve to understand they couldn't be done. And sometimes he succeeded. Overtaking Schumacher at the top of the hill at Spa: I wonder if even the Sennas and Prosts could have done that. The guy was so cool, never got excited.

"David Coulthard is the nicest guy, a real team player. In qualifying perhaps he doesn't have the killer instinct like Mika did, but on his day, on his track, he is a very fine racing driver. At the 2001 Hungarian GP it happened to be my 60th birthday, and Mika and David produced a beautiful leather jacket and put it on me. A really nice present, I thought. On the back of the jacket was the Harley Davidson badge, so I said jokingly, 'Now all I need is the bike.' They lifted me onto their shoulders and carried me to the back of the motorhome, and I heard the sound of a big bike being revved up, and there was a brand new shiny Harley-Davidson. They had bought it for me. I had a big lump in my throat, I couldn't say anything. It was one of the nicest things that ever happen to me, so generous for them to do. And they say F1 drivers have deep pockets and short arms..."

Is Bernie Ecclestone as terrifying as he seems? "I always got on brilliant with Bernie. He said to me, 'I envy how you can be friends with everybody.' I said, 'I'm not important like you, so I don't need enemies.' When I was at Fittipaldi and we were short of money I did a dodge to save on FOCA travel costs to Long Beach, and he found out. I was petrified, I thought, shit, Bernie will really make me suffer for this. In the paddock he pulled to me to one side and said, 'Ramirez one, Ecclestone nil. But it's only half-time...' He never held it against me, seemed to like me for it. It's how he is, he loves the game."

Jo's last race for McLaren was Indianapolis 2001. In the paddock afterwards, long-standing friends such as Emerson Fittipaldi and Placido Domingo drank champagne with him. Then the mechanics gave him their own send-off: he was tied to a tyre trolley and pelted with eggs. Now he divides his time between Spain, where he has built a house near Mijas, and London. Tragically Bea, his wife of 38 years, died of cancer in 2005.

Does he miss Formula 1? "Of course, very much. After 40 years on the inside, it is a strange feeling to be on the outside looking in. You don't want to abuse your welcome. I see old friends, they want to talk, but I know they are busy and I am taking up their time. But I still go to two grands prix a year, Barcelona and Silverstone. I know Lewis Hamilton from when he came to the McLaren factory as a kid, so I am up to speed."

He has been up to speed across five decades. Jo Ramirez has been part of the Clark era, the Stewart era, the Senna era, the Schumacher era and now the Hamilton era. He has given his working life to motor racing, and he wouldn't have had it any different. Even now, he is still a link in the chain.

Jo Ramirez was talking to Simon in July 2007.

BRIAN REDMAN

From mop salesman to
sports car greatness

History takes a lot of notice of Formula 1, and not enough notice of the rest. Here's a great British driver remembered by F1 only because he turned down an offer from Ferrari, and was lucky to escape with his life from an accident in which he was blameless. Yet in his professional career Brian Redman did 358 races. He was victorious, outright or in his class, in 94 of them, and finished in the top three 177 times. His tally of classic long-distance victories includes the Targa Florio, Daytona 24 Hours (twice), Nürburgring 1000Km (twice) and Spa 1000Km (four times). Now in his 70th year, he isn't living in quiet retirement: he promotes events for historic cars in the USA, and still races them with highly competitive flair.

More than 25 years of living in America haven't obscured Brian's no-nonsense North Country roots, so I suggest we lunch at the world's most famous fish emporium, the original Harry Ramsden's at Guiseley, north of Leeds. It's a shrine to fish and chips: crystal chandeliers, stained glass windows, sauce bottles on every table, and Engelbert Humperdinck's *Please Release Me* playing reverently through hidden speakers. We order cod, chips and mushy peas, and cups of tea. For afters there's Spotted Dick and custard.

Brian talks quietly, self-deprecatingly, with dry Northern humour. His unlikely start in motor racing, at 22, came at the wheel of a mop van. "The Patent Wringer Company employed two people, and me. I delivered mops all over the country in a Morris Minor Traveller. To get to my customers quicker I fitted a Shorrocks supercharger.

"One weekend in 1959 I removed the mops, took it to Rufforth and raced it. Then I thought, what I need is increased aerodynamic efficiency. So before a meeting at Linton-on-Ouse [a long-defunct airfield circuit north of Wetherby] I took the windscreen out and the back doors off. I thought it would be better if the air could go right through. The scrutineer took one look at it and said, 'Now, laddie, just take it away and put your screen back in and your doors on'. 'I can't,' I said, 'They're back home in Burnley'. So they had a stewards' meeting, and decided to let me run. In the race the head gasket blew. A friend towed me home behind his Healey 3000, in the dark, in the rain, no windscreen, at 80mph. On a short rope."

Next came an 850 Mini, stripped, highly tuned, no power under 4000rpm. "I was keen. I once drove it from Burnley to Goodwood, pouring rain the whole way, no motorways then of course, did a five-lap handicap, and drove it back to Burnley. Drove it to work next morning, too." Then there was an XK120 – "I raced it once, wore out a new set of Michelin Xs, and couldn't afford any more tyres" – and a Morgan. "I used the Plus 4 for every motorsport endeavour there was: racing, rallying, sprints, hillclimbs, trials. By now I was married to Marion, mortgaged, completely out of money, so I sold the Morgan and took up motorcycle scrambling. Then in 1965 everything suddenly changed.

"Gordon Brown, who had an ex-works XK120, let me drive it in a sprint at Woodvale on Easter Sunday, and I set BTD. A friend of his, Charlie Bridges of Red Rose Motors in Chester, had just bought the ex-John Coombs lightweight E-type, and Gordon put in a word for me. On Tuesday Charlie Bridges rang and said, 'come and test at Oulton Park on Thursday'. I'd never driven an E-type, but I knew Oulton. I felt this was my chance, so I probably drove it beyond my safe capability. I went 1.5sec under Jackie Stewart's lap record. On Saturday I raced it, and won."

That season the red E-type swept all before it, winning 16 out of 17 races. For 1966 Bridges bought a Lola T70 and the national wins continued, with some good showings in internationals, culminating in a Grovewood Award. He also did his first long-distance classics, at Monza and Spa.

"Peter Sutcliffe asked me to drive his GT40 in the Spa 1000Km, among the works Ferraris and 7-litre Fords. After first practice I wanted to give the whole thing up. I couldn't believe the speed. We were doing 200mph around the back of the old Spa on what were really narrow public roads, no barriers, just trees and farm buildings." Yet they finished a rousing fourth overall, and Peter asked him back in 1967.

"The next year was terrible. I'd been in the car for about half an hour when I suddenly ran into rain down at Stavelot, like a curtain. I couldn't see anything, the screen misted up and I couldn't reach it to wipe it. Then there were headlights in my mirror, and this yellow Ferrari P3/4 came by, Willy Mairesse, and he lost it right in front of me and had a huge accident. I was in the middle of changing into fifth, and found myself going sideways in neutral. How I missed all the wreckage I don't know. But we finished, sixth that year."

In 1967 Brian travelled throughout Europe racing an F2 Lola for Charles Bridges' brother David, and a GT40 at Le Mans for Lord Downe. And his efforts in privateer GT40s had been noticed. At the end of the season John Wyer asked him to partner Jacky Ickx in one of the Gulf Mirage GT40s in the Kyalami Nine Hours. They won, and Brian was signed for 1968. Then Cooper offered an F1 drive, and Brian took that too. "It was the start of the Big Time. But it was also the start of difficult times."

In motor racing back then, danger was ever-present. In April the death of Jim Clark devastated the world. It was followed a month later by the loss of Mike Spence, then Brian's F1 team-mate Lodovico Scarfiotti, and then Jo Schlesser. Brian and Marion now had two young children, but the money had to be earned. With F1 and sports car deals signed, there was still F2. Following a test at Modena, Ferrari offered a works Dino 166 for the Eifelrennen, on the tortuous Nürburgring Sudschleife.

"We were all in a bunch at the front, Ickx in the other Dino, Kurt Ahrens and Piers Courage in Brabhams, and me. A stone from Ahrens' rear wheel smashed through my goggles and hit me full in the eye. I flung up my hand and slowed, and peering through one eye I trundled back to the pits. Mauro Forghieri shouted at me: What's the matter? Put on your spare goggles. I hadn't got any, so they gave me a pair of Ickx's, which were dark green for bright sun and not much good for the dark bits. I restarted dead last, and drove like a maniac." He'd lost 2min 15sec, but he carved back up to fourth place, and broke the lap record. Even without a badly bruised eye, it would have been an astonishing drive, and Forghieri was beside himself with delight.

"At dinner that night he went away, came back, and he said, 'Bree-an, just now I speak with Signor Ferrari. You drive for us, Formula Due. At the end of the year, Formula Uno'. So I said, 'No thank you'. 'What you mean, no thank you?' I said, 'If I drive for Ferrari I'll be dead by the end of the year'."

But Brian was going brilliantly for JW, winning the BOAC 500 and the Spa 1000Km with Jacky Ickx, and coaxing a lot of speed out of the unwieldy Cooper. He was third in the Spanish Grand Prix, his third-ever F1 race. Next came the Belgian GP at Spa, and he qualified a strong ninth. On lap seven he had a huge accident at Les Combes. The Cooper smashed into a concrete barrier and slid along it, trapping Brian's right arm between the barrier and the chassis, and tearing off three wheels before cannoning into some parked cars, landing on top of them and bursting into flames.

"I was one of only about half of the drivers in F1 then who wore seat belts. Otherwise I would have been killed. John Cooper came to see me in hospital and said, 'What did you do?' I said, 'Something broke'. 'Now then, my boy,' he said, 'Don't worry, you'll be all right'. On Thursday morning *Motoring News* came out, and its report said that Redman claimed the steering broke. John phoned the editor and said, 'I demand a retraction, it was driver error'." But *Autosport* came out the next day with a photograph showing the front right wishbone in the act of snapping. Brian was vindicated.

He was out of racing for the rest of the season. His right arm was badly broken, and steel rods had to be inserted above and below the elbow – which are still there. He played himself back in with the Springbok Series for Chevron the following winter, but the arm was still giving him a lot of pain. He'd just signed for Porsche for 1969, so a specialist in Johannesburg did a radical operation, gluing in new bone taken from his hip. Six weeks later he did the Daytona 24 Hours, sharing a Porsche 908 with Vic Elford.

"I hadn't told Porsche about my arm problem, of course – just took the sling off when I got to the track. I had to drive on the banking at 200mph holding the wheel with my left arm, and bracing it with my knee. We were out after 12 hours with an engine problem that afflicted all the 908s. That saved me, because I couldn't have gone the distance. But Porsche never knew.

"Gradually the arm got stronger, and we had a great 1969. There were 10 rounds in the Sports Car Championship. 'Seppi' Siffert and I won five of them, including Spa and the 'Ring. In 1970 John Wyer ran the works Gulf-Porsche 917s, and I was paired with Siffert once more. It wasn't big money: I was paid £290 per race, and £420 for Le Mans and Daytona. And no prize money. We won Spa again, and Zeltweg, and in the 908/3 we won the Targa. We were leading Le Mans by four laps when Seppi missed a gear passing the pits. Those 917s would only go 200rpm over the limit without blowing, and you didn't have rev-limiters then. Le Mans is about the only long-distance race that really matters to the public, and I never won it.

"Spa I always found really frightening. Every time I went there I thought I was going to be killed. I used to lie in bed the night before the race with sweat dripping down my face, thinking, this is it." And yet Brian won the Spa 1000Km four times, and the Spa 500Km as well, winning the European 2-litre

Championship for Chevron after a huge battle with Jo Bonnier's Lola. Ex-JW team organiser John Horsman wrote that Redman was four seconds a lap faster at Spa in the Porsche 917 than either Siffert or Rodríguez. "Yes, I saw that. I rang John and asked him why they'd never told me. He said that if they had, they'd have had to pay me more! People always ask me if I liked Spa. After the race, I loved it. But before the race, I hated it.

"So 1970 was another good year. But at the end of that season I decided to retire. It wasn't because I was fed up with racing – I loved being paid to do something I liked. But within the space of three months we'd lost Courage, McLaren and Rindt. I said to Marion, 'They're coming down like flies. I'll be next. I've been offered a job running a BMW dealership in South Africa, and we're going'. So we went.

"But I didn't like the job, didn't like the politics – it was still in the days of apartheid. After four months we were back, and I had to earn a living. John Wyer had replaced me with Derek Bell, so I drove a Formula 5000 McLaren for Sid Taylor. Then Wyer asked me to drive with Siffert in the 908/3 in the Targa Florio, because Derek hadn't done the race before. John said to me, 'Redman, you start the race: I don't want Siffert and Rodríguez knocking each other off'. But Seppi had crashed the car in late practice, and from the start the handling was poor. I'd gone about 20 miles, was just turning into one of the few corners I actually knew, and the steering broke. I hit a concrete post right in the middle of the petrol tank, and it exploded.

"I shut my eyes, hit the seat belt release and leapt out. I was on fire, everything was on fire, but for a fraction of a second I saw the other side of the road and just ran that way. I didn't see anything after that. I was taken to some sort of first aid place. They bandaged me all over, hands, head. You never hear about the spectators who used to get hurt in the Targa, but a young boy was brought into the room – I won't describe the details, but he died while I was there. It was like your worst nightmare. Nobody at Porsche knew where I was. I couldn't communicate, and I still couldn't see, because my eyes were burned shut. Meanwhile Pedro Rodríguez and Richard Attwood had been searching all over Sicily for me, and about 10 o'clock that night they found me. They took me back to the hotel, Porsche's doctor got going with the pain killers, and next day they flew me back to Manchester.

"I wasn't out of racing for long. I did an F5000 race at Mallory seven weeks later, finished third. A week later I was on holiday in France with the family and somebody on the camp site told me Pedro had been killed. Three months later Seppi, whom I'd driven with in 18 long-distance races for Porsche, was killed at Brands." It was 36 years ago, but Brian goes silent for a while, staring out of the window at Harry Ramsden's car park.

"At the end of that miserable year Sid Taylor borrowed a CanAm BRM and asked me to drive it at Imola. The works Ferraris were there. It poured with rain – the Austrian Klaus Reisch hit the pit wall in his Alfa T33 and was killed – but the BRM was a Tony Southgate-designed car, and all his cars are good in the rain. I won my heat and the final, and then Ferrari got in touch, wanting me to drive the 312PB in long-distance races. Mauro Forghieri said, 'Bree-an, you are the only man we ever ask twice'.

"I was with Ferrari for two years, and for the first time I earned decent money: £20,000 a year, which was very useful then. In 1972 my team-mate was usually Regazzoni or Merzario, and in 1973 I was partnered with Jacky Ickx. The 312PB really was like a two-seat Formula 1 car, marvellous.

"At Spa in '72 my co-driver Merzario didn't like the circuit, and when I got back in the car Ronnie Peterson was right on my tail. I was going as hard as I knew, and we came to Les Combes. Since the Cooper accident I'd always taken an unusual line there, to give myself a bit more room if anything went wrong. And fleetingly I glimpsed something in the crowd, colours moving. That usually means people running or umbrellas going up – an accident just round the corner, or rain. So I got on the brakes a bit early, and suddenly I was on a wet road. The movement I'd glimpsed was people putting their umbrellas up. I just got round, but Ronnie hit the barriers. So that was a bit lucky, and we won.

"I did 19 races for Ferrari, and I never saw Mr Ferrari once. Back in 1968, when I'd had a test at Modena before that German F2 race, Forghieri said, 'see that man over there under the trees in a raincoat? That is Signor Ferrari'. It was his way of telling me to go faster. Next day at Maranello, Mr Ferrari was sitting there surrounded by his people. I hesitated by the door, and he got up – a tall, impressive man – and came over to me. He put his hand up to my cheek, squeezed it between his thumb and forefinger, and said: 'nice-a boy'. They were the only two words Enzo Ferrari ever spoke to me.

"During my second Ferrari year I was also racing in America in F5000 for Jim Hall. I was up against Jody Scheckter. I beat him five times and he beat me twice, but I missed a couple of races because of Ferrari commitments, so he was champion. It was a hard year, commuting back and forth across the Atlantic. At Le Mans, having flown straight in from the F5000 race at Mid-Ohio, I failed the medical because my blood pressure was too high, but then they took it again the next day and I was OK. At the end of the year I said to Marion, 'I'm not doing this any more, we're going to stay in America'. I drove for Jim Hall for the next three years, and won the F5000 title each year, against strong opposition from Mario Andretti.

"For 1977 the SCCA changed the rules, and F5000 became CanAm – effectively the same single-seaters but with full-width bodywork. The first race was at St Jovite. In Friday practice I came into the pits – we were substantially quickest at that point – and I said: 'The car's good'. They said, 'What do you want?' I said, 'Try a quarter of an inch off the front'. On the next lap, breasting a rise at 150mph, the car took off, flew 40 feet in the air, landed upside down and went hurtling on down the road, wearing a hole through my crash helmet as my head banged up and down. When they got to me, my neck was broken and my heart had stopped. Then the ambulance had a puncture on the way to the hospital, and they had to stop and fit the spare.

"When Marion flew in from England the next day, the first thing she saw at Montreal airport were newspaper pictures of the ambulance men changing the wheel by the roadside with the doors open, me lying inside and the headline *Redman est mort*.

"That was in June. By October I was walking. By January I was running slowly, and I looked around for a drive in the Sebring 12 Hours, not a winning car but a reasonably decent one so I could see if I could still drive – or if I still even wanted to drive. I got a ride in a Porsche 935 with Bob Garretson and Charles Mendez, and we won."

The fish and chips are long gone. We have another pot of tea, and the stories keep coming: the Lola-Chevrolet IMSA programme in 1981, the Bob Tullius Jaguar team for which Brian did some 44 races in the mid-1980s, and then the Aston Martin effort in 1989. "Richard Williams and Ray Mallock did a first-class job on a limited budget. The AMR1 was slow, but it was a lot of fun. At Le Mans, by a miracle, the car was still running in the final hour. There was no way we were going to get any higher than our 11th place, so I was a bit bored really. At Arnage there was a cheery group of British spectators, and they held up a hand-painted sign which said: *Give us some oppo*. On the next lap I did a nice slide for their benefit, and I nearly spun it. Next time round the sign said, *Now fastest lap*. And on the final lap it said: *Tea and crumpets with the Queen!*"

Since 1990 Brian has run his own business in Vero Beach, Florida, promoting historic races and track days across the USA. Nearly 50 years after a young mop salesman took his Morris Minor Traveller onto the grid at Rufforth, he's still racing in GT40, Lola F5000, BRM, Chevron and others, and is a regular Goodwood guest too. He's had a lot of success, a lot of drama, a lot of pain, and has mourned too many friends. Despite repeated attempts, he still hasn't managed to give up motor racing. But he's a survivor.

"After the Spa accident in the Cooper, in the hospital in Liège, the surgeon said to me, 'Monsieur Redman, I have to tell you something. We may not be able to save the arm'. And then he said, 'Why are you laughing?'

"I said, 'I'm laughing because I'm still here'."

Brian Redman was talking to Simon in September 2006.

KEKE ROSBERG

Getting to the top by believing
in hard work

According to Keke Rosberg, getting to the top in Formula 1 requires one of two things: "A lot of talent, or a lot of hard work. Nelson Piquet, for example, never wanted to work very hard, but he did have a great talent. Ayrton Senna was special, because for him it was both: he had the talent, but he also did the work. With me it wasn't talent. It was just a lot of hard work."

But anyone who watched Keke take pole position for the 1985 British GP as spots of rain were falling – grabbing the 1000bhp Williams-Honda turbo by the scruff of the neck, throwing it through Woodcote with fistfuls of lock, stabbing at the throttle – knows he had great talent, too. That lap still stands as Silverstone's fastest: less than 66 seconds for the 2.9 miles, an average speed a whisker under 161mph. They also remember his victory at Monaco in 1983, when he opted for slicks on a wet track, and obliterated the turbocharged opposition. Maybe they saw his second-ever F1 race, the Silverstone International Trophy in 1978. Who was this almost unknown Finnish refugee from Formula SuperVee, who'd grabbed a ride in the no-hoper Theodore? It rained that day, too. The great names crashed and, unbelievably, the Finn won.

"That day I thought I'd made it. I saw them all in the mud, the Petersons, the Laudas, the Hunts. I had Emerson Fittipaldi behind me for 20 laps and I beat him to the flag. Big time, here we come. I was young and naïve. I didn't know that's not how it works in F1. Nobody's memory lasts more than a fortnight, beyond the next race. It took me four more years to get out of shitboxes and into a decent car."

We're talking by the pool beneath the skyscraper apartment building where Keke and his wife Sina have their Monte Carlo home, with an uninterrupted view of the Mediterranean's most costly piece of coastline. But, apart from a double espresso and a glass of water, Keke doesn't take lunch: in his driving days he was a famous smoker, but since he gave that up he watches his weight. The trademark moustache is less luxuriant now, but he is the same small, chunky, urgent figure, sharp as a tack, talking fast with rueful, downbeat humour. He is a polyglot, taking phone calls during our chat in Italian and German, speaking fluent, idiomatic English in rapid, stabbing sentences, his vocabulary peppered with mechanics' slang.

His Monaco office is a walk away, and he goes there every day. His plane is at Nice Airport, ready to whisk him to his rural home in Austria, his development in Lapland, or his estate in the mountains above Marseille. Keke started with nothing, in a small distant country that had never produced an F1 driver. He was 33 before he got a good F1 drive, and at once he became World Champion. Before that, years of wheeling and dealing, hustling – and hard work.

"Both my parents did rallying, but gave it up because they couldn't afford it. I started karting at 16, and I had to finance it from the beginning. Even then I was selling stuff and importing engines from Italy. I was Finnish karting champion several times, but the big thing was coming fifth in the World Championship in Paris in 1970. I went to France with my dad, with one chassis and one engine, and we slept in a tent. Next to me was Hans Heyer with his mechanics, three chassis and 28 engines. I was leading the first final from pole, and the bastard engine broke.

"I wanted to go to university to do medicine, but I overslept on the morning of the big exam. I'd been studying until 5am. My one ambition was to be able to afford racing as a hobby. It never occurred to me that I could be a professional racing driver, like I never thought I could be an astronaut. I was working in computer software – I was married by then – and a colleague who was into Formula Vee persuaded me to try it. I found an old Veemax, but I only had a third of the money it cost, I borrowed a third from the bank. Then I persuaded my father to lend me the rest. He was not extremely thrilled. He gave me some sound advice: if you go racing you'll ruin yourself. He told me not to speak to him again until I paid him back. I did that at the end of the season.

"The second year, 1973, I bought a newer Formula Vee and pretty much won everything in Northern Europe. By this time my wife had left me. She thought I was crazy spending all my time and money on racing. I didn't even have a car. I drove the racing transporter to work every day, wearing my suit and tie. I worked nights as well at the computer company, not for extra money but for time off to go racing. I won the European FV Championship, and reckoned I had to go F3 for 1974. March invited me to England with talk of a works drive, and I thought, great, Rosberg is on his way. When I got there they asked me how much money I had. I said none. The conversation stopped there, and I drove home to Finland. I was just starting to learn how the motor racing world worked.

"So I drove down to Vienna and talked my way into a Formula Super Vee drive for Kaimann. I won five races for them, and we were third in the European SV Championship. Then I ran into a guy in the fashion business who wanted a racing team. I managed to convince him I knew how to make his team look good, he paid me some money, and for the first time I was earning my living from racing. The first pay cheque I got, I went to England and bought a new Jaguar XJ6. And some driving gloves from Les Leston. The team was based in Hamburg, so I moved to Germany. That was probably the hardest time of my life. I didn't speak a word of German, and it was a very lonely existence. But I won the German championship, and a big cheque."

That year Keke made a contact that was to prove vital. "An American race car dealer called Fred Opert wangled a Shadow

F1 drive in the Swedish GP for Bertil Roos, who'd been driving for him in the US. I didn't know Fred from the man in the moon, but I thought, this guy might be useful. So I wrote him a letter. That led to me driving for him in a SuperVee race at Watkins Glen, and we stayed in touch after that.

"For 1976 I got a ride with Jörg Obermoser's Toj outfit. It wasn't March, it wasn't Chevron, but hey, I was in F2. But the car wasn't much good. [*Autosport* called the Toj "cumbersome" and noted that Rosberg got his few results "through sheer bravery and bravado".] Then Fred set me up with a drive in the New Zealand series, and I won it. So in 1977 Fred and I got busy. As well as New Zealand we did European F2, the Argentine Temporada, Formula Atlantic in North America, F2 in Japan, Macau – 42 races in a year, in five continents. Fred didn't pay me. His job was to bring me a car, and my job was to find sponsors and get patches on my overalls. At the end of that long year it was back to New Zealand, and we won the series again."

The first sniff of Formula 1 came when sports car entrant Willi Kauhsen cooked up a scheme to buy a pair of Kojima F1 cars from Japan. "I tested the Kojima at Fuji. My first drive in an F1 car. But the Kauhsen thing never happened. Then in 1978 Teddy Yip came into Formula 1 with the Theodore. Eddie Cheever did the first two GPs for them, but he couldn't qualify. He told them the car was a shitbox. So I told them it was the most wonderful Formula 1 car I'd ever seen. Suddenly I had the drive and I was flying out to South Africa. At Kyalami I had my first meeting with Teddy and his Irish team manager Sid Taylor. Bejasus, what a character. I remember at Hockenheim Bernie Ecclestone raised hell because Sid washed out his underpants and hung them up on a line in the paddock to dry.

"So Kyalami was my first F1 race, and in first practice I had the biggest shunt of my entire career. A brake pad fell out going into Sunset and I rolled it up in the chicken wire. The poles came into the cockpit, I was lucky it didn't catch fire. They stripped the wreck in the paddock, and there was a huge hole in the monocoque. So they shoved it onto a truck and drove it to the local blacksmith's shop. A new bit of aluminium was riveted over the hole, then back onto the truck, back to the paddock, reassembled, and I qualified it. In the race the fuel tanks leaked, but otherwise it was fine. Two weeks later we were at Silverstone in the rain, and we won."

But even Keke's commitment and courage failed to get the Theodore through qualifying again, so it was put away and Keke found a berth at Günther Schmid's ATS team. In his first drive for them, in the British GP at Brands Hatch, he went from 22nd on the grid to an astonishing fourth place before the rear suspension broke. "The bloody shock absorbers fell out of the chassis. I'd probably been going too hard over the kerbs." Meanwhile Teddy Yip bought a year-old Wolf and painted it red and white to do the rest of the European season. "Then he lost interest, and I was back with ATS again."

Most newcomers would want to concentrate on the Grands Prix in their maiden F1 season, but while all this was going on Keke's relationship with Fred Opert continued. Alongside F1 he did F2 in Europe, Formula Atlantic in the USA, plus the F2 series in Argentina and Japan. He spent 420 hours in aeroplanes that year, plus an incalculable amount in airports. If it was a weekend, Keke would be racing somewhere.

"I'd hoped for a proper ATS deal for F1 in 1979, but Schmid said I was too expensive – I think I was asking $1000 a race. That was the level in those days at that end of the grid. I talked to every F1 team, but I got nothing. So I flew to America and signed to do Can-Am for Carl Haas. A couple of weeks later, when I was in Japan doing an F2 race, Haas called and said the deal was off. He'd decided to take Jacky Ickx instead, because Jackie Stewart had advised him that I was too wild. Fred Opert's brother, who was a lawyer in Boston, said. 'You've got a contract. Sue the hell out of him.' Which I did. But I still had to go racing, so I got another Can-Am ride with Paul Newman, who was running separately from Carl Haas in those days.

"Just when the Haas Can-Am deal had fallen out of bed I was offered two races in the ICI F2 March that Ron Dennis was running. Guy Edwards, who looked after ICI and was a good friend, offered me $12,000 to do Hockenheim and the Nürburgring. Then Guy comes on the phone and says, 'Sorry, Keke, I can't pay you.' I said to him, 'You bastard, you know I'm out of work, you know I've got to do those races.' So I did them for nothing. Years later I found out ICI had paid for those drives – the money had gone into Guy's operation but somehow never came out. Anyway, I won Hockenheim, both heats, and on the old Nürburgring I put it on pole by 4.5sec. [*Autosport* again: "Rosberg's staggering qualifying lap poses the question: when will somebody give this man a regular top-class drive?"] But in the race, in the wet, the throttle jammed open, and I hit the wall."

Meanwhile in the centre-seat Can-Am cars Keke showed himself to be blindingly quick. He took pole for every round except one, but thanks to engine unreliability he only won once. "I had a great time doing Can-Am. I loved the big cars, loved Paul Newman, loved his people. I promised Paul I'd concentrate on Can-Am and wouldn't go back to F1. Then James Hunt walked away from Wolf after Monaco. Peter Warr [Wolf team manager] flew to the Mid-Ohio Can-Am and offered me the seat. I said to Paul, 'I've got a bit of a problem. This opportunity won't come again, and I'd really like to take it.' And Paul said, 'I understand. You take it.'

"But I honoured my Can-Am commitments, so I was commuting back and forth for the rest of the season. I was a zombie by the end of it." At Laguna Seca he had a huge shunt in practice when a tyre exploded. He was trapped in the car with concussion and two broken ribs, but he raced next day in a borrowed car. "I was in bad shape, but the mechanics had worked all night to get the other car ready, so I wasn't going to say I couldn't drive. I'd hurt my wrists and had trouble holding the wheel, so they wrapped it with double-sided tape to give me some grip." From the back of the grid, he finished sixth.

"It was a tough time. I'd come back from a Can-Am, land at Heathrow and go straight to Silverstone for an F1 test, then on to the next Grand Prix, then back over the Atlantic for the next Can-Am. I travelled alone, going from hotel to hotel: these kids nowadays, they have their entourage with them. The Wolf was not very competitive that year, and I had to work my butt off in the car. But don't cry for me: I was working with Harvey Postlethwaite, Peter Warr, Jo Ramirez, all top people. I was in F1, and there are worse places to be in life.

"Then Walter Wolf sold up, and the team was taken over by Fittipaldi. I was now in a two-car team with Emerson, and I got on the podium in my first race for them, in Argentina. Two weeks later, in Emerson's home race at Interlagos, I got stuck behind him. He was blocking me on the inside, so I passed him round the outside of a fast left. He went ballistic. It was on TV, and all the Brazilian papers wrote how their hero had been overtaken. He said he'd have my balls. Next morning in São Paulo he called a meeting, me, Peter Warr, his brother Wilson, and started ranting at me. Wilson said, 'Sit down, Emerson. I've seen the TV coverage, I think you should shut up.' Pretty good, from his own brother."

For 1981 Fittipaldi stopped driving. "My team-mate was now Chico Serra, who became a good friend. But always there were car problems and money problems. At the end of that season I took a holiday in California, taking flying lessons, to give my brain a rest from motor racing. While I was there I had a phone call from Jeff Hazell at Williams. He said, 'Look, don't get the wrong impression or anything, but Alan Jones has decided to retire, and would you like to come down to Paul Ricard and have a test?' I said, 'I'll swim there if I have to.'

"I called a lawyer in London I'd used for contract work and told him Emerson owed me some money, not a lot, about $2300, and could he get rid of my contract with Fittipaldi? Luckily I'd reminded Emerson in writing that he hadn't paid up, done it all by the book. I landed at Heathrow, called the lawyer again, and he said, 'It's done, you have no contract.' I went to Williams for the seat fitting, and I said to Frank, 'I know this is only a test, but just for your information, I am a free agent.' Next morning we got to Ricard, they slapped on some qualifiers, I went out at 8am and got under the lap record. Went back to England, went to Frank's house, signed a contract, $250,000 for the first season. Plus freedom to keep making my own sponsorship deals, so I was earning well. Things were getting more professional in F1 now, so I started training. I ran for 45 minutes a day, I thought that was enough. I hated it, but my attitude was I was getting paid for it. I was still smoking, though.

"That first 1982 season was unbelievable. Everything happened. Today's F1 generation wouldn't even understand it. At the first race, South Africa in January, we had the drivers' strike, which in my opinion was completely disgusting. We should have found other means to get our due rights, even against Bernie. The whole strike thing was about Niki [Lauda], who'd come out of retirement, wanting to get back in the limelight. Niki was leading it with [Didier] Pironi, who was the GPDA representative. I wasn't a member of the GPDA. I decided I had better things to do with my time than listen to those guys arguing. They could never agree anything, and a lot of them didn't really understand what it was all about. But I did spend the night locked up in the hotel in Johannesburg, we all did, because we were tricked into getting into the bus to go off for a meeting. Certainly we needed a meeting, but we didn't know they were going to lock us in for the night. That was Niki's and Pironi's doing.

"The second race was Rio. It was a bloody hard day, incredibly hot and humid. Everybody was in trouble. Riccardo Patrese blacked out in the cockpit and spun off. Piquet won, and fainted on the podium. I finished second, and I earned those points. Then they disqualified Nelson and me because Brabham and Williams were running water tanks to cool the brakes, and of course to get the cars over the weight limit.

"Carlos Reutemann was my team-mate, a very charismatic guy. He was the Williams star, having his third season there. But I out-qualified him at Kyalami and Rio, and at Rio he ended up in the fences. Carlos was smart, I think he knew I was going to be quicker than him. On the Sunday night after Rio he told Frank he wanted to retire. I was second again at Long Beach, to Lauda, and then the fourth race was Imola, and the FOCA teams boycotted it. It was only April and we'd had the strike, the disqualification, the boycott, and my team-mate had walked out!"

Keke then got his head down and started to gather points: second at Zolder and third at Zandvoort, and at Brands he took pole ahead of the turbo Brabham-BMWs and Ferraris. But his car refused to start for the warm-up lap. He started from the back, passed eight cars on the first lap, and was sixth by lap 13, but then retired with low fuel pressure. By the time the teams arrived at Hockenheim Didier Pironi led the championship, and Keke was only fifth. But that Saturday morning Pironi had the accident that ended his career. The turbos triumphed on this power circuit, but Keke was third.

Then Austria, when Keke and Elio de Angelis crossed the finish line side by side. The Lotus won by the official margin of 0.05sec. "If I had a best mate in F1, it was Elio. I've often wondered if I would have behaved differently going into that last corner in Austria if it had been anyone else but Elio. It was a very fast corner, and Elio did a good job of blocking the inside. I could have tried the outside, but I could have ended in the wall. It was his first win, and I knew mine would come." It came 14 days later, at Dijon, when he beat Alain Prost's Renault turbo by 4sec. Now he led the table, and in the final round at Las Vegas his fifth place clinched it. In 1981 he'd scored not a single championship point, and five times he hadn't even qualified. In 1982 he was World Champion.

"I'd gone from zero to hero, and it all came so fast that my fame, and earning potential, were lagging behind. I was an unknown champion. So I went to work. I worked non-stop on building up my profile: TV talk shows, interviews, appearances all around Europe, working for new sponsors, working for existing sponsors to keep them happy. I was even on *A Question of Sport*.

"In 1983 I probably had my best season. The turbos ruled, but I took pole for the first round, in Rio. I was really insulted when Ken Tyrrell said to me, 'You must have been using special fuel to put that thing on pole.' I said, 'You obviously don't know Frank Williams if you think that.' This was from the man who was disqualified the following year for putting lead shot in his tanks! Frank would never cheat, it's just not in his vocabulary. Patrick Head neither. I would put my hand on the Bible for those guys. Anyway, in the race at Rio the car caught fire during my refuelling stop. I jumped out – the flames came up into my helmet and burned my moustache off – and I was just wondering whether my arse was on fire and should I roll about on the ground when Patrick grabbed me by the neck and shouted, 'Get back in the f***ing car!' They push-started me and I rejoined ninth, a lap behind. I got back up to second place by the end. Then two hours later – wouldn't you know it – they disqualified me for the push-start. That was Rio: second two years running, disqualified two years running."

Keke's Williams was usually first non-turbo home that year, and at Monaco it all came good. "It was wet as we went out onto the grid, but I told the team, 'I want to race on slicks', and they backed me up. I found a lot of grip, I don't know how, and I was leading by lap two. By the time the rain stopped I was clear." He was second in Detroit, too. "My driving never had a lot of finesse in it, which is probably why I was quick in street races. But I didn't have shunts – until my first McLaren test..."

For 1984 Williams had turbo power at last with the Honda-powered FW09. Keke finished second yet again in Rio, but the car proved difficult and unreliable. "The engine wasn't up to it, the car wasn't up to it. It wasn't an easy year for Patrick. He had the knowledge and experience to get engine and chassis to work as a package, but it was very difficult for him to get heard by Honda. One of the problems was the engine lacked rigidity. Austria was the only motor race in my life when I gave up. I came into the pits and said to Patrick, 'I cannot drive this. I am going to have the biggest shunt of my life in these fast corners with this thing twisting.' Patrick accepted it without discussion, because he knew that I would drive the wheels off anything. Also, with the Honda the power was on or off. You couldn't feed the power in at all, it just came in bang, which didn't help when the handling was so bad." Yet it was in the FW09 that Keke scored another classic victory, in searing heat between the concrete walls and on the bumpy, crumbling surface of the one-off Dallas Grand Prix.

"In 1983 and '84 my team-mate was Jacques Laffite, but for 1985 Frank signed Nigel Mansell. I was hurt that Frank would never discuss with me who was going to join. I didn't care if the guy was fast or slow, that wasn't the point. But we all operated really well together, Williams was a great place to be, and I didn't want anything to destroy that. Elio de Angelis, who'd been Nigel's team-mate at Lotus, said to me, 'This guy Mansell is poison.' I tried to tell Frank, but he wasn't interested. So I said, 'If he comes, I leave.' Frank said, 'No you don't, you're under contract.' And I was, so I had to accept it. But I'd already decided I wanted 1986 to be my last year, so I started talking to Ron Dennis early about going to McLaren.

"And then when Nigel joined, we had no problem at all. We got on fine. We were not great friends, but we worked well together. He did his job, I did mine, and it was a totally harmonious year." Keke took another street race win in Detroit, and he ended his four years with Williams with victory in the first Australian GP in Adelaide, another tough, hot race.

"Having said I was leaving Frank, I stuck to it. Ron was paying well, and all was sweet. But in the first lap of my first test for my new team I crashed. It was at Rio, on the long fast corner at the end of the straight. There was a bump in the middle which I'd always done in the Williams without blinking, but the McLaren got away from me and I was in the fences. At that moment [McLaren technical chief] John Barnard wrote me off. It was like I'd been branded, like burning a mark on a horse's ass. All season I struggled with understeer, and nobody seemed to be able to do anything about it. In 2005, at Patrick's 60th birthday party, I was seated next to Barnard, and I talked to him more that evening than I did in all of 1986. He said, 'I remember you complaining about understeer', and I said, 'Yes, why didn't you deal with it?' He said, 'I was going to Ferrari the next year. My mind was elsewhere. It didn't interest me.'

"But McLaren was a very professional operation, Steve Nichols and Tim Wright as race engineers, and I got on well with Alain [Prost]. I had some good races: at Monaco I qualified ninth because the understeer was so bad, but came up to finish second. But I hated the way F1 was going with the fuel: you just had 195 litres for the race, and the meter in the cockpit was always inaccurate. At Imola I ran out of fuel. Alain did too, but he spluttered over the line to win. Maybe his driving used less fuel than mine. There was no way I wanted to carry on in F1 when you had to drive to save fuel. That had nothing to do with motor racing.

"I was at the Paul Ricard test that May when Elio crashed. I was stunned. I went to the hospital in Marseille with Elio's sister and brother. I drove back to Ricard with Nigel Mansell, to carry on testing. Neither of us spoke, until suddenly Nigel said in the silence, 'How long is a piece of string?' I'll never forget that.

"I'd decided to go public with my retirement at the German GP, in my adopted homeland. After Elio's death it wasn't difficult to stick to the plan. I made the announcement on the Saturday morning, and in the afternoon put the McLaren on pole. I didn't want anyone saying I was retiring in the cockpit. It would've been good to win, too, and in the race I was leading almost to the end, but then the bloody fuel ran out again.

"My last GP was Adelaide. In your last race the most important thing is to come out of it in one piece. Even if you've never been scared before, in your last race you can't avoid it. I led from lap seven to lap 62, had a 28sec lead. Then flat out down the straight, 300kph, there was a huge bang. I thought the crankshaft had fallen off. So I switched off, parked it, looked underneath: no oil, that's strange. Then I walked away. I didn't realise it was a rear tyre until a marshal told me. I could have driven to the pits on the rim, got a new tyre, maybe won my last race. It was a big disappointment. But later they found both my front brake discs were finished. Another lap or two, I would have been in the wall anyway. After that I didn't feel so bad."

Retired at 38, Keke kept on working. Among other projects, he started a driver management business, notably looking after JJ Lehto and then Mika Häkkinen. "In 1989 I had a call from Piero Lardi. Would I consider driving for Ferrari? I thought about it and said, 'Yeah, that's something I'd like to do.' So he said, 'Fine, come and do a test for us.' And I said, 'You want me to drive, I drive. I don't come to show you whether I can drive or not.' They wanted to see whether I still had it. So that came to nothing.

"A year after that I was on my boat in Sardinia when Jean Todt called from Peugeot. He wanted me to race sports cars. I've always said only toilets have doors, but it was a big factory operation, and I decided to do it. In 1990 we developed the car, and we did a full season in 1991. Todt was 100 per cent, but there was too much of a French faction in the team, with Jabouille and Alliot and all. I was paired with Yannick Dalmas, and you couldn't get excited about the bloke, he wasn't going to set the world alight. But we won in Magny-Cours and Mexico.

"Those V10-powered cars were very quick. I was testing at Monza and the car exploded at 300kph on the straight. I thought someone had put a bomb in it, I thought I was dead. The injection had worked loose and sprayed fuel under the engine cover. The explosion tore my seat brackets out of the carbon-fibre chassis. When you're an old guy back from retirement that sort of thing gets your attention. The last round was at Autopolis in Japan: 16 tonnes of freight, 10 cases of best red wine, our own cook, and we were doing it for about 300 spectators. I said to myself, 'Why am I here?' Just to make money, which was no longer a good reason for me to go racing. So I retired again.

"But Mercedes persuaded me into doing DTM [the German touring car series] for a year, and that led to three years driving for Opel in DTM. I really did stop at the end of 1995, but by then I had started a racing team, which still runs two Audis in DTM today. Team Rosberg did seven years of single-seaters, too: my son Nico won the Formula BMW title in 2002, and did two seasons of F3. Out of that we started a suspension development and prototyping company in Germany, serving the road car industry."

Nico Rosberg's burgeoning F1 career is a source of delight to Keke, but he is no longer his son's manager. "I looked after him until late last year, when he signed his new Williams agreement. If a kid has his dad hovering around it's great for the dad, but terrible for the kid. He can't breathe, especially when dad has done it and knows everybody. Nico's grown up and found his own place, and it was time for Dad to go. But I still love going to the races, so I do F1 commentary for German TV."

Keke remains everything he was when he was in F1: uncomplicated, direct, aware of what he achieved, and yet modest and self-deprecating. Fame and money, when he finally got them, didn't change him. And he's still working hard. That, you feel, will never change.

Keke Rosberg was talking to Simon in May 2008.

ROY SALVADORI

Winning at every level, several
times a day

When I was first taken, as a small boy in the 1950s, to Goodwood, Silverstone and Castle Combe, Stirling Moss was of course the man we all wanted to see. But probably the second biggest draw in British motor racing, the darling of the crowds for his flamboyant speed and the ruthlessly determined way he drove to win, was Roy Salvadori. A typical national meeting would have separate races for F1, Formula 2, sports-racing cars big and small, saloons and *formule libre*. As likely as not the tall, debonair Englishman with the Italian name would be in all of them, in a variety of cars: invariably he would be challenging for the lead, and frequently he would be taking it.

Roy earned his living by racing other people's cars, and the combination of a strong work ethic and generous start, prize and bonus money meant that, by the standards of the day, he made a lot of money. But it also meant that he would usually opt for a busy British weekend with half a dozen races at two circuits, rather than an overseas Grand Prix that might offer international glory but less cash.

He invested his racing earnings shrewdly in his own motor businesses, ending up with both a BMW and an Alfa dealership, and when he sold out in 1971 he retired to Monte Carlo. So it's in his superb apartment on the start-finish straight of the Grand Prix circuit, overlooking the harbour, that his wife Sue serves us an excellent lunch. Sue, incidentally, must be the only girl in the world who is both the daughter of and the wife of a Le Mans winner: her father John Hindmarsh won for Lagonda in 1935.

Roy was born in Essex, of Italian parents, in 1922. In 1946 he went to look at an MG he'd seen advertised: he thought it was a sports car, but it turned out to be an R-type single-seater. He bought it anyway, took it to the first post-war British race meeting, at Gransden Lodge, and came second in his first race. "Maybe I should point out," he says modestly, "there were three starters and two finishers." The MG was followed by the ex-Dobbs Riley Special. He got it checked over by Monaco Motors of Watford and was horrified when the manager, one John Wyer, presented him with a bill for £15. But in those immediately post-war days old racing cars were cheap, and in 1947 he bravely bought, in half-shares with a friend, the ex-Nuvolari, ex-Kenneth Evans Alfa Romeo P3 Grand Prix car. "It scared both of us. The first race I did with it was Chimay, in Belgium, a very dangerous circuit, partly with a loose surface. The Alfa weaved all over the place, took up the entire width of the road. When you overtook another car you were never sure which side you'd pass it. Everything was very new to us: we didn't have any experience. The gearbox was playing up, so I did the whole race, start to finish, in top gear. I finished fifth. But it made a nice holiday."

A 14-year-old Maserati 4C followed, which Roy ran in the 1948 British GP at Silverstone, and in 1949 he campaigned a more modern 4CL Maserati which was prepared by Prince Bira's White Mouse Garage in Hammersmith. That car was destroyed in a fiery accident during the Wakefield Trophy in Ireland, and financial constraints kept Roy out of racing until 1951. By now competitive single-seaters were more expensive, so he bought a Le Mans Replica Frazer Nash.

"My first meeting with it was the May Silverstone in 1951. I was leading, a big thing for me then, ahead of Bob Gerard, Tony Crook and the other Frazer Nashes. So I was feeling pretty good about life. At Stowe we came up to lap a group of slower cars which were having their own battle. I tried to overtake them all, but it couldn't be done. I got on the loose stuff."

Thanks to a newsreel cameraman who happened to be on the spot, the horrifying accident that followed was later seen in cinemas up and down the country. The marker drums that delineated the airfield track were filled with concrete. The Nash hit them and cartwheeled into the air, over and over. Roy was half thrown out but caught his feet in the steering wheel and was flung around like a doll, with the car rolling over him. Among other injuries, he sustained a triple skull fracture and brain haemorrhaging.

"Crash helmets weren't mandatory then. I didn't wear one: they were expensive, and you saw the Italian stars like Farina in their leather caps, and you thought, that's the thing, that looks good. Anyway, at Northampton hospital they decided they could do nothing for me, and pushed me into a corner. They rang my parents, but told them I was unlikely to be alive by the time they got there. A priest was summoned and gave me the Last Rites.

"But I proved them wrong. I slowly recovered. My face was pretty bashed about, and I had a dreadful persistent ringing in my right ear. I've had to live with that ever since: I'm completely deaf on one side. In all my racing after that I could never really hear what the engine was doing. I just worked off the rev-counter and the gauges, and the vibration through the seat of my pants. I was never any good at Le Mans starts, because I couldn't hear the starter or when the engine caught. Once I brought my Aston into the pits complaining of a misfire, and when they opened the bonnet they found there was a rod out the side."

Three months after the Silverstone crash Roy was racing again, in an XK120, and during 1952 he raced that and the repaired Frazer Nash. The accident hadn't slowed him, but costs were mounting, and from then on he raced other people's cars. Wealthy Irishman Bobbie Baird offered Roy his Ferrari Tipo 500 for the 1952 British Grand Prix. This led to several more races in Baird's 2.7-litre sports Ferrari, which they shared in the

Goodwood Nine Hours. The rules said that no driver should do more than two hours without a break, so every two hours Baird was sent out to do one lap before Salvadori got in again. He got the Ferrari up among the works Jaguar C-types and Aston Martins, and then into the lead. A dead battery and a black flag for a faulty rear light dropped them to third by the end, but John Wyer, now Aston Martin's racing chief, was impressed.

"Bobbie Baird was such a nice chap. His father owned the *Belfast Telegraph*, a very big paper in those days. Bobbie had a drink problem, but they dried him out a couple of times, and the second time it worked. He married his nurse, Isobel. Then he bought a new 4.1 Ferrari, a terribly nasty car. In morning practice for a Snetterton meeting he turned it over. I was in the same session, so I stopped. He'd been thrown out, but he seemed to be all right, just winded. The marshals were looking after him, so I got back in my car and went back to the paddock. Then I heard he was dead: a broken rib had punctured a lung."

In 1953 Roy signed for Connaught in F1 and F2 events, and Aston Martin in major sports car races. When these commitments allowed he also drove for Ecurie Ecosse in its C-type Jaguars, and for Syd Greene in the Gilby Engineering 2-litre Maserati A6GCS. Syd was a tremendous enthusiast who was prevented from racing because he'd lost an arm in an accident. His teenage son Keith was as keen as he was, and went on to a life-long career in racing, first as a driver and then as a brilliant team manager. In 1954 Gilby added an F1 Maserati to the stable, and the green 250F was Roy's main mount in single-seater races for three seasons. Much of the money for the Maserati's purchase came from Esso, which also paid Roy a £10,000 a year retainer to remain loyal to its fuels and oils. A typically busy day was the June Snetterton in 1954, when Roy ran the two Maseratis and a C-type in six races and scored four wins, a second and a third.

"Sometimes I raced four or even five cars in one meeting. Some had left-hand changes, some right-hand changes. The

250F had a central throttle pedal. Torque curves, rev ranges, braking points, gearchange points, they were all different. I'd try not to talk to anyone between jumping out of one car and into another, to keep my concentration, but basically it was instinctive. I don't know how I did it, really.

"I'd clear about £27,000 in a good year, which was a lot of money in those days. I had a simple deal with Syd Greene: the mechanics got 10 per cent of all start and prize money, and we split the rest 45/45. But Esso would pay a big bonus for a win, because they liked to use it in their press advertising. Second place was no good to them, so it really mattered if you won. But at Aston Martin John Wyer would pool the start and prize money and split it equally between the drivers, so we all got the same amount whether we won, or finished fourth, or retired.

"I did have a reputation as a hard driver with certain people. I wouldn't be hard with most of my team-mates, but there were some tough drivers about, and you just had to hit back. If you were being deliberately baulked, you had to let them know you were quite prepared to put your car where there might be a shunt. If you did that often enough they'd respect you."

A memorable confrontation was Roy's tussle with Ken Wharton's V16 BRM at the 1954 Easter Monday Goodwood. The BRM was chucking out oil and fuel, and Roy in the Gilby 250F was being badly held up, but he couldn't get past. Getting angrier and angrier, he tried to force his way past at Lavant Corner. "Ken was a hard driver too, and he wasn't going to let me through. We collided, and we both spun. We both restarted, but my clutch exploded a lap later, bits of shrapnel came out through the bodywork, and Ken won the race. We didn't have a nasty scene afterwards or anything like that. We just didn't talk to each other – which in the friendly atmosphere of motor racing then meant just as much, really. Later the Duke of Richmond & Gordon sent me a silver cigarette box and on it was engraved 'In acknowledgement of a splendid show at Goodwood'. So I thought, well, he realises I was robbed of that race – until I found out he'd sent exactly the same box, with the same inscription, to Wharton!"

A stand-out Ecurie Ecosse drive came in the 1953 Nürburgring 1000Kms. Roy did the first stint, with the C-type not particularly happy over the bumps, but soon after his co-driver Ian Stewart took over he came in to say the car was handling so badly that it should be retired. Roy got in again and drove to the end. "It was completely falling to pieces. Every 14-mile lap I'd come round thinking, I'll stop this time, but then as I approached the pits I'd say to myself, I'll just try one more lap. I wouldn't say I liked the Nürburgring. I respected it. You'd look forward to a race there, and once you got there you'd wonder why you'd been looking forward to it. Anyway, we finished second, and then as Wilkie Wilkinson of Ecurie Ecosse was taking the C back to the paddock the front suspension collapsed. The fuel tank had come adrift, too, and was only being held in place by the body."

Roy's contract with Aston Martin, having started in 1953, endured more than a decade. He had a great relationship with the often terrifying John Wyer. "He was marvellous. You really wanted to do well for him. He was very methodical, kept detailed notes of every race, with extremely frank comments about the performance and behaviour of every driver. It was a wonderful team – drivers like George Abecassis, Peter Collins, Reg Parnell. We used to party pretty hard. I can't believe what hooligans we were. At one hotel a sofa got pushed through a plate glass window and the police were called. Fortunately the copper who interviewed me didn't seem to know much about motor racing, so I gave my name as M. Hawthorn of Farnham. Parnell was the instigator of a lot of it. He was bloody quick, too, such an under-rated driver – he could sort out most of the Aston team. George was great company. He used to say, 'When I crash an Aston Martin, I get a bollocking from Wyer. In the war, when I crashed my aeroplane, I got a medal.' You can never replace these people.

"At Le Mans in 1955 the rule was that, whatever order the Astons were in at the end of the first lap, we should stay like that, so we didn't race each other and wear our cars out. Well, Peter Collins and I had the most terrific dice, swapping places all round the circuit, and then when we approached the pits we would sort ourselves into the right order so it looked like we were behaving ourselves. On one lap I was trying so hard I spun at Arnage, and Peter waited for me while I got going again, roaring with laughter. Peter was such a nice chap.

"The sports car race at the 1956 May Silverstone was a bit of a story. There were four DB3S Astons for Stirling, Peter, Reg and me. There were six D-types, including Mike Hawthorn and Des Titterington. My DB3S was actually my own car, which I'd bought from the works on the basis that they could borrow it back when they wanted. Des and I made joint fastest practice time. Stirling's contract gave him the pick of the cars, but when he asked John Wyer to try mine John pointed out that he would have to ask me, as it was my car. Well, he didn't ask me: if he had I'd have let him have it. But he asked me to try his car in practice, and I told him I preferred it with the 6.50 tyres – he'd opted for the 6.00s. He was changing down for Stowe, and I was taking it in top. The downside of that was that unless you got it right you'd be understeering off the circuit, whereas in third you'd be right in the power band and you could just floor it to get some pull from the back.

"Stirling led away from the Le Mans start, but I screwed myself up and went by on the inside under braking for Stowe, and unfortunately I pulled two works D-types through with me. Then at the next corner, Club, a D-type came nosing up the inside. I assumed it was Mike, so I moved to the right, so he would have to go round on the outside. I knew Mike would know the score, he'd know Salvadori wasn't going to let him through on the bloody inside. But he kept coming and I thought, 'Oi, Hawthorn, you're making this a bit dangerous.' What I didn't realise was that it wasn't Mike, it was Titterington. Then the Jaguar spun in a cloud of rubber smoke, and Collins and Parnell in our Astons and an Ecosse D-type crashed into him. It was a four-car pile-up."

Salvadori went on to win from an aggrieved Moss, and there was an enquiry afterwards, as some felt that Salvadori had squeezed Titterington at Club. "The only verdict they reached was that we should all be more careful on the first lap. Well, it's no bloody good telling a racing driver that, is it?" But Roy took no part in the enquiry because, having also won the small sports car race earlier in the day in a works Bobtail Cooper, he was once more in Northampton hospital. Fighting for second place with Archie Scott-Brown's Connaught in the Formula 1 race, the Gilby 250F had broken a driveshaft, locking up the rear wheels, and the car hit the bank at Stowe and overturned.

The high point of Roy's Aston Martin career was of course the 1959 Le Mans 24 Hours. "I didn't really like Le Mans, but I loved the week we'd have there, staying at Aston's hotel at La Chartre. In 1958 I'd been partnered with Stuart Lewis-Evans, who was probably seven inches shorter than me, but for 1959 I was with Carroll Shelby. We were the same height, so we could make ourselves comfortable in the car. But Carroll was suffering from a stomach bug, so I drove for 14 of the 24 hours. We were in the lead by 10pm, but four hours later the car developed a dreadful rear-end vibration. I stopped at the pits but they could find nothing wrong, so I continued, but it got worse and the car was bouncing all over the road. I went slower and slower. I thought it was probably transmission, which was always the DBR1's weak point. When I came in for my fuel stop they discovered that the offside rear tyre had lost part of its tread. We'd now lost the lead to the P Hill/ Gendebien Ferrari, and I had a terrific row with Reg Parnell, who said, 'You silly bugger, why didn't you realise it was the tyre?' That upset me and I must have said something, because there was a very tense atmosphere in the pit until John Wyer calmed us all down.

"The Ferrari was now three laps ahead, and we needed to make up the lost ground. What you have to do if you want to drive as fast as possible at Le Mans is stick rigidly to the rev limits and not make any duff gear changes, but be absolutely flat out as far as braking and cornering are concerned. That's because brakes and tyres can be replaced, but the engine and gearbox can't. If you look at the lap times, even while we were saving the mechanicals, you'll see we were going like hell. We whittled away, kept the pressure on, and then at 11am on Sunday the Ferrari blew its engine."

After 10 years of trying, Aston Martin had won Le Mans. If it could win the Tourist Trophy at Goodwood, it could take the World Sports Car Championship from Ferrari. Roy was paired with Stirling Moss for this race: Stirling led from the start, Roy consolidated that lead during his stint, and when he brought the DBR1 in to hand back to Stirling they were three minutes ahead of the sister car of Carroll Shelby and Jack Fairman. "I made sure I'd left the car in first gear for Stirling, and then as I was about to get out of the car I felt wet on my back. The fuel was coming out of the hose before the mechanic had got the filler cap open. Then we were on fire. I leapt down the bonnet, kicking the mechanic who was changing the front wheel on the head, and rolled over and over on the little strip of grass between the pitlane and the track. Then an ambulance man wrapped me in his coat and got the flames out." Stirling took over the Shelby/Fairman car, drove it for the rest of the race and won. His burns bandaged, Roy watched from the pits as Aston took the title.

He began the 1957 F1 season with a BRM contract. "Raymond Mays could really lead you up the garden path. He was very charming when he wanted to be, made you believe he could make you World Champion. Because BRM had had a lot of braking problems, I specifically agreed with Ray that only Lockheed should be allowed to develop and modify the brakes. First time out at Goodwood I spun in practice when a brake locked. Then on the warm-up lap they all locked on. It happened again on the first lap of the race. The marshals couldn't push the car and had to heave it off the track. Ray promised me Lockheed would be summoned to sort out the brakes before the next outing, which was Monaco. In qualifying there the brakes were still jamming on and I failed to qualify. At the hotel I bumped into the Lockheed rep, who said BRM had made their own modifications to the braking system and had not involved Lockheed. I found Raymond Mays, told him what I thought about it, and left the team forthwith."

He had a couple of Vanwall drives at Rouen and Reims, and then concentrated on his rides with Cooper, which was doing more and more F1 events with 1500 and 2-litre Climax power. He and Jack Brabham made a good team, and in 1958 Roy's little 2.2 Cooper was second in the German GP, third in the British GP and fourth in the Dutch. Any pleasure he might have felt from the second place at the 'Ring, his best-ever Grand Prix finish, was wiped away by the death of his friend and former team-mate Peter Collins; but that season he was fourth in the World Championship behind Hawthorn, Moss and Brooks. "In the Cooper team old Charlie Cooper kept it all together. He was the businessman, the disciplinarian, and he always told John what to do. When we got back from a race on Monday, Charlie would ask John to hand over the start money, then he'd go through John's pockets to see if he'd kept any back."

Aston Martin was now developing its DBR4 Grand Prix car, and Parnell approached Roy and Jack Brabham to drive it. They agreed verbally, but then Coventry Climax told Cooper that it was preparing a full 2.5-litre engine for the new season, and John Cooper tried to get Jack and Roy to stay. Jack agreed, and of course went on to be 1959 World Champion. Roy, having given his word to his old friends at Aston Martin, stood by his verbal agreement.

But the nimble little rear-engined Cooper made the Aston out of date almost before it appeared. Apart from second place in its first outing at the 1959 May Silverstone, the DBR4 was never competitive. Nor was its 1960 replacement, the lighter, all-independent DBR5. In 1961 Roy drove for the Yeoman Credit team of F1 Coopers, and in 1962 for the Bowmaker-backed Lola team alongside John Surtees, which produced a string of retirements. But he was as busy as ever in British racing. At Crystal Palace he raced four cars in four races – Yeoman Credit Cooper and E-type, Cooper Monaco and Jaguar 3.8 for Coombs – and won all four. Then at Oulton, in the 3.8, a tyre burst at Cascades and he went upside down into the lake.

"When I undid my seat harness I was floating inside the car. My chest was exploding and I started to swallow water. I thought, what a way for a racing driver to die, by drowning. I was trapped until a marshal got one of the back doors open and pulled me out." Soaked and black with mud, he was given a lift back to the pits by 3.8 rival Graham Hill, put on some clean overalls and went out to practise the F1 Lola for the Gold Cup. He qualified on the third row, but a broken throttle cable put him out of the race.

"When we raced at Oulton Park we used to stay at the Chester Country Club. You never booked in those days: you just arrived. One year [private entrant] Tommy Atkins told me I had to behave myself and get a decent night's sleep before the race. So I took a single room and went to bed early. I'd just got to sleep when there was a knock on the door, and the hotel manager said, 'I've got a young lady here who says she does your timing, can she sleep on your floor?' In she came, and I'd just got off to sleep again when there was another knock. It was Jim Clark, complete with girlfriend, with nowhere to sleep. They squeezed in, too. I got no more sleep that night because Jimmy snored.

"Another time we were having a bit of a party and I counted 41 people in one hotel bedroom. The lady in the next-door room was knocking on the wall saying, 'My husband's a racing driver, he needs to sleep. If you don't quieten down I'll send him in to sort you out.' After a while there was a knock on the door and

Graham Hill came in, very pompous, but in no time at all he was having a beer. In the end a tearful Bette came in and asked him to come back to bed."

Having driven privately-entered DBR1s at Le Mans in '60 and '61 – he finished third in 1960 with Jim Clark – Roy was offered Briggs Cunningham's Tipo 151 Maserati for the 24 Hours in 1962. But he couldn't squeeze his tall frame into the Maserati's coupé body, so he shared Briggs' E-type instead, and they finished fourth overall and won their class. In 1963 he was in a Cunningham E-type again.

"On Saturday evening I was going through the Mulsanne kink, which was just about flat in the E – you had to feather the throttle just a bit – and suddenly I felt the car sliding. Oil." Bruce McLaren's Aston Martin had blown its engine comprehensively moments before. "Several people had already gone off, so I was a late comer, so to speak. There were cars up the bank and in the trees. An Alpine was on fire on the other side of the track – that was a Brazilian called Bino Heinz, he was burned to death. I hit the bank with a huge impact, and somehow I was shot out through the E-type's back window onto the road. I was lying on the tarmac and there was another driver nearby, unconscious [Jean-Pierre Manzon, whose René Bonnet had also gone off]. I was drenched in fuel because the tank had ruptured, and I remember the E-type's horn going off, this weird sound, and then it all flared up. I was lying in the road soaked in petrol, my car was burning and the flames were coming along the trail of petrol towards me. But I literally couldn't move. Finally I stretched my hands out, managed to get my fingernails into the grass verge and pulled myself up this little earth mound. That's all I remember. In the early hours Sue came to the hospital and sneaked me out, drove me home to England."

Through the early 1960s the hectic British racing schedule continued in cars as diverse as Ferrari 250LM, Cooper-Maserati and AC Cobra. His last works Aston Martin drive came with the team's swansong in the Coppa Inter-Europa at Monza.

Roy's Project 214 Aston battled wheel-to-wheel throughout the three-hour race with Mike Parkes' Ferrari GTO until, in the closing laps, Roy outfumbled Mike among the backmarkers and won what Wyer regarded as the finest victory of his career. Wyer then left Aston for the Ford GT40 programme, and asked Roy to be involved in its development. "The early GT40 was a big disappointment. There was something peculiar about it: it wasn't a nice car, and I had no confidence in it," says Roy. "We eventually discovered the aerodynamics were all wrong, and the back wheels were coming off the ground. I reeled off all my complaints to John Wyer, and he sighed heavily and said, 'Anything else, Salvadori?' I said, 'You don't believe me, do you? I'll give you a demonstration.' So I took him round MIRA, and I showed him how the doors were lifting so much at 150mph that I could put my hand through the gap. He said hastily, 'Put your hands on the wheel, Salvadori, drive the thing.' I said, 'Look at the bloody bodywork, it's swelling.' Then there was this explosion and the front bodywork disintegrated, all there was left were shreds of fibreglass and the remains of the wire fixings. But I did drive a GT40 in my last race, at Goodwood in 1965. I finished second to a CanAm McLaren, and won the GT category."

In 1965 the Chipstead Group, with which Roy was involved, bought Cooper, and he found himself racing manager of the Cooper F1 team. It was the twilight of the team's F1 days, but they had young lion Jochen Rindt, and when John Surtees fell out with Ferrari in the middle of the 1966 season they had him, too.

"We managed to get on with John Surtees, which was an achievement in itself. He was so angry with Ferrari, so determined, that he went well for us. So did Jochen, so did Pedro Rodríguez. Some of Jochen's races with the car were fabulous. But John Cooper couldn't bear it that we were paying Rindt £50,000. He didn't understand that by having Jochen, who was a brilliant driver and a rising star, we were much more attractive to sponsors. We weren't paying the money, the sponsors were. If we'd run an unknown driver we wouldn't have got that backing."

Talking to Roy evokes an era of motor racing that has disappeared: the friendships, the rivalries, the parties, the accidents. Roy himself is surprised that he's still here to tell the tales.

"I never reckoned I'd be around to retire. I was sure it was all going to come to an end with a big accident. All of us used to think that. We wouldn't have been human if we didn't. I'd given myself a span, I thought I knew exactly when I was going to buy it. I just hoped my accident was going to be a big one so I didn't have to linger. You knew it was bloody dangerous, but you didn't want to stop.

"Anyone who can come back from a painful accident and still be as fast as he was before must either be brave or thick. I suppose in my case it was a bit of each."

Roy Salvadori was talking to Simon in November 2007.

JODY SCHECKTER

The Formula 1 approach to
organic farming

If you're a top Formula 1 driver, you are a driven man. As well as all those skills and physical attributes, you are motivated by abnormally high levels of determination, self-confidence, persistence and stubbornness. Putting yourself under pressure and exposing yourself to risk is part of your daily life. But when the time comes for you to leave the cockpit, what then?

Former racers cope with life after F1 in different ways. Money is usually not a problem, so there's rarely an economic requirement to do a conventional job of work. Some find it impossible to break their addiction to the circus that has dominated every second of their life for a decade or more, so they parlay their knowledge and reputation into a role on the other side of the pitwall – with varying degrees of success, because history has shown that the egotistical qualities of a driver do not always sit easily with building and managing a team. Some remain involved in motor racing as TV commentators, or as club officials, or as consultants of one sort or another. Some invest in other people's businesses outside the sport, which may make them richer and may make them poorer. Some do nothing much at all, apart from enjoying their wealth, and telling anyone who will listen that motor racing isn't as good as it was in their day.

Jody Scheckter is different. As a racing driver it took him just 12 years to go from a teenager hammering an old Renault saloon around the local tracks of his native South Africa to World Champion for Ferrari. Then, without regret, he turned his back on racing and started a new business from scratch in the USA, developing weapon training systems for law enforcement and the military. While he was building up Firearms Training Systems Inc, almost nobody he dealt with knew anything about his past as a racing driver: and Jody was happy with that, for his previous life no longer concerned him. With single-minded enterprise and ceaseless hard work he built a company worth hundreds of millions of dollars. Then, at the end of another 12-year cycle, he sold the company and came to England. At the age of 46 he was now a very rich man, but there was no question of opting for an easy life. The racing driver's determination, stubbornness and the rest of it were still a crucial part of his make-up. A few years before, his second wife Clare had given him a book about organic farming, and that pointed him towards his third career. He immersed himself in the subject, researched it in endless detail, and then bought Laverstoke Park, a 2500-acre estate in Hampshire. He then set about developing his purchase into a showpiece farm, which has won international awards and been called the University of Organics.

"It's a passion which has become an obsession," says Jody ruefully as his farm runabout – a Mercedes GL 4x4 – takes us on a rapid cross-country tour of his huge operation. "The key is bio-diversity, and following nature. Modern farming is chasing profit, and the animals are bred to grow bigger faster. We're going in the opposite direction. We go for smaller and slower, because it tastes better. There are only 45 pure uncrossed Angus cattle left in the world, and we've got 13 of them here. There are probably 500 pure-bred Herefords left in the world, and we've got 80. We have 1000 head of buffalo, which is most of the UK population. Our sheep, our chickens, all are feeding totally naturally. I employ a full-time Doctor of Microbiology working in our own laboratory here, which is the only one of its type in Europe, so we can get the soils and the grasses, herbs and clovers back to how they used to be. We hired the world's top animal psychologist to help us design our abattoir, so there is no stress on the animal when we kill it. We purify our own water – no chlorine, no fluoride – and within two years we want to be running all the farm machinery on non-fossil fuels, like rape seed oil. We want to be totally self-sustaining."

He shows me his recently planted vineyard, 28 miles of vines within 45 hectares, which will produce champagne. He also has 130 organic acres on another site 40 miles away producing fruit and vegetables, with three acres of glasshouses. He supplies meat, vegetables and salads to the very best restaurants, like Le Manoir aux Quat' Saisons and the Fat Duck; in the more affordable world Waitrose is now stocking his buffalo burgers and buffalo milk. Other plants on the estate are making salamis and cured meats, organic ice cream, and buffalo cheese. As we drive round, Jody dictates messages to himself on his BlackBerry as new ideas occur to him. This is still a driven man, bringing the same determination to perfecting his soil as to a perfect lap of Monza in a Ferrari 312T4.

Bordering the estate is Laverstoke Park itself, a pillared 18th-century stately home standing in rolling, manicured parkland, with the River Test running through the grounds. Here I find that Jody has not entirely closed his mind to his first career: there is no evidence of his racing days in the house, where the walls are hung with modern art, but lined up in one section of the immaculate stable block, gleaming on polished tile flooring, is almost every single-seater he ever raced, from his Formula Ford Merlyn to his World Championship-winning Ferrari T4. His Can-Am Porsche 917 is away being restored, but here are his F2 McLaren, his McLaren M23, the original Wolf; only the P34 Tyrrell is missing.

Our lunch in the lofty dining room, with floor-to-ceiling windows overlooking the park, naturally consists entirely of Laverstoke produce: a green salad, roast lamb with parsnip and beetroot all tasting as they used to when I was a child, and apple crumble with custard made from buffalo milk. Over the meal Jody allows his mind to slow down for a while, and looks back over those 12 years of racing.

"In my early days I was very wild. I only did a little bit of karting and a couple of 50cc bike races, but when I was 18 and apprenticed at my dad's garage in the Eastern Cape I got my hands on a beat-up old Renault R8. I had no money, but I scrounged the bits and pieces I needed to prepare it for racing. The rules said I had to have a rollcage, so I bent one up out of exhaust tubing. I didn't think about the safety aspect. I locked the diff, which meant I got a reputation for going sideways – got black-flagged for it in my first national race, because they thought I was driving dangerously. We'd take it on a borrowed trailer 1200 miles to Rhodesia and back for a race, do the trip in 20 hours non-stop. I was doing my National Service in the middle of this, so I'd get leave to go racing, and get my cousin, who was a dentist, to give me a doctor's certificate for the Monday if I needed to mend the car after the weekend. Then I supercharged it, which made it rather a handful, because it still had standard brakes and cut-down road springs.

"But it got me noticed, because I got a ride in a Mazda in the Springbok Series and won my class in the Kyalami Nine Hours. Then Ford offered me a loan car, a Lola, for the five-race Formula Ford Sunshine Series. A lot of European drivers came over for it, but I finished third in the series. The prize for the best-placed local driver was a ticket to Europe, and I won that. I'd just had my 21st birthday.

"So in March 1971 I arrived in England. It was just before the big Race of Champions meeting at Brands, and I needed an FF car. Colin Vandervell was selling his Merlyn, the one Emerson Fittipaldi had used in 1969, and Vandervell had won everything with it in 1970. I didn't have a workshop, I didn't even have any spanners, so Colin delivered it to Brands and I bought it. It was a wet weekend and I'd never driven a single-seater in the wet, but I put it on pole and led the race. Two laps from the end I got over-excited and spun at Bottom Bend. But I came back to

Jo Ramirez spent his working life in motor racing as mechanic, engineer, team manager, and friend and confidant to many drivers. (James Mitchell)

Ramirez and the rest of the McLaren team celebrate Alain Prost's first victory for McLaren in Rio de Janeiro in 1984. (sutton-images.com)

Brian Redman with film star Steve McQueen during filming of McQueen's movie Le Mans *in 1970.* (LAT)

Redman's glittering sports car career included two years as a works Ferrari driver – here at the Nürburgring in 1972 with the 312PB. (LAT)

Keke Rosberg went from zero to hero when he left the also-ran Fittipaldi team for Williams in 1982, and won the World Championship. (LAT)

Probably the toughest win of Rosberg's career came amid the concrete barriers and stifling heat of the 1984 US Grand Prix in Dallas. (LAT)

After a long and fruitful racing career, Roy Salvadori became team manager of the Cooper F1 team. Jochen Rindt started his F1 career under his guidance in 1965. (LAT)

Salvadori raced, and won, in every type of car from Formula 1 downwards. Here he leads Graham Hill in a typical Jaguar 3.8 battle at Silverstone in 1962. (LAT)

Jody Scheckter spent his last two F1 seasons with Ferrari, winning the World Championship in 1979. (LAT)

Scheckter gave the distinctive six-wheel Tyrrell P34 its only victory in the 1976 Swedish Grand Prix at Anderstorp. (LAT)

The son of a famous pre-war racer, Hans Stuck enjoyed a racing career that lasted for more than 40 years. (LAT)

Brands Hatch, 1977: Stuck's BMW 320i turbo leads away from the start in pouring rain. His premature retirement after an accident earned him and co-driver Ronnie Peterson the wrath of BMW. (LAT)

Professor Sid Watkins revolutionised medical facilities in Formula 1, earning the respect and affection of everyone in the sport. (James Mitchell)

Prof Watkins at work, as he and his crew tend to Takuma Sato after the Japanese driver crashed his Jordan in the 2002 Austrian Grand Prix. (sutton-images.com)

Tom Wheatcroft's towering enthusiasm for motor racing drove him to be a circuit owner and an F1 entrant, and to build up a superb museum collection. (James Mitchell)

Wheatcroft counted the day of the 1993 European Grand Prix on his own Donington circuit as the best day of his life. Here he congratulates winner Ayrton Senna on the podium. (sutton-images.com)

finish second, half a second behind the winner. That was what got me up the ladder so quickly – not so much because I was fast, but because I was spectacular.

"Later in my career that became more a negative than a positive. I could usually drive around a problem, so a car's set-up didn't make much difference to me. If it was understeering I'd throw it around, if it was oversteering I coped with that. I don't know whether my car control was natural ability, or if the Renault with its locked diff had something to do with it. But other drivers were better than me at sorting out a car in practice, so they'd have an easier time in the race. Also my short-term memory wasn't great: I wasn't good at passing on exact details of car behaviour. Other drivers, the Alain Prosts of this world, could sort a car out better than me.

"That first year in FF I got a job at Merlyn: they let me cut and weld up brackets. There was an F3 chassis sitting around which had been built for a French customer who'd run out of money. So I got Merlyn to lend it to me, and I went to Holbay and persuaded them to lend me an engine. Firestone South Africa gave me some tyres, and I went F3 for the second half of the season. I won at Mallory and Oulton and Thruxton, I think. There were some shunts too, like at Crystal Palace when Dave Walker, Colin Vandervell and I were three abreast fighting for the lead and our wheels got tangled, and we all went off. At Mallory Roger Williamson and I went into Devil's Elbow together: he went off and I won. He was the local hero there, so words were exchanged afterwards. The Escort Mexico championship was running for the first time that year, too, and Ford put me in a car. That was fun. One meeting my car blew up in practice, or I crashed it, one or the other, and so I went to the pub. I'd just downed my first pint when another of the Mexico drivers offered me his car. It's the only time I've gone racing after a drink.

"Both Surtees and McLaren got in touch offering me Formula 2 for 1972. I wasn't sure about possible personality clashes at

Surtees, so I chose McLaren. Phil Kerr was in charge there, and Teddy Mayer and Tyler Alexander. It was just a one-car F2 operation, and at first we had serious handling problems with the car [the Ralph Bellamy-designed M21]. It had this mighty twitch when you got near the limit. In F2 you raced against current Formula 1 drivers, and at first I wasn't competitive at all. It was depressing. Finally they found the rear shock absorbers were imbalanced, and once that was sorted, bang, I was competitive. I won Crystal Palace and went well at Rouen, and for the first time I started to think I could make it in F1.

"I also did some testing for McLaren, and I remember going to Goodwood with one of the turbo McLaren-Offy Indianapolis cars. They'd just finished putting it together and hadn't put the rear wing on it yet, but they wanted me to do a few shakedown laps to make sure it ran OK. So their F2 wild guy gets in, and once I got it on the straight I put my foot down, the turbo came in, and it just spun around and went straight into the bank. Very embarrassing. I had to buy the lads at the factory a lot of beer after that.

"Things came to a head when Lotus offered me an F1 ride in their second car for the last five races of the season [intending to replace the struggling Dave Walker]. McLaren wouldn't let me do it, but it put some pressure on them, so they agreed to run a third M19 alongside Denny Hulme and Peter Revson for the last round of 1972 at Watkins Glen."

It was barely 18 months since that first Formula Ford race at Brands, and it was a remarkable F1 debut. Jody qualified on the third row ahead of newly crowned World Champion Emerson Fittipaldi, and at the start he shot into third place. At half distance he was still fourth behind Stewart, Cevert and Hulme when a sudden shower of rain blew across the circuit. Jody was the first to drive into it and spun into the dirt. It took two laps for him to restart, but he brought the car home ninth, and his best lap was the second quickest of the race, a fifth of a second slower than Stewart.

But the 1973 season dawned unpromisingly. The McLaren Formula 2 programme was no more, and Phil Kerr told Jody that, with Hulme and Revson still under contract, there would only be occasional F1 drives. One of them was at Kyalami, where the organisers offered good start money for the local boy. He qualified his last year's M19 on the front row and led the race briefly, running second to Jackie Stewart for 27 laps, and holding a strong fourth until, with four laps to go, his engine failed. In July Revson was committed to the Pocono USAC race, so Jody was in an M23 for the French GP. He qualified second-fastest, starting between World Champions Stewart and Fittipaldi on the front row – this was still only his third F1 Grand Prix, remember – and led the race from the start until, with 12 laps to go, Fittipaldi tried a move on him as they were lapping Beltoise's BRM. Jody kept the door firmly shut, Fittipaldi ended up in the guardrail, and Jody was out with a broken wishbone.

"Fittipaldi came to find me in the pits and delivered a heated monologue at me about newcomers not holding up the World Champion. He went on and on, and when he got to the end I pointed out that he'd had 42 laps to get past me, and if we found ourselves in the same situation in the future I'd do exactly the same again.

"I'd gone pretty well in my first three Grands Prix, but unfortunately what happened in the fourth rather wiped everybody's memory of what had gone before. This was the famous Silverstone shunt. After the morning warm-up we decided to put a harder left rear on the car, because Silverstone is mainly right-handers and I was sliding a lot. So that tyre was unscrubbed. At the end of the first lap I was fourth, right behind Denny, and coming into Woodcote I passed him on the outside. I thought, now I can really get going. And that's when it swapped ends on me. I went across the grass on the outside, went across the road and slid along the pitwall, then bounced back into the middle of the track. I looked up and cars were crashing all around me, crashing before they hit me. I ducked down in the cockpit and when it went quiet I looked up again, and there was another wave of cars crashing, so I ducked down again. Then I jumped out, went over the pitwall, and Phil Kerr grabbed me and said, 'Go into the motorhome, hide away and don't come out.' Everybody was looking for me. All three of John Surtees' cars were written off, so he wanted to find me and kill me. I'd taken nine cars out in all.

"I escaped from Silverstone and flew to New York, because I was due at Watkins Glen for the Can-Am round. First I had to do a press conference in New York, and just as I was thinking, thank goodness I'm out of England, the first thing the guy asked me was, 'Tell us how you broke all those cars in England.'

"With no full-time F1 drive I'd lined up F2 with Rondel, but after two races I pulled out of that. Ron Dennis was trying to run five cars – three for Frenchmen because of the Motul sponsorship, and two for Tim Schenken and me – and I didn't think it was going to work. So I signed up to do F5000 in America with Sid Taylor in a Trojan, and the Can-Am Series with Vasek Polak's Porsche 917 turbo. Sid's car turned up at each round of the L&M Series on a trailer towed by a tired old truck, when everybody else had smart transporters and motorhomes. But I won the series, after a season-long battle with Brian Redman. As for the 917, it had 1100 horsepower – some of the time – but it didn't have any brakes, because the pads used to glaze after two laps. On the uphill right-hander at Road Atlanta people were saying, 'Jeez, Scheckter brakes late.' In fact I was braking early, but the car wasn't slowing and I was flying past everybody. I did 19 American races between May and October, and I sat on a lot of aeroplanes."

Although Jody's three-year contract with McLaren had a year to run, the team still couldn't offer him a full F1 season for 1974. "It was a political thing with the main sponsor: there was still apartheid in South Africa then, and they didn't want a South African driver. But I did the last two 1973 rounds,

Mosport and Watkins Glen, and I'd had approaches from several teams. I talked to Ken Tyrrell at Watkins Glen, in the motel after Friday practice. He made me an offer, we agreed in about three minutes flat, and shook hands. It was a big secret that Jackie Stewart was going to retire, but I knew I was going to be partnered with François Cevert. That was the team for 1974.

"Next day, 10 minutes before the end of morning practice, as I accelerated out of the pits Cevert came past. When I got to the Esses the front of his car was in the middle of the track. The rest of it was in the guardrail on the left, sort of wrapped over it. I stopped and jumped out of my car and ran over to him, because fire was a big thing then, so it was an automatic reaction. I got to the battery and I remember it was sparking like anything, so I went to grab his seat belt buckle. And immediately I turned around and walked away. I'll never know what I saw in that cockpit; to this day I don't remember because it's just blanked out in my mind. Other drivers had pulled up and were running over, and I stopped them and said, 'No. It's finished.'

"He was the first person I'd known who had died. I couldn't believe that a guy had died and everybody just carried on, like nothing had happened – not so much the F1 guys, and of course Tyrrell withdrew from the race, but everybody else. Suddenly it came home to me, hey, this is dangerous." In the race, his last for McLaren, Jody was running fifth ahead of Fittipaldi and Revson when a wishbone broke. It gave him a spectacular moment but no further damage.

Jody spent three seasons at Tyrrell, with Patrick Depailler as team-mate. "Everybody says Ken got hold of me and calmed me down, but I think I'd learned by then that you're not going to win a championship by crashing. Ken was a great guy, and we had a good relationship, but what made it difficult – and I didn't realise it at the time – was that I wasn't Jackie Stewart. Jackie had won everything and they'd say, Jackie would do this or Jackie would do that, but I was me, I wasn't the same as Jackie. The first year with Ken was great, and we finished third in the championship, but it deteriorated from there. I found them very old-fashioned from a technical point of view after what I'd seen at McLaren. The 006, the car Jackie drove in his last year, I couldn't get on with it at all. It didn't seem to have any grip. I was sliding the car around and Ken said, 'You've got to drive it more delicately.' But I was slower like that, so I went back to how I was driving it before. Then we got the 007, and that was a good car. After Monza I was fighting for the title, one point behind Regazzoni and two ahead of Fittipaldi. But at Mosport the brakes failed and I hit the wall, and at Watkins Glen a fuel line broke, so we ended up third."

In 1975 Jody won his home Grand Prix at Kyalami in the spare 007, having crashed heavily in practice, but that was the high point in a difficult year. In 1976 the Tyrrell team astonished the world by introducing Derek Gardner's revolutionary six-wheeler: but Jody's enthusiasm for the P34 was muted. "I just didn't believe in it, I didn't believe in the theory, and the tests we did with it were wrong. Testing at Paul Ricard they ran with a narrower rear track, so of course it was faster down the long straight. The braking was supposed to be better: well, it was when you were braking in a straight line, but as soon as you turned in, the little wheels slid and you had to come off the pedal, so there was no advantage there. And it broke all the time."

But history shows the P34 was much better than that. Jody did 12 GPs with it, and only retired twice: the shunt in Austria, when a wishbone broke and the car turned sharp right into the barriers on a 160mph curve; and Japan, when the engine overheated. He was in the points at every other race. He scored the six-wheeler's only victory in Sweden, and was second at Monte Carlo, Brands Hatch, the Nürburgring and Watkins Glen, and took third in the World Championship behind the battling James Hunt and Niki Lauda.

"Yes, I suppose I got more results with the six-wheeler than I'd remembered. And you could do anything with it: it reacted like a car with a very short wheelbase, you could slide and correct it. But there were breakages. At Anderstorp, where I won, a front wheel flew off in practice. We had a little window in the cockpit sides, otherwise we wouldn't have been able to see what the front wheels were doing. I drove into the pits on five wheels and Derek Gardner put his head down into the cockpit and said, 'What's up?' I said, 'I think I've got a bit of understeer.'

"Patrick Depailler was great, but mad. He got arrested driving to the French GP at Dijon, flat out down the wrong side of the road. Ken had to get him out of jail so he could start the race. He was very French. I remember saying to him, 'Patrick, that corner, what are you doing there?' And he'd say: 'It ees quite flat.' I'd think, shit, he's taking that flat? I'm lifting off there, no way can I do it flat. It was about halfway through the season before I realised he was talking French English – to him, '*Quite* flat' meant *not* quite flat.

"At the end of 1976 I felt I had to leave Tyrrell. There weren't a lot of options, but Walter Wolf came along talking very big, said he was going to conquer the world. In fact he only delivered 80 per cent of what he promised, but that was still more than anybody else was offering. So I said, 'OK, I'll come, but I want some people to come with me.' He agreed to it all. I took Roy Topp, my mechanic at Tyrrell, and I got Peter Warr as team manager, because he had a winning record at Lotus."

Harvey Postlethwaite was carried over from the previous season's unsuccessful Williams/Wolf relationship and designed a neat, elegant and very effective car. "The conceptual work was Harvey, but Patrick Head did a lot of the suspension. Patrick came out to South Africa with me for testing, and we really got on well. Then he told me he was leaving to join Frank Williams. I said to him, 'God, no, don't do it. That Frank Williams is a complete loser.' Shows how much I knew..."

In the intense heat of Argentina's high summer, the Wolf made history by winning first time out. Jody qualified halfway down the grid after various new-car problems in practice, but he moved strongly up the field until he was on the tail of Carlos Pace's leading Brabham-Alfa. "It was very, very hot, but I just kept to my steady pace, and I could see Pace was in trouble, taking some funny lines. He was near collapse from the heat, and being sick in his helmet, and I went past him easily. I was always very fit, did weights, running up and down hills with heavy stones in my hands, that sort of stuff. Less sophisticated than it is now, but I had stamina.

"We should have won Long Beach, too. I was leading Andretti and Lauda with eight laps to go when I got a slow puncture in the right front. It got worse and worse, and I kept thinking, I'll go in the next lap, but I kept going. In the final laps Andretti and Lauda both went by, but I got to the finish in third place." Second at Kyalami, third at Jarama, and then a flag-to-flag victory at Monaco: at the season's halfway point Jody was leading the championship. There was another victory in Canada and more podiums at Hockenheim, Zandvoort and Watkins Glen. Wolf's maiden season ended not only with Jody runner-up to Lauda in the Drivers' Championship, but with Wolf fourth in the Constructors' Championship – running a single car.

For 1978 the ground-effects WR5, boxy where the WR1 had been shapely, was not in the Lotus and Williams class. There were four podiums, but by July the news of Jody's departure was out. "Nearly every year Ferrari said, 'We want to talk to you,' but nothing had ever come of it. But in May I was ushered in to meet the Old Man, and the first thing he said was, 'How much money do you want?' I said, 'I'm too young to talk about money,' and we got on well after that. Enzo Ferrari was tough, a tough, smart guy. But when it came down to it I said, 'I don't want to talk now, it's early in the season, I'm busy racing.' 'No,' he said, 'we want to sign you up now.' So I said, 'If you want me now, that's my price.' We settled on a retainer of $1.2 million, a lot of money 30 years ago. Plus prize money on top, and other bits and pieces."

Jody was the contracted number one, with Gilles Villeneuve, in his second full season both in F1 and with Ferrari, the number two. But after the first five rounds of 1979 Gilles was leading the championship. Then Jody took the lead with back-to-back wins at Zolder and Monaco, and stayed there. At Monza, in front of the delirious fans, Jody and Gilles finished one-two, and Jody was World Champion.

"All my life I've never needed anyone to push me, I've always been self-motivated. But having Gilles as a team-mate did probably push me to get more out of myself. Gilles could have won the championship, but he always wanted to be the hero, always wanted to be the quickest guy. Wherever he was he wanted to win, win the corner, win the lap, do the most wheelspin out of the pits, and that's what gave me the confidence to beat him. At Monza he was trying qualifying tyre after qualifying tyre, trying to get the best time. I told Ferrari to give me the hard race tyre, I was doing engineering, engineering, engineering, to get the car right for the race. I still qualified quicker than him. Everybody thinks Gilles let me win at Monza, but it's not true. We were running one-two and Jacques Laffite was chasing us in the Ligier, but as soon as he dropped out I backed off and cut my revs, and Gilles did the same.

"Gilles was a great guy, and we got on really well. He was very hard-working, really worked at the testing. But he liked the daredevil image. If there was a chance of some wheelspin or a doughnut in front of an audience, he would do it. We both lived in Monaco and I used to go with him to Maranello by car. I'm a nervous passenger, but he was well-behaved all the way – until we got within two miles of the factory, then he'd start to show off. Above all he was honest. A very honest, honourable guy, honest to the point of being naïve. That thing with Didier Pironi [at Imola in 1982, when Pironi reneged on a pre-race agreement and took victory from him]: he just thought everybody else was as honest as him. He called me after Imola, he was furious and upset, and of course he was killed in practice for the next race.

"Actually, he was serious about safety. Everybody thought the wheel-banging battle with René Arnoux at Dijon, when they were fighting for second place, was the best thing in the world. But we talked about it afterwards, and I said, 'The crowds love it, but it's stupid what you're doing. You're going to kill yourself' – because, you know, we used to have one or two drivers killed every year in those days.

"Mauro Forghieri was the technical boss at Ferrari, but for me he was more the team manager. Marco Piccinini was the political team manager, but Forghieri made things happen. But he had some very awkward ideas about design, and didn't seem to want to understand the wing car concept. At Silverstone we were slow: I qualified 11th, Gilles 13th. The problem was that the V8s were getting more air through the underside of the car, their ground-effects worked properly, whereas we had our wide flat 12 – which was made worse by having the exhaust pipes going through the only place that the air could come through. But Forghieri didn't want to do anything about it. After Silverstone the Italian press were going mad, like they always did, and so Mr Ferrari called a meeting. I said to Gilles, 'Let's speak with one voice on this; the car needs to be modified.' In the meeting I said, 'We shouldn't be fighting among ourselves, we should be fighting the other teams.' Gilles said the same, and Mr Ferrari agreed with us, so Forghieri modified the exhausts. We took it to Monza and we had another 300rpm, and more downforce. It was a performance jump.

"Winning the title for Ferrari at Monza – I remember the sea of people at the end, but what I really felt after a year of being up and down was the relief. It was just a relief to get it over. I didn't get too emotional or excited when the crowd were going mad, and that maybe helped me the following season, when they weren't going mad!

"For 1980 everybody else moved forward and we stayed still. The T5 just wasn't competitive. Gilles was quicker than me most of that season. It wasn't that I wasn't trying hard: when

I got to the track I put just as much into it as I ever had. But now, if I woke up in the middle of the night, I wasn't thinking of understeer and oversteer. Subconsciously I had probably lost some of my edge. If you've been around for a while and you've been fighting at the front, and then you find yourself fighting for 18th place, it's very hard. So early in the season I decided to retire. I had done what I wanted to do. We'd had accidents and deaths, and I saw some people not really caring much about that. The magic of F1 had gone for me. In July I told Mr Ferrari I wanted to stop, and then I announced it to the press straight away. But I carried on doing the testing and the races to the end of the season.

"Renault approached me with a serious offer to carry on for them, at any money. I didn't even consider it. I'd made my decision. I stayed living in Monaco, and I spent a year trying to put together a Race of Champions series around the world, using identical DFV-powered Ford Sierras. I was lining up sponsorship and TV coverage, but in the end it didn't happen. I was probably too naïve and greedy. Then I saw an advert in a magazine for the weapons training system, had some ideas, moved to Atlanta, and Clare and I started that business at our kitchen table."

In the 1990s Jody became involved in the racing careers of his two sons by his first marriage, Toby and Tomas. "It was the worst time. I found myself grubbing around in the Brands Hatch paddock changing gear ratios and humping tyres, which I'd been doing 30 years earlier. If you're driving you can always drive harder, but with Toby and Tomas I always felt I couldn't do anything useful, although I did try to help Tomas on the engineering side. Toby isn't racing any more, but Tomas is in his seventh season in Indycar. I go to a couple of races each year to see him." And he goes to the occasional Grand Prix with Honda – but only because he supplies the team with organic food.

Twelve years in racing, 12 years in weapons training, and now the Laverstoke project is in its eighth year. "By that measure,

I've got four years to go here. After that, who knows. But I don't want to end up on a beach. It's not just that I get bored, it's worse than that. If I'm not busy, I feel useless. I'm getting a bit better about it as I get older, but not much." Whatever Jody focuses on for his next 12-year project, you know he'll attack it like an F1 driver: still the driven man.

Jody Scheckter was talking to Simon in February 2008.

HANS STUCK

Plying the family trade over
five decades

It's intriguing how often sons of racing drivers become racers themselves. In Formula 1 Nico carries on the work of Keke, as did Jacques for Gilles – although so far only Damon and Graham have achieved a World Champion son of a World Champion father. Sometimes grandsons follow to make a third generation, or brothers and cousins. The remarkable Andretti and Unser dynasties spring to mind.

In the campsites around the Nürburgring Nordschleife, they'll tell you about *Die Stuckrennfahrerdynastie*. Hans Stuck von Villiez drove for Auto Union in the 1930s, winning Grands Prix and dominating mountain hillclimbs. Including the interruption of World War II, his racing career lasted 39 years. His son, Hans-Joachim Stuck, beat even that. When he hung up his helmet this year his cockpit time, covering F1, endurance racing, GTs and touring cars, had spanned 43 seasons. Now his two sons, Johannes and Ferdinand, are busy GT racers in Europe.

Hans-Joachim is known to the German-speaking world as Strietzel, an untranslatable nickname referring to a type of local honey-cake. At his christening an aunt exclaimed that the plump new baby looked just like a Strietzel. The plumpness left him early on – he became and still is a tall, rangy individual who often had difficulty fitting his height into tight cockpits. But the name remained. Although he has a place in Florida, where a close neighbour is former team-mate Derek Bell, his main residence is in Austria. It's a breathtaking mountain-top house he had built 10 years ago close to some of the Tirol's most fashionable ski resorts, made almost entirely of wood harvested from Porsche-owned forests in southern Germany. A central staircase curves around an immense tree trunk that supports the whole house, and panoramic windows on all sides reveal jagged peaks that march from horizon to horizon. That's where he welcomes me, once I have received the slightly grudging approval of his enormous Rottweiler/German Shepherd cross. He shows me historic photographs and trophies from his father's racing days, including a tiny working musical box in delicately worked filigree silver, part of the spoils of victory in the 1934 Swiss GP. The basement garage cut into the mountainside contains great cars from his own career, from his first BMW 700. Then we bump down the mountain in his runabout for the rough local roads, a Land Rover Defender.

Lunch is in a village *gasthof* where his banter with the owner shows they are old friends. He takes only a small plate of thinly-sliced raw steak and apple juice. His conversation is machine-gun rapid, punctuated by uproarious laughter and realistic car noises as he reloads with the next anecdote. Even in the already straight-faced world of 1970s F1, with Stuck a practical joke was never far away. His fellow German Rolf Stommelen was, says Hans, rather serious. "On a race weekend while he was having dinner, a group of us stripped his hotel room. Took out all the furniture, the bed, even the light bulbs, rolled up the carpet. Hid it all away. When he and his lady go up to bed they open the door: only bare floorboards." Snorts of laughter between gulps of apple juice.

In the 1920s the young Hans Senior had a farm south of Munich. The farm's milk was sent into the city every day by train, but Hans realised profits would be better if he delivered it himself. "He got an ancient Dürkopp and drove it like a maniac to Munich every morning. His friends teased him about his old car, so he bet them he could drive up a steep local mountain pass, backwards, faster than they could in their cars, forwards. He switched the gearbox around so he had one forward gear and four reverse gears, and he won the bet. So he got the taste for car sport, and he started to do hillclimbs seriously."

Noting his success, Austro-Daimler put him in a works car. For them he won a string of hillclimbs and championship titles, and embarked on a circuit career. Then Austro-Daimler pulled out, so Hans bought an SSKL Mercedes, hurling the big car up the hills he now knew intimately and becoming 1932 Alpine Champion. He also shipped it to South America and won the Brazilian Hillclimb title.

Stuck had got to know Austro-Daimler and Mercedes designer Ferdinand Porsche, and when Adolf Hitler came to power in 1933 Dr Porsche was ordered to outline his plans for a world-beating Grand Prix car – a rear-engined, 4.4-litre supercharged V16. Stuck was present at the meeting, and was the first to test the new P-Wagen. In March 1934 he set world speed records at AVUS, and in July at the Nürburgring he scored Auto Union's first major victory in the German GP. The next day he was obliged to drive the winning car on the public roads from Berlin to the Auto Union factory at Zwickau: schools were closed and thousands lined the route to cheer him. He went on to win the Swiss and Czechoslovakian GPs, and would have been European Drivers' Champion had such a thing existed. He also powered the difficult V16 monster, with its rear swing-axles, up the steep, narrow passes of his beloved hillclimbs, winning another Mountain Championship.

The funds set aside by the Third Reich for motor sport domination were split between Auto Union and Mercedes-Benz. According to the late Chris Nixon's superbly-researched work *Racing the Silver Arrows*, Alfred Neubauer of Mercedes offered to double Stuck's retainer if he would swap teams. Stuck talked the proposal over with his friend Rudi Caracciola, who as the star of Mercedes not surprisingly persuaded Hans to stay put. But, while Stuck was the only one of Auto Union's 16 drivers to remain with the team throughout their six seasons' racing, he would never again experience the same level of success. He won the 1935 Italian GP at Monza, was second in the German GP to Nuvolari, and led at Avus until a rear tyre exploded at 180mph. In 1936 he had big accidents at Pescara and at Monza, and in 1937 his best finish was second to Hermann Lang at Spa. In hillclimbs he continued to dominate, but at the end of 1937, by which time the brilliant Bernd Rosemeyer was Auto Union's new star, he was fired.

Stuck's own explanation for this was that he allowed Rosemeyer to see his contract. Rosemeyer felt he was being underpaid, and asked Stuck's advice. Each Auto Union contract contained a clause forbidding the signatories from discussing it with anyone else, but Stuck, sympathising with young Bernd's plight, told him he was going out for a walk, and hinted where in the house his contract could be found. A few days later Auto Union finance director Dr Bruhn told Stuck that Rosemeyer had asked for more money, and he knew why. Stuck's contract was terminated.

A few weeks later Rosemeyer was dead, killed in a 270mph record attempt on the Frankfurt-Darmstadt autobahn, and soon Stuck was back in the team. He was third in the German GP, and was lying second to Nuvolari at Monza when his engine failed. And he was European Mountain Champion again. But there were no more race wins up to the outbreak of war.

When peace returned Stuck raced an 1100cc Cisitalia, and built the AFM F2 car with Alex von Falkenhausen, working in the garage of Stuck's house in Garmisch. He was third in the 1950 Solitude GP, but once again there was more success on the hills. He raced a Porsche Spyder in South America, winning on the new Interlagos track, and in '57 he started a relationship with BMW. He took class wins in its elegant but heavy sports car, the 507, and in the little 700 coupé he claimed the German Hillclimb title at the age of 60.

In 1948 Hans had married his third wife, Christa-Maria. Their son Hans-Joachim was born in 1951. "I wouldn't have been interested in cars without my father. When I was a toddler I would hang around the garage while my dad and von Falkenhausen worked on the AFM. One day they couldn't find the small spanner they needed to adjust the valvegear. They searched high and low, but in the end they put the bonnet back on, started the car up – and *Wheee!* this little spanner shot out of the exhaust pipe. I was in a world of my own, and I'd pushed the spanner into the exhaust, thinking I was helping to prepare the car. When I went with him to his races and hillclimbs, I got the smell, I got the infection, and from then on my only target was to be a racing driver.

"My father taught in the race driving school at the Nürburgring, and I was just nine years old when he first let me drive a couple of full laps in one of the school cars, seat right forward, sitting on a cushion. After that I did a lot of laps. Another instructor was the BMW tuner Hans-Peter Koepchen. When I was 18 he said to my father, 'I've watched your lad. I want to put him in for a race.' My father was worried, he knew a racing driver's life can be very hard with injuries and money, but it was too late already. There was a 300km single-driver race on the Nordschleife, and I did it in a Koepchen 2002, no seat belts, no overalls, just shirt and jeans and open-face helmet. I already knew the track, every kilometre. But each time I went over a big jump the throttle cable came undone. I had to keep stopping to reconnect it, but I still finished third in class. Then Koepchen put me in the Nürburgring 24 Hours with Clemens Schickentanz. We won it outright. It was so different in 1970: no catering, no motorhomes, nowhere to change or shower, no girls to massage you. The state of the art then was sitting on a camp chair in the old pits for 24 hours, eating chips and drinking Coke."

Hans also sampled the hillclimbs at which his father had excelled. "They were fun weekends. When you stand around for 15 hours and do five minutes of racing, there is plenty of time for funny stuff. And it's good training, because in a race, if you make a small mistake, you can recover. In a hillclimb, if you make the smallest error you can never get the time back. You have to be very precise, starting on cold tyres, trying to memorise the track. Some drivers would sneak out in their road cars on Thursday and Friday to do extra practice. They'd paint black bars on the white reflector posts by the road, braking points, two stripes for second gear, three for third. So when it got dark we'd go out with white and black paint and change them all, removing some stripes, adding others."

More and better touring car drives began to come his way. In 1971 he scored wins in BMW 2800, Simca 1100 and Opel Commodore. He nearly had a second win in the Nürburgring 24 Hours, starting from pole and holding a big lead until, with an hour left, the engine blew. For 1972 Jochen Neerpasch, Ford of Germany's racing boss, signed him to drive the works 2600RS Capris. He and Jochen Mass won the Spa 24 Hours, and three more wins at the Nürburgring and a string of other victories earned him, at 21, the title of German Champion.

"For 1973 Neerpasch left Ford to go to BMW, and he wanted to take me with him. He was one of the first to focus on how cockpit concentration is allied to physical fitness, and in January he summoned all the team drivers to fitness training in Switzerland – gym, cross-country skiing, weightlifting. Some of us weren't too sure about this stuff. Chris Amon was in the team, and he was anything but fit. We had to report to the factory in Munich and pick up brand-new BMW road cars, then drive to the hotel in St Moritz. Of course it developed into a flat-out race on those twisty mountain roads: eight cars started and only five arrived. Neerpasch was furious. I did the season with the CSL coupé, usually with Chris in the longer races. We won the Nürburgring Six Hours, but we had bad luck everywhere else. At Kyalami Jacky Ickx and I were leading the class, and a front wheel fell off. I came into the pits on three wheels and a brake disc, *Screeech!* They rebuilt the front corner, and we finished the race.

"I'd had my first single-seater race at Hockenheim in 1970, in an F3 Eifelland March, and I didn't enjoy it. I didn't fit in the car, and I got caught in somebody else's accident." A car spun mid-pack and several others piled in. Hans' March flew, landed on its nose between a post and a startled photographer, and caught fire. In 1971 he had a single F2 ride in an Eifelland Brabham at the 'Ring, but was taken off by Vittorio Brambilla. But in '73, with March now using the BMW engine in F2, Neerpasch organised with Max Mosley half a dozen rides for Hans. He didn't finish in any of them, but he ran near the front often enough, particularly at the 'Ring in the wet, to show he was comfortable in a single-seater now. "I stuck up above the rollover bar, I had trouble fitting my knees under the dash, and I had to cut the toes off my boots to work the pedals. Otherwise I was OK."

This led to a works March F2 drive for 1974. Then, days before the first F1 round in Argentina, Jean-Pierre Jarier walked away from his March seat and signed for Shadow. Overnight Hans was summoned to Buenos Aires to squeeze into the March 741. "I had never even sat in an F1 car before. My first try was in official Friday practice. I was going through a fast fourth-gear right-hander thinking, this is pretty good, and *Eeeeowww!* Niki Lauda's Ferrari came past on the outside. I was 10 seconds off the pace. So I went to see Carlos Reutemann. It was his home circuit, so I thought he was a good guy to ask. 'Excuse me, my name is Hans Stuck, and I am new to F1. Can you please tell me how to drive round this circuit?' We did 10 or 12 laps in his road car and he gave me a lot of good advice, which was very nice of him. On Saturday my times were much better, and in the race I was running 11th when the transmission broke."

At Kyalami Hans qualified seventh and finished fifth, and a month later he was fourth at Jarama, making his mark in what was at best a midfield car. In F2 he won four rounds and had three more podiums, but was pipped to the title by consistent team-mate Patrick Depailler. He was also scoring more wins in BMW's touring cars. In all, he did 31 events that season.

"For 1975 Teddy Mayer approached Jochen Neerpasch, who was pretty much acting as my manager now, to see if I could drive for McLaren in F1. But Jochen wasn't keen, because BMW were going to race touring cars in America, and he persuaded me that would be better: maybe I was wrong, but I have no regrets. I had a great time in the US, and my team-mate was often Ronnie Peterson.

"Ronnie and I got on so well. Our relationship was just perfect. But I knew if I could beat Ronnie's times I could ask Neerpasch for more money. So we just tore the cars up like throwing bread to the birds. At Brands Hatch we shared a 320 turbo. After a couple of laps it started to rain and I lost it, chucked the car over the guard rail and into the woods. It was wrecked: bodywork gone, parts hanging off. I walked back to the pits and told Ronnie, and we jumped into our road cars and drove away, Ronnie to his place in Maidenhead and me to Heathrow to catch an early flight home. Monday morning Neerpasch's secretary called: 'Mr Stuck, please come to the office at once.' I was living in Munich then, so I got there in 10 minutes. Jochen was sitting there, face as long as a metre. 'Where were you yesterday? They stopped the race because of the rain, we got the car back, there was only bodywork damage, we fixed that in minutes. We put the car back on the grid for the restart, and we had no drivers. You're lucky that both of you had left, because if it had been one of you he would have been fired. You're both fined 10,000 marks for leaving the circuit without permission.' I got straight on the phone to Ronnie. 'Listen, you won't believe this. This is the best story of all!'"

Hans continued to drive for March in F1 when his BMW schedule allowed. He qualified seventh at the Nürburgring, ahead of reigning champion Emerson Fittipaldi and eventual winner Reutemann, only for his engine to fail on lap three. Two weeks later, in the chaotic rain-sodden Austrian GP, he qualified fourth and ran near the front until he slid off into the fences. He did a full F1 season for March in 1976, finishing fourth at Interlagos and at Monaco. But the race he remembers most fondly that year is Watkins Glen. "I qualified sixth, but had a clutch problem at the start and got away almost last. At the end of lap one I was 23rd. By half-distance I was fifth, and that's where I finished, with Lauda's Ferrari and Mass' McLaren about five seconds in front of me."

In March the following year Brabham's Carlos Pace died in a light plane crash. "At once a lot of talk, who will be John Watson's team-mate? The flat-12 Brabham-Alfa looked like a winner, and the next race at Long Beach was less than two weeks away. Then Bernie [Ecclestone] calls me in. 'Do you want to drive for me?' Of course I say 'Yes'. 'How much do you want?' I say, 'Last year with Max I earned $80,000. I'm not a rich man, and I need to take care of my mum.' [Hans Stuck Sr had died, aged 78, a few weeks before.] At that moment the phone rings on Bernie's desk and he picks it up. 'Ah, Arturo. *Si, si.* How much? Thirty? OK, I'll get back to you. *Ciao*, Arturo.' Then he says, 'That was Merzario. He will race for me for $30,000, plus some money for the points. You want it, or not?' 'I'll do it,' I say. I sign the contract for $30,000, and five days later I'm in a Brabham-Alfa at Long Beach.

"The next month, after qualifying at Monaco, we're having dinner, all in a good mood because Wattie's on pole and I'm fifth on the grid, four-fifths of a second slower. And Bernie says, 'Now we're friends, I'll tell you something. In my office when we were talking about money, it wasn't Merzario on the phone. It was my secretary in the next room, I told her to call me.' That's Bernie.

"I always got along with him extremely well. When you work for Bernie he is very demanding, which is good for me: I'm always better when I'm put under pressure. That season there were some problems with the car and the engine, but I finished ahead of Watson in the championship. I was on the podium at Hockenheim and Zeltweg, and in the points at Jarama and Zolder and Silverstone. Then at Watkins Glen I qualified on the front row. Before the race Bernie said to me, 'Next year Lauda comes to us from Ferrari, and Parmalat are our new sponsors.

Parmalat only want winners. You win this race, and you'll stay with me.' John Watson had only won one Grand Prix then, and Bernie had to choose between us for 1978.

"It was raining hard when the race started. I out-accelerated James Hunt's McLaren, which was on pole, and pulled out a good lead. I felt very comfortable. Then on the third lap the clutch cable broke. But it wasn't a problem because gearchanges were easy without the clutch if you got the revs right. Then the rain stopped, the track started to dry, and I began to think I'd have to stop for slicks. How could I get out of the pits without a clutch? While I was trying to work that out I slid off the road and into the barriers. *Babaaam*. That was that. For 1978 Brabham had Lauda and Watson.

"So I went to Shadow. Not a great season, I only scored points at Brands Hatch, but my team-mate was Clay Regazzoni. A fabulous guy, good driver, very fast, we had some great fights. He had the right mentality, and we both liked to have fun. When he arrived at a circuit for a Grand Prix, his first question was never, 'Where is the car?' It was always, 'Where are the girls?'

"For 1979 I joined ATS, Günther Schmid's team. It all seemed good: me as sole driver, spare car, lots of testing, good money. The car wasn't so bad, but Schmid always wanted to control everything. He had a problem with himself, a terrible temper, he was always angry. Once he didn't like the new front wing the guys had fitted. He told them to take it off, and then he jumped up and down on it in the pitlane to destroy it. He'd made his money out of ATS wheels for road cars, and at Monaco he said, 'Now we must race on ATS wheels.' We thought he must know what he was doing, because he was a wheel manufacturer. After 30 laps I was up to eighth ahead of the Brabhams of Piquet and Watson, and along the waterfront a wheel broke, flew in the air, bounced off a lamp post, and *Kersplosh!* into the water by Schmid's yacht, in front of all his guests.

"In the last race of the season, at Watkins Glen, I came through from 14th on the grid to finish fifth. Those two championship points were the first ATS had ever scored, and it got Schmid into FOCA, which was worth a lot of money to him in transport to the races and so on. But he didn't say, 'Good job, Hans.' He was angry: 'Why didn't you finish fourth?'

"ATS was the end of F1 for me. I knew I could get good drives in sports and touring cars, earn a good living, have more fun. I did Le Mans 18 times, the Daytona 24 Hours 16 times, all the other long-distance races. In 1985 I joined Porsche." Hans drove the immortal 956/962 Porsches at Le Mans seven years running, winning two years on the trot and scoring a second, two thirds, a fourth and a seventh, a superb record. On six of those seven occasions he drove with Derek Bell, and Al Holbert joined them for their back-to-back victories in 1986-87. "Whenever Derek was in our car I never had to worry for a single second. Fast, reliable, he didn't break anything, and very good at adapting if anything was going wrong. Holbert was brilliant too. Two more favourite co-drivers were Thierry Boutsen and Danny Sullivan. I was third again at Le Mans in '94, and second in '96, both times with Thierry. He is quite serious, quite Belgian, and I am not so serious, but our sizes in the cockpit were the same, and he was very fast. Danny was with us in '94, a lovely guy. Who doesn't like Danny? We used to call him 'spin and win'.

"When I joined Porsche Professor Bott, head of development, said: 'Mass is living in South Africa, Bell is in England, Ickx is somewhere, but you live two hours from Stuttgart. We need you to be on call for development testing.' I did more kilometres at the Porsche test track at Weissach than anyone, setting up the works cars, setting up customer cars. Norbert Singer was one of the few guys I ever worked with who would build a new car and it would come to the track already very nearly 100 per cent. I learned so much in my years with Porsche. At the races Peter Falk was the perfect strategist, and my engineers were great: Walter Näher and Roland Kussmaul, who was also a very good rally driver. But the first GT1 was a terrible car, because it was almost a normal 911 with a 962 back end bolted on. It never felt in one piece, it was like somebody was sitting in the back and steering, although at Le Mans in 1996 Thierry, Bob Wollek and I brought it home second overall, first in class. The later GT1 was much better, but it was a heavy mother to drive.

"I did a lot of racing in the States. In 1988 Audi sent me over there with the big four-door 200 turbo saloon, massive horsepower and four-wheel drive. With the centre differential we could change the percentage of power front to rear, adapting between street circuits and ovals. We could go from 50/50 to 20/80, which was almost like a nicely balanced rear-wheel-drive car. It was totally cool. In 1990 Audi did DTM, and against Mercedes and BMW I thought we had no chance, but we still won the title because there was so much engineering in the car. Then there was the ITC in 1995, when I drove for Opel. Those cars were incredibly complex: cooling shutters that closed to increase straightline speed, moving weight ballast under braking, self-adjusting rollbars, paddle gears developed by Williams, and you could pre-programme it all to each circuit. Going testing we had an engineer from Cosworth for the engine, another from Williams for the transmission, somebody from Bosch for the ABS braking. At the end of a race you had so much data you couldn't analyse it all, but when it went right it was amazing. Like on the street circuit at Helsinki, narrow and twisty between concrete walls. I won both heats."

Hans' favourite series of all was the wild BMW M1 Procar programme that supported Grands Prix in 1980/81. "The best ever, nothing has ever compared with it. A whole field of identical BMW M1 coupés mainly driven by F1 guys, with big prize money so everyone really went for it: the close racing, the noise – open-exhaust straight-sixes, *Mmmmm!* – it was usually better than the Grand Prix. Neerpasch organised it, he spent a ton of money on it. The five fastest F1 guys from Friday qualifying were put in the works cars to compete with privateers: I was always in a privateer car because at ATS I never qualified in the top five. They were put at the front of the grid, so I could never start above P6. But I won at Monaco, Zandvoort and Monza, and I won the privateer section both years. The second season I was in the Project 4 car run by Ron Dennis. He was my mechanic – 'Hey, Ron, hurry up, take the front rollbar down a couple of notches' – but he prefers to forget those days now.

"I raced a special spaceframe M1 with Nelson Piquet in the '81 Nürburgring 1000Kms, and we were leading when it was stopped by poor Herbie Müller's fatal accident. I had my worst accident in that car, in the Kyalami Nine Hours. During the night something broke and I hit the wall at 250kph (155mph). The car broke in half, I was sitting with the steering wheel in my hands and the front of the car was somewhere else. Since that crash I have a false nose."

The stories of 43 years' racing continue to pour out, always with guffaws and sound effects. Victory in the Nürburgring 24 Hours again, this time with a BMW 320 diesel: "Four-hour stints between refuelling stops, *chugchug*. That's how we won it." Winning the German truck championship: "So much fun. Just the tractor unit, very short wheelbase, 1500 horsepower, constant oversteer, smoking tyres. They weigh 5.5 tonnes, and you sit up high over the front wheels, so it's hard to feel what you're doing. The speed limiter is set to 160kph (99mph). Five or six trucks all flat out down the straight inches apart, *Rrrrrrrr!*, swapping paint, and it's all about who's going to brake last."

And the abortive Grand Prix Masters series of 2005/6: "I hadn't driven a single-seater for 15 years, but I loved it. Big tyres, big wings, paddle shift, and all my old friends – Emerson, Merzario, Danner, Laffite. At Kyalami 16 guys all changing in the same room, going bowling the night before, a pit walk for the crowds and us all signing autographs. This is what F1 should be like. Drivers together, friendly, and for the public. And close racing. Not DRS and flaps and closed motorhomes and all this shit. I shared a pit with Nigel, he was great with the public, then as soon as we started practice he was just like the old Nigel, moaning all the time. Then the race started, and

Wheeeoww! he was off. His battle with Emerson was brilliant, he beat him by 0.4sec."

In 2007 Hans was hired by VW as Motorsport Ambassador, covering all the Group's brands from Skoda to Lamborghini. "In 2009 I did the Langstreckenmeisterschaft at the Nürburgring, a 10-round series on the old Nordschleife, races of four hours, six hours, 1000Kms, and the 24 Hours. Eleven classes, everything from Golfs and Fiestas up to full-race Porsches, 250 cars on the track at once, a real demolition derby. And huge crowds camping all round the track, lots of beer. I came into the Schwedenkreuz in an Audi R8 on a dry track and went into a curtain of heavy rain. I hit the guard rail backwards at 225kph (140mph). They stopped the race because of the weather, so I got second place. It was a big impact, and two weeks later I didn't feel well. I got on my motorbike and rode 50kms to the hospital. They gave me a CT scan and said I had a blood clot on the brain and I was probably half an hour away from falling over dead. I was there 11 days, longest I have stayed in a hospital. They made two big holes in my skull, and they fixed it. That's why, look, I have this big dent in my head. But I am not George Clooney, so it doesn't worry me.

"But I don't do historic racing. In 1993 I raced the 1973 Mark Donohue Can-Am turbo Porsche 917/30 at Laguna Seca. I love the Laguna track, and I loved that fantastic huge Porsche, so much power, but massive throttle lag. You put your foot down, you count, you keep counting – suddenly *Beeeoowahhhh!* But after that I made a decision. You drive an old car, tube frame, feet out in front, modern rubber giving more forces on the chassis, who knows if everything is still right. And some people in historics now are really crazy guys. I demonstrate, like Goodwood Festival, but I don't race, like Goodwood Revival. If you race at all you have to race hard.

"When I drove my father's Auto Union at AVUS it was amazing. All so heavy, brakes, steering, gearbox. Sitting far forward, close to the wheel, zero ergonomics. How did they do it for a four-hour GP at the 'Ring? I took it up to 145mph, and then I was scared, I didn't want to go faster. He did 200mph around the Avus banking, and no crash helmet.

"Since I was nine years old, I have probably driven more laps of the Nordschleife than almost anyone else on earth. When I am bored, like when I was lying in the CT machine having my head scanned, I just drive laps of the 'Ring in my head, every gearchange, every apex. My first race was there, so this year I decided the 24 Hours should be my final race. I did it in a Lamborghini with my two sons Johannes and Ferdinand. Our target was just to finish, not to win, because we were against some big teams. At the end of the race I did the last stint. Ferdinand brought the car in, and as I got in I thought, 'after 43 years, this is the last time you ever race a car'. The commentator must have been talking about it, because as I drove round I could see banners and signs everywhere in the crowd, 'Goodbye Strietzel', and 'Thank You Hanschen'. As the race ended I was crying tears, my sons too, everybody was crying. I was able to end my time as a racing driver on my most beloved track with my two beloved sons.

"I still do some taxi-driving: round the 'Ring in an R8 race car with passengers paying big money for charity, classic rallies like the Mille Miglia. But no racing now, and no regrets. For 43 years the stopwatch ruled my life. Now I only use a stopwatch to boil an egg."

Hans Stuck was talking to Simon in September 2011.

SID WATKINS

In Formula 1's ruthless environment,
a universally loved figure

In the relentless theatre of Formula 1, the members of the complex cast – drivers, team chiefs, designers, organisers, circuit owners, officials – may be liked, admired, respected, even feared. But rarely are they loved. However, love is not too strong a word to describe the F1 paddock's feelings towards a man who, for no fewer than 424 Grands Prix, was an indispensable part of that cast.

Even more remarkably, it didn't represent his proper job. He was just a motor racing enthusiast who used his days off from a very demanding vocation, saving lives and healing wounds, to deal with lives and wounds in F1.

Professor Eric Sidney Watkins, OBE, BSc, MD, FRCS, has had a brilliant career as one of the world's foremost neurosurgeons, practising in the UK and USA. For some 30 years he was a pillar of the Royal London Hospital. He performed unnumbered operations, and developed groundbreaking new procedures. He launched the Brain & Spine Foundation, and led vital research into Parkinson's tremor, movement disorders, intractable pain and cerebral palsy. But he also happens to love motor sport, and during 26 seasons as F1's doctor he completely revolutionised the principles and procedures of driver safety. Thanks to him, lives were saved and injuries lessened. No Grand Prix, race or practice session, could start without him. To everybody in Formula 1 he was affectionately known as 'Prof'.

Sid is a lover of other good things in life, too. Since his retirement from the regular F1 grind five years ago he has more time for them: fishing, good whisky, the novels of John Buchan, his children and grandchildren, his house in the Adirondack mountains in upstate New York, and his Scottish home on the side of a steep hill overlooking the River Tweed. That's where I go to meet him. A mere lunch won't give us enough time to plumb a serious bottle of Glenmorangie (or for some scurrilous off-the-record stories, racing and medical, after the voice recorder is turned off). So he and his wife Susan invite me to spend the day and stay the night.

The house is superb: an early 18th century manse which Susan has flawlessly restored from a wreck, with the same attention to period detail that a Ferrari expert might bring to rebuilding a 375MM. It has tall, gracious rooms, separate studies for Sid and Susan where each can write in peace, an Aga-warmed country kitchen, and a fishing tackle room for Sid. A subterranean tunnel, carved through rock when the house was built, runs from the wine cellar under the terraced garden to a balcony overlooking the river. Susan is a respected historian, with acclaimed books on Elizabeth I and Mary Queen of Scots among her works. Her authorised biography of Bernie Ecclestone, when it is published, should be extremely revealing.

Sid came from humble beginnings. His family were miners, and his father first went down the pit aged eight, as a candle boy. But young Wally Watkins was determined not to spend his life at the coal face, and his means of escape was the bicycle. He became a professional racer, eventually riding for the Raleigh works team, and during the 1920s he scraped together enough money to set up a bicycle shop in Liverpool. The family of six, including Sid, the youngest, lived over the shop. Sid and his brothers went to the local school in Bootle – "a rough area then," Sid remembers. "The local copper used to take two Alsatians with him on the beat. One day, when I was about eight years old, our teacher asked the class what we wanted to do when we left school. The other kids had the usual ambitions – fireman, engine driver – but I said I wanted to be a brain surgeon. I don't know where it came from. All the others laughed at me, of course."

Young Sid was bright. He got a scholarship to Bootle Grammar School but, when he told his father he wanted to be a doctor, it didn't go down well. The bicycle shop had become a small garage, and Sid was expected to muck in. Undaunted, he got a scholarship to Liverpool University to read medicine. "The brain was my goal from the outset. In 1952 I qualified as a doctor and went into general practice, but my father still wanted me as a source of cheap labour. So I used to do morning surgery, then house calls, work in the garage during the afternoon – tuning twin carbs with my stethoscope – and then get cleaned up for evening surgery.

"National service got me in 1953, so I became an army doctor. I joined a physiological unit in West Africa with the rank of captain, doing research into heat exhaustion: went out there weighing 14 stone, and came back weighing eight stone. Then I did general surgery in Weston-super-Mare, and in 1958 I joined the Radcliffe in Oxford under the great American brain surgeon Joe Pennybacker. I'd already started to go to races as a spectator, with a colleague who was nuts about motor racing and had a Lotus-Climax. He introduced me to Dean Delamont, the RAC Competitions boss. Dean persuaded me to go to kart races as the medical officer, and then to car meetings."

In 1962, when Sid was 34, he was appointed professor of neurosurgery at the University of New York in Syracuse. With an introduction from Delamont, he applied to Watkins Glen to be one of the circuit doctors for the US Grand Prix. "They had a small medical centre with no equipment. The first job before practice started was to sweep out the dead flies that had accumulated since the last meeting. If someone got hurt they couldn't do anything at the track, so the ambulance had to go to the nearest hospital. Sometimes that was closed, and they had to drive another 60 miles to one that was open. I arranged to take a team from my hospital in Syracuse to the race, so we could get an instant consultant's opinion for any injury. I attended regularly at Watkins Glen for the Grand Prix, and for the Canadian race when it was at Mosport and at St Jovite."

At the end of 1969 Sid returned to England to become Professor of Neurosurgery at the London. "Soon Dean got me involved in the British Grand Prix. When I'd first worked at Silverstone the medical centre was a primitive hut, staffed by Red Cross people. There'd be some ambulances and doctors, but nothing very sophisticated. When I took a proper team up to the British Grand Prix in 1973 – another neurosurgeon, an anaesthetist, a cardiac doctor, an orthopaedist and a nursing sister – I was told we weren't necessary for an F1 weekend, and our presence would be more appropriate at a club race where they had more accidents. So to stay out of the way of the locals I staffed the Louis Stanley Medical Unit with my people, and in the saloon race before the Grand Prix there was that huge pile-up, involving Dave Brodie, Dave Matthews and Gavin Booth. We found ourselves dealing with head injuries, a leaking lung, facial injuries, a broken femur. Then the Grand Prix started, and Jody Scheckter spun coming out of Woodcote and there was another pile-up. Fortunately only Andrea de Adamich was injured: he had a dislocated ankle, which we put back in the Stanleywagon.

"I continued to staff the Stanley unit at the British GP each year, and then in 1978 Bernie Ecclestone, whom I'd never met, called me at the London and asked for an appointment. I agreed to see him that evening at 7pm. He consulted me about a minor medical matter, but I realised that was just Bernie seeing what he made of me. Then he came to the point. He'd decided that F1's medical facilities weren't good enough. They varied widely from race to race, and he wanted the same levels of competence at each track. He proposed that I should go to every Grand Prix, and he said he'd pay me $35,000 a season for the 16 races. I was impressed by Bernie at once, his decisiveness, his clarity of thinking, and I said I'd do it. Then he said I would, of course, be responsible for my own travel and accommodation expenses. Typical Bernie: he did it very cleverly, and I just walked into it!

"The following Wednesday I flew to Anderstorp for the Swedish GP. It was the race when the Brabham fan-car appeared and caused such a furore. I got a lift from the airport to the circuit with John Watson. In those days I paid my own way, booked my flights, made my own arrangements. Often I'd arrive at a circuit with no hotel to stay in, and had to scrounge a room from one of the teams. But, to be fair to Bernie, after a couple of years he said, 'I don't think we're paying you enough,' and put my fees up.

"At first there was pressure on me to set up a mobile team and take it to every race. But that would have brought all sorts of problems with professional licensing and insurance from country to country, and we wouldn't necessarily have had any privileges at the different hospitals. So it became my job to harass the locals at each race to get the nearest decent hospital standing by with surgical staff ready, and improve the level of response. There was a lot of opposition, of course, not so much from the local medical teams as from the circuit people, who didn't want to spend money on more staff and better facilities at the tracks.

"That first year at Hockenheim the medical centre was an old converted bus with only two doctors to staff it, neither of whom was an anaesthetist. The bus was parked out in the paddock and the crew camped overnight beside it. If a helicopter was required they had to call in the Autobahn traffic team, who might well be busy elsewhere. Then, as the grid was lining up on race day, they wouldn't let the chief medical officer into Race Control. I told Bernie, who said he'd stand in front of the cars on the grid and, unless he saw me give a thumbs-up from the Race Control window, he would get the drivers out and send them all home. The organisers, shocked, relented at once. The following year Hockenheim had a well-equipped new medical centre and helicopter availability all weekend."

Less than three months after Sid's first race in his new role came Ronnie Peterson's accident at Monza. Sid's procedure in those pre-medical car days was to follow what was going on from Race Control. When Peterson's accident happened he fought through the crowded paddock to the medical centre at the back of the paddock and got there just as Ronnie arrived in the ambulance.

"He had more than 20 fractures in his legs and feet. We stabilised him and took him on a stretcher to the helicopter and they flew him to the Ospedale Maggiore at Niguarda. I had to stay for the race. I also had to deal with Vittorio Brambilla, who was unconscious after being hit on the head by a wheel in the same accident, and Hans Stuck, who had concussion. For the restart Jody Scheckter went off on the warm-up lap and destroyed a lot of Armco, which had to be replaced. By the time the shortened race finally got done it was almost dark. I went to the Lotus motorhome to see Colin [Chapman] and Mario [Andretti] and they'd heard that Ronnie was being operated on. I would have treated him conservatively, but the blood supply to his legs had started to fail. At Niguarda they decided they had to straighten his legs to get the blood vessels working again. Mario set off for the hospital in his Rolls Royce, with me trying to keep up in my Fiat Panda hire car. We went across some fields and down a farm track because Mario said he knew a short cut to the motorway. We initially joined it going in the wrong direction, but the race traffic was so bad I was able to keep up with him. When we finally got to the hospital they were just finishing the operation. I thought the signs were that he would be OK, and I telephoned Ronnie's wife Barbro in Monaco and gave her some reassurance. But during the night he developed multiple blockages in the arteries to his brain, lungs and kidneys, emboli from bone marrow in his circulation, which was fatal. It was a terrible tragedy.

"I felt that the initial response to the accident had been a shambles. Reports of how long it took for the ambulance to reach the scene ranged from 11 to 18 minutes. I agreed with Bernie that I was going to have to take a much more active role. I wanted to be in a car, with life-saving equipment on board, to get to an accident in the shortest possible time, and run behind the field on the first lap.

"We had this two weeks later at Watkins Glen, an estate car with no rear seats, me in the front and the anaesthetist, Peter Byles, sprawled on the floor in the back. We borrowed a pair of helmets, Jody Scheckter lent me a set of overalls, and Peter got some overalls from James Hunt. He rather enjoyed giving autographs and kisses to the less knowledgeable female American spectators who saw the name on his overalls. The driver allocated to us was obese and sweating heavily, and obviously nervous. When the race started he set off in vain pursuit, hit the kerbs at the chicane and took off, landing very forcibly. We managed half the lap before peeling off, and just reached the medical centre before the field, led by Andretti, caught us up. After that Bernie made sure we had a proper car and a proper driver – usually one of the F1 chaps who hadn't qualified for the race, but at least knew his way around.

"Later on I had regular, trusted drivers at each track. Phil Hill was my driver at Long Beach, for example, and I've been driven, among others, by Niki Lauda, Carlos Reutemann, Derek Daly and Alex Ribeiro. Vittorio Brambilla used to drive me at Monza. He would greet people with a bone-crunching handshake and a big grin and say, 'I am the Monza gorilla!' When he first turned up to drive the medical car I asked him if he had fully recovered from his 1978 head injury. 'OK, OK, Doc,' he said, adding proudly, 'And I have another big head injury since then!' He enjoyed getting the medical car into sideways slides in the wet, looking across at me with a broad grin.

"My usual driver at the Australian GP was Frank Gardner, phenomenally quick, and wonderful in the wet. So precise:

he'd spend time getting himself just right in the car, arms there, legs there, thumbs on the steering wheel rim, never around the spokes. Then he'd take off. The first time he drove me, in Adelaide, our medical car was a new Ferrari, and we had some trouble squeezing all the equipment in. We did a few practice laps to get used to the circuit, and afterwards he said, 'This old girl hasn't got any brakes any more.' They had to rebuild the brakes before the race.

"At the London in those days there were just two neurosurgeons, and we worked alternate weekends. I fitted that in with the Grands Prix, and for the long-haul races I just took more out of my holiday entitlement. I didn't have any holiday for years. I did 26 weekends at the hospital and 16 weekends at the races, so I was a busy boy.

"Initially the FIA were not fond of my activities, because I was appointed by FOCA. The FIA president, Jean-Marie Balestre, never opposed any medical improvements, but he didn't like anyone who was not part of the FIA exerting power. Then one year in the hotel in Montréal he swallowed a piece of steak the wrong way and went blue in the face. A chap at an adjoining table jumped up, did the manoeuvre around his chest and expelled the steak, thus saving his life, but in so doing he cracked a rib. In the middle of the night Madame Balestre phoned my room saying her husband was in pain, so I went and gave him a local anaesthetic and some painkillers. My reward came when I got to Zandvoort for the next race and found the FIA were now booking and paying for my hotel room.

"In 1981 Balestre set up the FIA Medical Commission, and I became its president. We began to hammer out standards for medical centres and procedures at every circuit. Balestre was a very smart chap, actually, but he was very short-tempered and would fly into a paroxysm of rage about small things. Nelson Piquet, who was very mischievous, used to tease him unmercifully. Once Piquet said he'd found Balestre's hotel key in the pitlane, and gave it to him. It had a metal tag attached which said, 'Admit one prostitute to the room of the president.' Another time Balestre was making an endless pompous speech at one of the drivers' briefings, and Piquet was standing beside him with a litre bottle of mineral water, pouring it into the pocket of Balestre's blazer. Everybody could see what he was doing, but it was a while before Balestre became aware of the wetness seeping through his trousers.

"I quickly got to know all the drivers on a personal level. I became a sort of father figure – although later I suppose it was a grandfather figure. They regarded me as one of them, in the sense that they knew I was at the back on the first lap, and I'd be with them as soon as possible if anything went wrong, in practice or the race. Gilles Villeneuve used to joke about it – he'd say, 'I hope I never need you, Prof.' That was the first thing that went through my head when he crashed at Zolder in 1982.

"Gilles was unconscious when we got to him but his pupils were working. He wasn't breathing, but he had a pulse, so I put a tube in and ventilated him until we got him to the medical centre. We kept him ventilated in the helicopter until we got him to the hospital in Liège. The X-rays confirmed that he had an irreparable neck fracture, and it was obviously going to be fatal. We kept him on a respirator until his wife arrived. We told her what the situation was, and she was very brave and dignified. Then we switched him off." Sid enunciates the medical details professionally, with apparent lack of passion, but the quietness of his voice confirms his deep sadness and heartfelt regret. Has seeing so many race accidents ever made him dislike the sport, or feel that it is foolish?

"No. I've lived my life with head injuries, motorcycle accidents, car crashes. Most of them are equally tragic. I was always very upset when a racing driver got killed. It was particularly upsetting because they were my friends. Luckily we didn't lose many. And it did get better."

The tragedies get remembered, of course, but Sid's successes should be, too: the tracheotomy performed on Mika Häkkinen at the trackside in Adelaide in 1995, which saved his life; Martin Donnelly's dreadful accident at Jerez in 1990, which so nearly killed him but saw him, under Sid's care, eventually make a complete recovery; and so many more potentially very unpleasant incidents which received his prompt action, like Gerhard Berger's fiery crash at Imola in 1989.

"Jody Scheckter I was very close to. He could be argumentative and sulk a bit, but he really cared about safety, and was outspoken about it. If anyone was hurt he was always on the phone wanting to know how they were. Nigel Mansell: well, I had a lot of amusement with him. He had this penchant for appearing injured when he wasn't. In Australia he drove gently into the barrier, got out of his car and limped to a nearby ambulance. James Hunt spotted it at once on television: 'Look, he's limping on alternate legs!'. But sometimes I didn't find it so funny. At Spa in 1990 somebody nudged him at the start and his Ferrari went into the barrier before La Source. As our car passed him I could see him slumped in the cockpit, head down, so I shouted to my driver to stop. There was another accident ahead and they red-flagged the race, but I ran back up the hill to him first. As I ran there was a sound like a pistol shot: I'd snapped a tendon in my leg. I was in some pain but I hobbled to the Ferrari's cockpit and Nigel was still motionless, his helmet down. So I tapped on the helmet and shouted, 'Nigel?' He looked up, opened his visor, and I said, 'What's wrong with you?' 'Nothing,' he said. I said a very rude word and limped back to the car and we went to check on the other accident ahead. Then I was driven to the medical centre to get my leg strapped up.

"All the drivers were good chaps in their different ways, and I got on well with all of them. The only one I didn't like was Didier Pironi. He was a surly fellow. He wasn't grateful for anything we did for him after his Hockenheim accident. When we got to him he knew his legs were terribly injured, and he implored me to save them. I said to him, 'There's no way your legs are coming off. Even if they're very bad, they're not coming off today.' But after we'd flown in the helicopter to Heidlberg and we were getting ready for a very long and complicated operation, I was surprised to hear the consultant surgeon say bluntly to him that an amputation might be needed. I repeated to Pironi that I would not agree to such an action at that point, whatever might be necessary later. Later he complained to Bernie that he'd heard me say, while he was in the car, 'Let's take his leg off. It will be quicker for getting him out,' which of course I hadn't. I said to Bernie, 'No, it was his head I wanted to cut off.' I'm delighted to say that Pironi went on to make a good recovery, although he never returned to Formula 1. Of course he died in that powerboat accident five years later.

"I knew Ayrton [Senna] better than any other driver. We were very close. He came to stay with me up here in Scotland, and we fished together. He gave a talk at my stepson's school, Loretto, and was so patient and inspiring with the boys, answering all their questions. A bishop who was visiting the school at the same time remarked on how spiritual he was. Among his various projects for the poor of Brazil, he funded a programme for medical support for people in the upper reaches of the Amazon. We'd agreed to go together and see it in action at the end of the 1994 season...

"I was staying with him in Brazil once on his farm, and there was a terrible storm. All the electricity and phone lines were down. I'd promised to phone Susan at a certain hour, so we set out for the nearest village to try to phone from there. We drove through the storm on waterlogged roads for a long time, finally got to the village and found a garage with lights on. Ayrton explained to the man there that we wanted to use his phone to call Europe. The man recognised Ayrton, but at first he refused. Ayrton gently explained that if I used my BT phone card it wouldn't cost him anything. Magically the word had gone around and every child in the village had gathered at the door. While I made my call, Ayrton stood in the rain signing autographs by the light of a street lamp until every child had one.

"I knew Michael [Schumacher] pretty well, too, and it's interesting that the two greatest drivers in recent years were both capable of misbehaving on the track. Ayrton seemed to undergo a personality change when he got in the car. I don't know how he justified to himself something like that incident in Japan with Alain Prost in 1990. He was telling everybody it was an accident, but that night he admitted to me in private that it was deliberate. He said, 'I backed off a little bit, let my left front go close to his right rear, we touched, and off he went.' From the medical car I saw him jump out in a flash and run back to the pits in case there was a restart, while poor Prost was still slumped dejectedly in his cockpit. I can't think of anybody else who was quite so deliberately naughty.

"I said to him once, 'You don't have to drive so quickly when you're in front, you just have to be in the lead. You don't need to be a lap ahead.' Later he said, 'Sid, I always think of your advice when I see your medical car as I go round the circuit. But by the next corner I've forgotten it!'

"That weekend at Imola he was dreadfully upset by Roland Ratzenberger's accident on the Saturday. We'd had such a good run, you see. Some big accidents, some big injuries, but nothing life-threatening apart from airway obstruction, and I was always there quickly enough to deal with that. The last fatality at a Grand Prix had been Ricardo Paletti in Montréal, 12 years before. Rubens Barrichello's accident on the Friday had been bad – he'd had an airway obstruction, too – but our procedures had all gone well on that occasion. After Ratzenberger's accident on the Saturday Ayrton got into the medical centre at the back, jumped over the fence, and came in to ask me what was going on. When I told him he broke down, and wept on my shoulder. I suggested he should withdraw from the race. Actually, I said he should give up for good. He'd proved he was the best driver in the world, he'd been World Champion three times. 'Give it up,' I said, 'let's go fishing.' Then he composed himself and said, 'Sid, there are things we can't control. I cannot stop. I have to go on.' That was the last thing he said to me.

"Mario Casoni was driving for me that day. When he got me to Tamburello and I saw it was Ayrton it wasn't as difficult as it might have been, because I was too busy to think about anything except the job in hand. But I did regret that I hadn't leaned on him more, not to race. We got him out of the car and, even in the heat of the moment, I noticed he felt terribly light as I cradled him in my arms and laid him down on the Tarmac. I cut the strap to his helmet, got that off, got an airway in, and then I could look into his eyes, and that told me it was going to be a fatal accident. He had a terrible head injury. Then he made a funny noise, like a sigh, and that's when I think brain death occurred.

"We called the helicopter, and Ayrton was flown to the Ospedale Maggiore in Bologna with the intensive care anaesthetist. There was no point in my going, because there was nothing more to be done to influence the situation. I took his helmet back to the medical centre. I hadn't been able to examine it fully when the police seized it. Later it was returned to Ayrton's family, and they quite properly had it destroyed. As soon as the race was over, and I'd checked out some mechanics who had been injured in the pits, I went in the helicopter to the hospital. Everything had been properly managed there, but it was clear there was no hope. Ayrton's brother Leonardo and his manager were there, and I explained the situation to them, and I spoke on the phone to Ayrton's brother-in-law in Brazil. There was nothing more for me to do, and I got a lift back to my hotel. Of course the TV kept on playing and replaying the whole nightmare."

Senna's death sent shock waves around the world. Including testing accidents for Lehto, Lamy, Alesi and

Montermini, there had been six big F1 accidents in a matter of weeks. Eleven days later Karl Wendlinger had his practice accident at Monaco. The next day FIA president Max Mosley announced a new Expert Advisory Group, made up of Sid as chairman, race director Charlie Whiting, safety delegate Roland Bruynseraede, technical advisor Peter Wright, an F1 driver and an F1 designer.

"Our brief was initially to look at car and cockpit design, crash barriers, circuit configurations. We've always had a pretty clever committee down the years, with drivers like Gerhard Berger, Michael Schumacher and Mark Webber, and technical people like Harvey Postlethwaite, John Barnard and Pat Symonds. We commissioned proper research, and we worked on side penetration, wheel tethers, impact absorption front and rear, collapsible steering, leg protection. The crash testing was very expensive, but McLaren made a chassis available to us and we came up with solutions very quickly. In the early days I'd wanted to put a head protection cushion behind the driver's head, and the FIA recommended it. But you don't get anywhere in F1 if you recommend something. If it weighs a few ounces they won't put it in. So it has to be mandatory. And nobody will accept a change that you just think would be a good thing. You have to prove it.

"Max Mosley, who'd taken over from Balestre as FIA president in 1993, made the funds available to get all this work done. Poor old Max, he's had to live through a lot of garbage recently, but I have to say he's been tremendous in supporting our safety work and pushing it through. Things have come a long way. When I started, one in 10 accidents resulted in death or serious injury. Now the ratio is one in 300. Think of Robert Kubica's accident at Montréal last year. I was watching the race with Lauda on TV in the paddock and Niki said, 'What do you think?' I said, 'He'll be unconscious. At the very least.' Well, he was only briefly unconscious. He was cracking Polish jokes as they lifted him out."

In 2004 Sid retired as F1's medical chief at the races. "I handed over to Gary Hartstein. In some ways I had a sense of relief, not because I didn't want to do the job any more, but because of those endless long flights. I calculated I spent up to 140 days a year at the circuits, but I also spent 82 days physically in an aeroplane. Also, F1 has changed completely since the 1970s. There isn't the same sense of fun. Back then, even though there was tragedy, there was fun. The security is so high now, and the drivers, quite understandably, don't want to be bothered with all the people in the paddock. So they just do the disappearing trick. I used to have dinner with the drivers, enjoy their company, but in the end they would just go back to their rooms, have room service and go to sleep. Eventually that's what I did too."

Sid is still president of the FIA Institute of Motor Sport Safety. "We meet every three months, and we have a couple of scientific gatherings each year. We've developed a new type of safety barrier for use where there is little room for runoff, to stop a car from 200kph with acceptable rates of deceleration. After a lot of scientific testing using dummies, it was installed at Monza, at the second chicane and at the Parabolica. And it's not just about circuit racing. I took a look at a round of the World Rally Championship, and found it was like F1 in the 1960s. So we set up a research group. If a car hits a tree sideways it wraps around the tree, and the energy comes into the cockpit. It kills people. Now we've got new side protection in rally cars, which I believe has already saved lives. There's a karting group too. There were some karting deaths in children, and we've established that an adult-style crash helmet doesn't work properly on a child's head, even if it's the right size: there's a danger of neck injury. A lot of data was gathered by X-raying the heads of children from six to 18, and now we've got some new helmets for children of different ages."

Sid is 80 now, but his energy is still prodigious. When we met he'd just flown in from an Institute meeting at

Indianapolis. "We co-operate closely with the Council for Motor Sports Safety in the USA, and we had NASCAR people there too."

Today there are already many drivers in F1 who do not know Professor Sid Watkins. But each time they line up on the grid they have reason to be grateful for his 30 years of dedicated work, his unruffled common sense, his down-to-earth determination to make things better. Generations of drivers still to come, and in fact every motor sport enthusiast, should also feel grateful. Thank you, Prof.

Sid Watkins was talking to Simon in September 2008.

TOM WHEATCROFT

Indomitable wheeler-dealer driven
by enthusiasm

Larger than life: that well-worn phrase might have been coined especially for Tom Wheatcroft. His presence fills any room with energy and bonhomie. Tom likes to laugh, and finds much to laugh about. Actually, 'laugh' is too paltry a word to describe the process that begins deep inside the man as a rumbling, whirring noise, like some giant starter motor winding up a large-capacity engine of mirth, and then erupts and engulfs everyone within earshot.

As well as the laughter there is the passion, an all-consuming love of motor racing machinery and motor racing people. It still burns as brightly as it did more than 70 years ago when Tom, a penniless 13-year-old, bicycled 30 miles from his home in Leicester to Donington Park, found a hole in the hedge, and crawled through to see, hear and smell racing cars for the first time. It is the stuff of legend that some four decades later Tom Wheatcroft bought the long-derelict track, surmounted apparently insuperable obstacles to bring it back from the dead, and made it the scene of the European Grand Prix.

As well as circuit owner and promoter, he has been a Formula 1 entrant, team sponsor, and benefactor of young drivers. And his passion has also benefited countless numbers of enthusiasts through his extraordinary Donington Collection, the finest and most complete display of historic racing cars in the world.

Childhood wasn't easy for Tom. He was only two when his father died, and at four he was badly injured playing in a timberyard when a pile of huge logs fell on him. There were worries about brain damage, and he was kept off school. "The doctor said I'd never be able to take any pressure," Tom remembers. "He were wrong about that!" – and the laugh begins to rumble, *rrrrrr rrrrrr*. So he filled his time searching rubbish dumps for discarded wood, which he chopped up and sold as kindling for a shilling a bag. He finally went to school for the first time when he was 12.

"I did a lot of fighting. Fighting is a weakness. If a lad's fighting, he's missing something and it makes him want to fight. My weakness was I'd never been to school, and my mother couldn't give me the chances I thought I should have. Four of them at school took the piss out of me, and I give them all a hiding. We were friends after that."

But Tom only stayed at school for 18 months. He was still 13 when he "went on the buildings" as an apprentice plasterer. He had an insatiable appetite for hard work, and by the time he was 16 he could plaster an average 1000sq ft house in a day. Soon he was riding to Donington on his own 350cc Rudge. He never missed a meeting, and of course he saw the famous German onslaughts in 1937 and 1938. "You had to be there to know what it were like. The W125 Mercs and the V16 Auto Unions were doing 170mph by halfway down the straight. The noise and the smell and the speed – we'd none of us seen anything like it before. The nitro made your eyes water. And when they took off over the Melbourne hump, two foot off the ground, you just didn't believe what you were seeing."

Then came World War Two. At 19, having barely ever left Leicestershire, Tom found himself posted to Burma, then India, Iran, Iraq, North Africa, Italy, Belgium and finally Germany, driving tanks. His hair-raising war stories underline the toughness of the man – and his ever-present willingness to challenge authority. After several narrow escapes he was back in Leicester in 1946 with a German wife, Lenchen, and the first of his seven children. With his £50 gratuity he set himself up as a jobbing builder, sowing the seeds of a giant business that, within less than a decade, would be riding the post-war boom and completing a house every day.

Donington was no more, of course, but in 1950 Tom took a rare day off to go to the British Grand Prix at Silverstone. Since then he's never missed an F1 race on British soil. In 1956 he made his first foreign foray, driving his smart red Daimler Conquest roadster down to Sicily to watch Fangio lead home a Lancia-Ferrari 1-2-3 in the Syracuse GP, and soon he was a regular European spectator. The F1 circus was smaller then, and Tom was befriended by *Autosport* editor Gregor Grant.

"Gregor were ever so good to me. There'd be parties, and he'd say, 'Tom, d'you fancy coming to a do tonight?' Mimmo Dei, who ran Scuderia Centro Sud, he had a party at the Italian GP one year, in a big house just outside the Monza gates; very grand. Of course I weren't invited, but Gregor sweeps in and introduces me to the host, 'This is Monsieur So-and-so', makes me sound important, and they bow at us and in we go. Afterwards I said to Gregor: 'How d'you get invited to such a wonderful do? Everybody were there, Fangio; everybody.' And Gregor says, 'Oh, I wasn't invited.' If I'd known I would never have dared go in. He took me around, I were like a spaniel dog beside him, and he got me the courage to chat to anybody. And I'd sometimes bring his reports back to the *Autosport* offices, to help out.

"I loved Gregor. He knew what were going on, but he were a terrible liar. He'd tell nine of the biggest lies you'd ever heard, and then the 10th one, the wildest of the lot, would turn out to be true. We're eating in a fish restaurant in Monte Carlo, and he says, 'Tom, I've found a car. It's four doors away from where we're sitting. It's the remains of the Lancia that Ascari crashed into the water here in 1955.' 'Come on, Gregor, you've got your eyes crossed. I bet you a tenner you can't show me that car.' So he took me up the road, and we went into a lock-up, and there it was. I went back later and couldn't find the bastard thing. It came out of the water and they put it in that lock-up, but then it must have got stolen... *rrrrrr rrrrrr*.

"Fangio were a lovely man. If you had a pound or a penny, he treated you the same. We got to be friends down the years, and he came to Donington a few times. I went to his 80th birthday party. He drove me from Buenos Aires to his home town in the country, and the whole place turned out to welcome him, kids, old men; everybody. He sent me his helmet for my collection. It were during the Falklands War, and the customs people intercepted it and wanted to destroy it. Fortunately I got that sorted. I've got Nuvolari's helmet from when he won at Donington in 1938, and Ascari's helmet, Hawthorn's and a lot more.

"Rob Walker were a real gentleman, just like it said in his passport. I got to know his team ever so well. I used to go back to the paddock at night and fetch the mechanics some beer. His wife Betty always had a tin of her home-made chocolate brownies that she'd hand around in the pits. Once I were coming back from the Nürburgring in me 300SL Gullwing and there was his Facel II broken down by the side of the road. He were going to leave it there for someone to collect, but I said, 'You can't leave the booger here; I'll tow you.' Towed him about 80 miles on a short rope... *rrrrrr rrrrrr*."

In 1963 Tom decided he wanted a painting of one of his favourite cars, the Ferrari 125. A top motorsport artist of the day quoted him £900. Then, flicking through the classifieds in the back of *Motor Sport*, he saw a real 125 for sale – for £1000. The 1949 Italian GP winner, it had been in Australia ever since Peter Whitehead took it there for the Tasman Series, and now it had a Chevy V8 engine in it. Tom bought it sight unseen. Later he tracked down the original engine (in an Australian powerboat!) and had the car rebuilt to original spec. By 1973 he had bought and restored 30 more grand prix cars.

"I've always been lucky. I can always come up with the right figure to do a deal. A deal's got to be a two-way street: you've got to leave some cake for the other man, otherwise he'll never deal with you again. I've dealt with Bernie Ecclestone for more than 20 years, and it's always dead easy with him. I've sold him several cars, like I sold him a V16 BRM, and we always do a deal in two minutes. Always over the 'phone, always unseen. First car he tried to buy was the Thinwall Special. I had both of them, one complete and one in bits. I told him I weren't selling the complete one but he could have the one in bits. 'What sort of bits?' 'Big bits, Bernie. Engine's all complete, we've took the sump off and had a look. Chassis, fuel tanks, it's all there.' He says, 'What's your figure?' '£350,000, Bernie.' 'Now, Tom, you've got your figures mixed up. All that money for a load of rust?' 'No, Bernie, I'm not charging you for the rust.' *rrrrrr rrrrrr.* The cheque were in the post next day.

"Bernie will always use you when he can. I were in the Silverstone paddock and he came up and said, 'Talk to me here, Tom, where the BRDC blazers can see us, because I'm doing their new British GP contract.' He wanted them to think he were bringing the race to Donington. *rrrrrr rrrrrr.* With me he's always been 100 per cent. When he closed the Brabham factory down he rang up. 'Tom, there's a lorry load of stuff here, don't know if it's any good or not, but you can have the lot. I'll send it up.' We get on like a house afire."

There are now over 150 cars in the Donington Collection, many of them unique. To see some of the marques lined up is heart-stopping – the BRMs, for example, running chronologically through 27 seasons of failure to triumph and then mediocrity, from Mk 1 and Mk 2 V16s to P201. Or the full glorious set of Vanwalls, from Thinwall Special to the final rear-engined car, and including the unraced streamliner. Some are unrealised dreams that were never raced, like the 1969 4WD Cosworth. Tom has a story about every one: how he found lost and hidden cars, how he married engines that had been parted from chassis, who he dealt with and how each deal was done. In the 1960s and 1970s old racing cars were worth very little, but now the Collection's value is simply incalculable. The ex-Nuvolari Maserati 8CM, for example, cost Tom £9500. As one of the most original 1930s grand prix cars in the world, it is now almost priceless. Post-war F1 cars were routinely bought for £2000 and restored for £4000 more. But, while Tom is the shrewdest of buyers, his acquisitions have all been driven by the love of each car and its history, and not by any thought of investment value.

Tom also believes in driving his cars. Most of them, restored and maintained by Hall & Hall, are fully raceworthy. Even the wondrous Bimotore Alfa is ready to go, on both engines. Every so often Tom invites a few close friends up to Donington for "a little play". And Tom plays hard, and has had his share of hairy moments: the one-off Tec-Mec had just been fully restored when Tom somersaulted it, escaping serious injury but instigating another rebuild.

Although almost all his cars are single-seaters, Tom wanted a Bugatti Royale. None of the six that exist could be bought, so he spent 10 years and £2 million having a perfect copy built from scratch: engine, chassis, body, interior, every detail correct. While he was at it, he had five spare blocks cast and four spare chassis made, to salt away for possible future use. Now he has commissioned Crosthwaite and Gardner to make a batch of five Mercedes-Benz W125s – and Bernie has already ordered the first car. "Some people may not like it, but this way everyone can see and hear and smell a W125 really being raced."

From collector to entrant was an inevitable step. In 1970 Tom backed Derek Bell in the Tasman Series and then, briefly, in F1 with a Brabham BT26A, before helping him into Team Surtees. He also ran Derek in Formula 2 with a BT30 and the *équipe* finished second in the European Championship. Then at the 1971 Monaco GP, watching the F3 final from his balcony at the Hotel Metropole, Tom found himself following the charging progress up the field of a young driver from his home town of Leicester. Roger Williamson was doing his first season in F3 on a shoestring, and Tom noted the March 713's smoky engine. So he stumped off to the distant F3 paddock, where he found Roger already embarking on a roadside engine rebuild.

"He'd got the engine on the never-never from Holbay, and he couldn't even afford the first payment. I introduced meself, and right from the start we just got on ever so well." There was an immediate rapport between them, and perhaps Tom recognised something of himself in the quiet, unpretentious but totally determined 23-year-old.

Tom's gift there and then of a fresh engine grew within a few weeks into full backing for a concentrated onslaught on British F3, in which Roger became virtually unbeatable. Over the next two seasons he won three championships, and the top Grovewood Award. His trademark attacking style, head down in the cockpit, showed at its best when the odds were stacked against him. F2 followed in 1973, with a typically Williamson display at Monza: Roger was pushed off at the first chicane by Vittorio Brambilla, restarted dead last, and came through to win by 17sec. Already there was interest from the Formula 1 world and, following an impressive BRM test, Tom was summoned to lunch at The Dorchester with Louis Stanley. Not surprisingly the pompous Stanley and the no-nonsense Wheatcroft didn't speak the same language. "He tried to buy Roger. I told him Roger weren't for sale. Things got heated, and I got up and left the table. As I went I said, 'You've spoiled my day, Louis.' He called after me, 'You can call me Mr Stanley.' 'I'll try to remember that, Louis.' *rrrrrr rrrrrr*."

Tom had much more respect for Ken Tyrrell, who also wanted to sign Roger. With Jackie Stewart's retirement looming, Ken needed a young team-mate for François Cevert. Meanwhile, Tom hired an F1 March for Roger's first grand prix, at Silverstone. This was the year of the Scheckter induced pile-up at the end of lap one, so his debut was brief. Two weeks later came the Dutch GP.

"The day before we left for Zandvoort, Roger came over and said he had something to ask me. 'Is there any chance of me staying with you, instead of going with Tyrrell?' 'Now, Roger,' I said, 'you've got to make your name. Ken has forgotten more about F1 than I'll ever know. I'm not good enough for you.' 'But we said that about F3, and we said that about F2, but we did it. I want to stay with you.' So we rang up McLaren there and then and we ordered two F1 cars, so we'd have a spare. Teddy Mayer agreed we'd get all the works know-how – if they learned anything, we'd get it. So there I was, all set to run an F1 McLaren for Roger, do it properly. I know he had it in him to go right to the very top."

The ghastly events of that Zandvoort race are all too familiar. Roger qualified 18th out of 24 starters, but he was already up to 13th on lap eight when, in a fast fifth-gear right-hander, his left front tyre delaminated. The barrier that he hit was anchored in sand and bent back on impact, launching the car, which finally came to rest upside down several hundred yards down the track. Roger was almost certainly completely unhurt, but trapped inside. The car's nearly full tanks ignited, and the marshals nearby, improperly clothed to deal with fire, did not go to his aid. David Purley, who'd been chasing Roger, stopped and rushed into the fire, but despite frantic efforts he couldn't lift the car off him single-handed. Neither of the two fire extinguishers he grabbed from the trackside worked. The race wasn't stopped, and by the time a fire truck got to the scene several minutes later the car was burnt out, and Roger was dead.

"It were the worst day of my life. He didn't have a break on his body, you know. He were conscious in the car, shouting to Purley to get him out. The police came and arrested me – as the owner of the car, under Dutch law I were implicated in his death – and I had to verify him and everything. I spent the night in a cell, and it were 10 o'clock next morning when the British consul got me out. Then we had to fly him home. I just felt so sad. I loved Roger like a son. People said I should sue, but I wasn't interested. It wouldn't bring Roger back. But I were very ill after that: it knocked a lot out of me. I started to get over it, and then a year later, when farmers were burning stubble after the harvest, I saw the smoke rising across the fields like I did from the pits that day, [and] it all came back. I were ashamed; had to have some words with myself. You have to learn to live with it but I still think of Roger every day."

It wasn't quite the end of Tom's days as an entrant. He commissioned Mike Pilbeam to design a Formula Atlantic chassis and then an F2 version – initially with a straight-six Abarth engine – which was raced by Brian Henton and Bob Evans. But by now Donington was consuming more and more of Tom's time. In 1971 he'd heard that the site of the old circuit, which was an Army transport depot during the war and had been lying fallow ever since, might be for sale. Within days he had bought it. That was only the start of a six-year pitched battle, with endless planning problems and trenchant local opposition conspiring to block his dream of running motor racing there once more. But Tom has quite extraordinary tenacity. "I'm an awkward bastard. I'm determined in everything I do. I'd known Donington as a lad, and I wanted the place to live again. The more I were blocked, and fobbed off, and lied to – and the more days we spent in court with my legal bills mounting by the minute – the more determined I became."

On May 28 1977 the first race meeting took place, 38 years after the last one. Even that was nearly stopped by protesters claiming right of way over an ancient footpath that crossed the track. Meanwhile the new Museum building had been built near the main entrance, and before long international events came back to Donington – the British Motorcycle GP, and rounds of the World Sportscar Championship. But of course Tom wanted an F1 race, and finally he got it: the European Grand Prix in April 1993. That wet weekend, when Ayrton Senna scored perhaps his greatest victory, has gone down in history.

"I shouldn't have been there. I were very ill in hospital because I'd just had a heart attack, then I'd had an operation, the whole do, but on the Saturday I told the specialist I had to go because I had a grand prix on. I got to the track and I saw Bernie. I could see from the way he looked at me he thought he'd better get his money quick before I snuffed it. *rrrrrr rrrrrr*.

"Then on the Sunday someone said I should drive the W154 Mercedes in the demonstration laps before the race. After all the struggles to get the race to happen, I wanted to do it. The specialist were very unhappy: he said I were mad, but he told me whatever I did not to let any cold air get to my chest, to wrap a silk scarf around my mouth. Off we went, and it were raining heavy. I couldn't see much, and I'd never driven the W154 before, but down through Craner Curves we went, and I thought, 'This is grand'. Then all of a sudden I can't breathe. I pull the scarf off my mouth, and when the cold air goes in it's like a hundred little bayonets inside me lungs jabbing to come out. Then I realised I was off line, and I thought, 'you booger, you're going to stuff it'. I tried to brake, and then we were in the gravel. They hooked me out with a tractor and I carried on for my four laps, got it back to the paddock, and I were just finished. I were gone. They lifted me out of the car, took me to the medical centre, took my overalls off, put oxygen in me. I tried to fight it, then I passed out. I didn't think I'd make it to the podium to present the prizes, but I did get there, and once I was up there with Senna, wearing me top hat, I felt strong as a bulldozer – 18 years old again. Then I went home to bed.

"Of course, because of the dreadful weather and the cold, we only got 50,000 spectators. Between you and me, I lost £4.2 million that weekend. But it were bloody wonderful. At the FIA prize-giving in Paris that year we got the trophy for the best-organised race. Really tickled me up, that did. Max [Mosley] come out of the curtains one side of the stage, Bernie come out of the other, trophy were so big it were all he could carry. When I went up for it, everybody stood and cheered. Afterwards Bernie come up and he said, 'Tom, you can run the grand prix next year. I can get rid of Silverstone.' I said, 'No thanks, Bernie. It's proved two things to me: the circuit's no good for a grand prix unless I put the structure in and spend the money, and you can't run two grands prix in one country. Even with good weather I'll still lose £2 million, maybe two and a half."

Donington's new lease has been much in the news and, says Tom, has been misunderstood by some. "We haven't sold Donington. Us Wheatcrofts still own it. After 14 months of negotiation, we've granted a 150-year lease on the whole place. That covers the museum as well, and the new people have to operate the museum and pay the labour, and there are very strict conditions in the lease about cleanliness and upkeep. The cars mean so much to us as a family, we'll never let them go. And the cars in the museum that are on loan to us: some of them have been with us for over 30 years, and we have a great relationship of trust with their owners. They're all still under our control. I'm president of the new company, and my son Kevin is very much involved. They can't even take one car out of the museum to photograph it without his say-so."

A crucial provision in the lease caters for Tom's wish to take any of his cars out of the museum from time to time and exercise them on the track. For the rest of us, that wondrous collection, and the track where once Auto Unions and W125s roared, are there to enjoy. They are the true legacy of this great enthusiast's lifelong passion, which all began when a young lad found a hole in the Donington hedge and squeezed through it, 72 years ago.

Tom Wheatcroft was talking to Simon in May 2007.

INDEX

INDEX

INDEX